WRITING WORKPLACE CULTURES

WRITING
WORKPLACE
CULTURES
An Archaeology of Professional Writing

Jim Henry

Southern Illinois University Press
Carbondale and Edwardsville

Copyright © 2000 by the Board of Trustees,
Southern Illinois University
All rights reserved
Printed in the United States of America
03 02 01 00   4 3 2 1

Library of Congress Cataloging-in-Publication Data

Henry, Jim, 1952–
　　Writing workplace cultures : an archaeology of professional writing / Jim Henry.
　　　　p. cm.
　　Includes bibliographical references and index.
　　1. English language—Rhetoric—Study and teaching. 2. English language—
　　Technical English—Research. 3. English language—Business English—Research.
　　4. English language—Rhetoric—Research. 5. Technical writing—Research. 6. Business
　　writing—Research. I. Title.
　　PE1404 .H398 2000
　　808'.042'07—dc21　　　　　　　　　　　　　　　　　　　　99-088861
　　ISBN 0-8093-2320-6 (cloth : alk. paper)　　　　　　　　　　CIP

The paper used in this publication meets the minimum requirements of American National
Standard for Information Sciences—Permanence of Paper for Printed Library Materials,
ANSI Z39.48-1992. ⊗

For Jim and Thelma,
my first teachers

CONTENTS

Preface   ix

Introduction: Changing Modes of Composition 1

Part One. Writers in Theories and Practices (Mapping the Dig)
   1. RESEARCHING THE DISCURSIVE SELF 15
      Reading Writers Narratologically 19
      Exploring Discursive Selves Beyond Academic Borders 22
   2. WHAT IS A WRITER? 29
      Profiles of Professional Writers 34
      What Will Writers Be? 43

Part Two. Research on Discursive Work in Organizational Settings (Uncovering Shards)
   3. IN FIELDWORKPLACES: RESEARCHERS' SITES OF STUDY 49
      Writers' Work and Positions in Private Businesses and
         Corporations 54
      Writers' Work and Positions in Government Agencies and
         Institutions 57
      Writers' Work and Positions in Professional Associations
         and Societies 60
      Writers' Work and Positions in Educational and Nonprofit
         Institutions 62
      Writers' Work, Fieldwork, and Subjective Work Identities: Syntheses
         from Shards 64
   4. ORGANIZATIONAL FEATURES OF WORKPLACE WRITING CULTURES 69
      Dynamics Between the Individual and the Organization 72
      Dynamics of Collective Procedures and Writing 78
      Organizational Goals 86

From Organization Charts to Discursive Digs: Imagining New Unities in
   Subjective Work Lives 88
5. DISCURSIVE FEATURES OF WORKPLACE WRITING CULTURES 91
   Discourse Forms 94
   Discourse Effects 102
   Taking Inventory 106

Part Three. Implications and Applications (Links to Other Shards, Other Sites)
   6. REPRESENTING DISCURSIVE WORK IN THE ACADEMY 111
      The Content(s) of Postmodern Composing 114
      Melding Composition with Discourse Studies 120
      Designing Professional Writing Curricula 127
      Pondering Discursive Shards and Imagining New Writing Vessels 136
   7. REPRESENTING DISCURSIVE WORK IN THE WORKPLACE 139
      Representing Authorship 142
      Representing the Domain of Professional Authorship 146
      Representing Writers' Expertise 149
      Representing Writing's Interests 158
   8. INTERVENING IN CULTURAL PRODUCTION AND REPRODUCTION 161
      Discursive Sites of Intervention 165
      Organizational Sites of Intervention 172
      Reforming Discursive Formations and Recapturing
         Intellectual Dominion 179

Appendixes
   A. Researchers' Professional Writing Backgrounds 187
   B. Researchers' Topics in Self-Assessment as Writers, Sites of Research,
      and Research Topics and Themes 189
   C. Writers' Work and Positions by Nature of the Organization 211
   D. Researchers' Abstracts of Workplace Ethnographies 221

Works Cited 247

Index 255

PREFACE

In the twentieth-century United States, writing in the workplace and writing in academic settings coevolved perniciously. In the high-volume production workplace of the early century, writing requirements at most levels of organizational pyramids were relatively simple: workers had to interpret executive commands. enact them properly, and report on this execution. Writing instruction in the academy, at most institutions, followed the so-called Harvard model: students produced demonstration essays or research papers, usually on a belletristic topic (because English departments had staked claim to writing instruction in a student's "general education"), elaborated in the hermetic environment of a classroom, to be submitted to one instructor as the sole arbiter of their worth. Because this worth was most often based on formal qualities of communication, academic writing instruction furnished the workplace with writers adapted to the relatively simple writing tasks demanded of them by the high-volume economy.

Pernicious was the reduction of *writing* to something akin to communicative packaging, as most students learned it and as most workers exercised it. The educational philosophy driving this model was that of liberal humanism, which held that writing *about* belletristic authors would improve people morally and aesthetically, perhaps endowing them with the wherewithal to oppose workplace realities found to be insalubrious. (In theory, graduates of Harvard and similar institutions, who would occupy the top levels of organizational pyramids, would thus feel a moral obligation to improve life in the workplace.) The reality for most workers was that the discursive environment of most job settings offered little possibility for critique, opposition, or even innovation because the very understanding of writing as produced by composition epistemology was so thin. The organizational purview of most people writing in the workplace, moreover, was so restricted by high-volume structures and practices that they would not have been able to muster a broader scope for their writing even if composition instruction had provided them with fuller understandings of it.

In the last three decades of the century, a sea change took place. In the academy, the shift to "process pedagogy" in composition instruction opened the door for fuller understandings of writing and for richer development of writers' (and writing's) potential. Theories of "subjectivity" as shaped by discourse also advanced understanding of writing dramatically: social constructionist theory states that realities are shaped by the language practices undergirding them, and postmodern theories of discourse hold that discourse is the very material from which realities take form. Theoretically, with each new entry into discourse, with each foray into a genre, with each word on the screen, writers inscribe cultures and shape their own psychological realities. These new understandings of discourse not only acknowledged the power of writing to shape individual subjectivity, they also implored inquiry into the interrelationships of writing with power and of writing with value. Yet here the perniciousness endured, because writing instruction remained under the dominion of English departments and subject to a paradigm that reproduced the discursive status quo: students continued to produce singly authored display essays on belletristic topics in a hermetic classroom, to be judged by one instructor—an apt surrogate for a future manager in a high-volume mode of production.

The high-volume mode of production, however, had dissipated with the sea change. The nation had entered a high-value mode of production, which meant that organizations with pyramidal structures would lose their competitive edge through sheer lack of brain power in decision making, problem solving, and solution brokering (thousands of heads are better than one). The personal computer also figured in this sea change, because workers' engagement with discursive processes and products in the workplace could now be configured in dramatically new ways that would enable a realization of the potential of writing and of discourse in the lives of workers and in the lives of organizations. Yet the perniciousness endured, wrought on the one hand by workplace executives' failure to realize the potential of writing for organizations in the information age and on the other hand by the academy's relentless shaping of learning forums and of writing instruction to reproduce the status quo—despite purported opposition to the status quo among most faculty.

The time is ripe to turn the lenses of discourse theory to workplace writing, long denied such attention because of its seeming transparency and its "instrumental" functions. Some of this work has already begun, primarily by researchers in technical and scientific writing, but circumspection endures on both sides of the ivory walls: workplace writers and managers often deem academic theory too removed from the exigencies of everyday work life, and academics often see the workplace as either too mundane or too exploitative to merit their attention or collaboration. This book addresses both audiences with the promise that their understanding of workplace writing practices and articulations with broader discourse processes can benefit from its reading. Academics in general and compositionists in particular can enrich their understanding of the writing subject's formation in workplace cultures, the better to reshape writing instruction, writing research, and writing philosophies. Workplace executives and managers can glean ways to restructure and reconceptualize writing to generate greater value for their organizations, for workers, and for the larger cultures that use their services and products. Workplace writers and students can discern ways to elaborate their writing practices and broaden their discursive knowledge.

As a source book for such an array of readers, *Writing Workplace Cultures: An Archaeology of Professional Writing* covers much ground. From 1993 to 1999, practicing professional writers (and aspiring writers) composed workplace ethnographies of writing as part of a graduate course I designed, Cultures of Professional Writing. These researchers received instruction in ethnographic theory and methodology, fieldwork methodology, and cultural analysis. Using a workshop format, they produced analyses of discursive processes and products in workplace cultures. They also agreed to serve as my subjects in teacher-research on writers' subjectivities as shaped by the discourses of the workplace and the academy. Their work and my analysis of it form the foundation of this book.

As a teacher-researcher committed to an informed intersubjective methodology in which my students would devise their own research questions and topics and in which I would share my ongoing analyses of their work, I struggled to develop adequate representations of what they had done. Aware of recent ethnographic thought that lobbies for constant reflection on the politics and poetics of representation, striving to enact postmodern tenets that call us to resist totalizing accounts of any cultural trends or practices, I sought a way both to highlight the *petits recits* that these researchers provided and to represent their work in ways useful to them, their teachers, and their workplace colleagues. My solution has been to conceptualize this book as an archaeology, in which researchers' findings and researchers' self-representations figure as so many shards to be scrutinized by readers according to their own theoretical frames and local contexts. To this end, researchers and their research are represented from various perspectives and in various dimensions, aided by tables in the appendixes summarizing the researchers' backgrounds, their sites of research, writers' organizational positions, and their kinds of work. Researchers' abstracts, which represent both findings on local discourse practices and researchers' positions with respect to those practices, are also included to support heuristic readings.

The introduction expands my above comments on the coevolution of academic and workplace writing in the century with a particular eye to composition theory and practice, emphasizing the potential of social constructionist theory and poststructural understanding of language practices for reconfiguring writing practices in the workplace and the academy. The value of exploring subjectivity in everyday workplace discourse practices is emphasized, and the theoretical connections with Michel Foucault's work in *The Archaeology of Knowledge* are set forth. The rest of the book then is organized into three parts.

Part one, "Writers in Theories (Mapping the Dig)," opens with chapter 1, "Researching the Discursive Self." This chapter summarizes some recent research in composition studies on the new "subject" of composition and lays out a narratological framework for analyzing subject formation within discourses; sample "shards" are considered for the light they shed on subjectivity. Chapter 2, "What Is a Writer?" opens the Foucauldian framework for understanding subject positions in discourse and presents the eighty-four researchers represented in this book, all the while delineating cultural forces that deny these researchers full enjoyment of the status of "writer" even though they write full-time. Appendixes A and B support readings of this chapter with data on researchers' self-representations as writers.

Part two, "Research on Discursive Work in Organizational Settings (Uncovering Shards)," presents much of the documentation for the claims made in this book. Chapter 3, "In Fieldworkplaces: Researchers' Sites of Study," discusses the various sites of study and writers' work in these sites, by category of organization, all the while making the case for construing all professional writing sites simultaneously as sites of fieldwork. Appendix C, "Writers' Work and Positions by Nature of the Organization," supports readings of this chapter. Chapter

4, "Organizational Features of Workplace Writing Cultures," presents features of writing identified by researchers over all seven years and draws syntheses across these features. Chapter 5, "Discursive Features of Workplace Writing Cultures," provides a similar development of discursive features as identified by researchers Chapters 4 and 5 present numerous lists of specific organizational and discursive structures and practices, providing additional shards for readers' uses.

Part three, "Implications and Applications Links to Other Shards, Other Sites)," prompts heuristic thinking, too, as it draws implications for the academy, the workplace, and collaborators on knowledge production in both. Chapter 6, "Representing Discursive Work in the Academy," posits discourse studies as a means of re-presenting writing instruction to colleagues in the academy, the aim being to reconfigure composition epistemologies and practices in light of this archaeology and recent composition thinking Chapter 7, "Representing Discursive Work in the Workplace," posits a domain of professional authorship as writers' workplace realms, in which they manage multi-authored documents with an eye to local cultural norms and values, contributors, end users, and our larger culture. Chapter 8, "Intervening in Cultural Production and Reproduction," situates the work of the researchers in this book within the ideological context of Washington, D.C., and makes the case for collaboration among academics and workplace writers to identify and promote measures to add value to workers' lives and to the organization's life.

Obviously, this project has entailed a lot of collaboration among many people. My thanks go first and foremost to the eighty-four graduate students who composed ethnographic analyses of workplace cultures as the basis for this book. They appear throughout the book under pseudonyms, and so I shall not name them here. Their analyses were aided greatly by my colleagues who have visited our course each spring to probe the topic of cultural analysis from a variety of perspectives. Since the inception of the project, the following colleagues have visited at least one class session: Debra Bergoffen, philosophy/women's studies; Zofia Burr, women's studies/cultural studies/creative writing; Pat Caretta, career services; Dulce Cruz, composition studies/Latina/o studies; Joel Foreman, English/social and organizational learning; Cindy Fuchs, film and media studies/cultural studies/English; Ted Gessner, organizational psychology; Robert Holt, organizational psychology; Kara Incalcatera, organizational psychology; Roger Lancaster, anthropology/cultural studies; Marilyn Mobley McKenzie, African-American studies/English; Tom Moylan, cultural studies/English; John O'Connor, English/computers and composition; William Rifkin, social and organizational learning; Michelle Smith-Bermiss, African-American studies/English; Beverly Stennett, career services; Susan Trencher, anthropology; Margaret "Peggy" Yocom, folklore/English/cultural studies. My colleagues in the English Department at George Mason University have provided support and encouragement throughout the project; Chris Thaiss and Terry Zawacki in particular have aided me through critical response to chapter drafts. Two anonymous reviewers for Southern Illinois University Press also provided valuable critiques. Finally, Meg Moss aided me with the graphic design of the figures in the book.

WRITING WORKPLACE CULTURES

INTRODUCTION:
CHANGING MODES OF COMPOSITION

> Modes of composition have changed because the discipline's
> research agenda has shifted from the search for structures to
> theories of practice that explore the interplay of both structure
> *and* agency.
>
> —Renato Rosaldo, *Culture and Truth*

The discipline Renato Rosaldo refers to is anthropology. As one of the
contributors to James Clifford and George Marcus's widely referenced
Writing Culture: The Poetics and Politics of Ethnography, Rosaldo
helped usher in an era of reflexivity in ethnographic writing. To achieve
this reflexivity, ethnographers have turned their scrutiny to the ways
and means of textual representation of cultures, to the "poetics and
politics" of ethnographic work and ethnographic products. The work
of the ethnographer no longer consists of composing a written account
that pretends to mirror flawlessly a local reality, in which members of
the culture are cast as types and the researcher as an instrument of science—objectivity personified. In the postmodern scene, all composition is contingent, all composers politically and discursively positioned.

The shift in research agenda that Rosaldo describes applies to many
disciplines in the postmodern academy, in particular to those in the
humanities and social sciences. Much of the deconstructive work of
the 1980s and 1990s has enabled fuller understandings of the ways in
which structures identified through earlier "objective" research were
inevitably also products of the research frame and researchers' methods (and thus always partial), leading researchers in many fields to focus their efforts not on further reifying structures but on examining
practices within and against them. With the increased complexity of
cultural practices resulting from the shifts in national economic and
social structures, changes in organizational structures, and the sheer
volume of information moving among these structures in the informa-

tion age, questions of agency have assumed centrality in postmodern research. For researchers and for researched subjects entering a new century, many postmodern theoretical tenets have become a part of daily life. Witness the fragmentation of cultural unities believed to be nearly immutable (e.g., job security in certain organizations earlier allied with purported national interests), blurred boundaries among domains of life (in particular, those of work and leisure), hyperacceleration of cultural processes (through digitized information, its networked flows, and its Web dissemination), and a pastiche of synchronic representations of realities supplanting the more linear and hierarchical (most notably in mass media). Discerning agency as practiced among structures in this scene looms a task as vital as it is challenging.

Composition has been one of the many fields to rise to this challenge. In the 1970s the shift in research focus from students' written products to their writing processes (framed then for the most part as cognitive processes) prepared the ground for the ensuing shift in the 1980s to a focus on writing contexts (mostly academic classrooms). This in turn opened the way for some researchers to focus on agency as circumscribed by cultural and discursive practices. Susan Miller, for example, proposed "disclosing connections between specific social and textual superstructures and highlighting how writing situations construct their participant writers before, during, and after they undertake any piece of writing" (198), and Lester Faigley suggested that students be invited to explore "how agency can be constructed from multiple subject positions" (224).

Undeniably, one of composition's most endearing traits is its resolute and persistent connection to teaching practices, as indicated by the comments of Miller and Faigley. Yet the history of teaching composition in American postsecondary institutions has grossly undermined the potential of inquiry by composition researchers or by writers themselves into their agencies and subject positions. James Berlin's comprehensive history of twentieth-century postsecondary writing instruction in the United States traces the dominance of "current-traditional" rhetoric, which "makes the patterns of arrangement and superficial correctness the main ends of writing instruction" (*Rhetoric and Reality* 9). Sharon Crowley extends the critique, noting shortcomings of such instruction in the realms of purpose and audience as well as the narrow range of subject positions offered to writers:

> In current-traditional pedagogy, students' papers are not constructed as messages that might command assent or rejection. Nor do current-tradi-

tional teachers constitute an audience in any rhetorical sense of that word, since they read not to learn or be amused or persuaded but to weigh and measure a paper's adherence to formal standards. Hence the current-traditional theory of discourse is not a rhetoric but a theory of graphic display, and so it perfectly met the humanist requirement that students' expression of character be put under constant surveillance so that they could be "improved" by correction. (*Composition* 96)

Such instruction has dominated curricula since the turn of the century, when the so-called Harvard model grounded in current-traditional rhetoric and spearheaded by Francis Child gained enormous influence among curriculum designers at many institutions across the country, leading them to conceptualize composition as he had: an endeavor consisting of mastering forms, engaging little disciplinary content knowledge (Russell 50). The research paper had earlier emerged as a form of writing quite valuable in initiating new members into their chosen realms of discursive work, yet this component of writing instruction had been in its turn sapped of relevance through curricular reforms at the time. As Donald Stewart notes, early-twentieth-century curriculum reforms witnessed writing instruction wrested away from departments of rhetoric (many in demise) by English departments concerned primarily with the belles lettres. Student composers who might earlier have pondered the discursive "I" as it assumed membership in a discipline while researching topics valued by the discipline and dear to their own concerns now were faced with researching topics in literature, like it or not. Whether justified through current-traditional rhetoric's tenet that composition's focus should be primarily formal or through liberal humanism's belief that the values gained through the study of literature automatically took priority over values that might be nurtured through other discursive work, the end result was that studying composers through the years—at least until the resurgence of disciplinary writing courses in the 1980s—rarely got the chance to compose positions (and selves) in the discursive realms of their future active lives. Coincident with the loss of this written discursive experience, notes William Riley Parker, was the loss of parallel spoken discursive experience, since composition instruction focusing on literature lacked the oratorical component found earlier in departments of rhetoric (349).

David Russell observes another important effect of the reconfiguring of research writing when taken over by English departments devoted to belletristic pursuits: "Its pedagogical uses narrowed, moving from apprenticeship to production" (85). That is, composers not only were deprived of discursive subject positions in their future active realms but were in the process positioned primarily to produce. This shift eerily presaged the Taylorization of American industry in the early 1900s. Spearheaded by the studies of Frederick W. Taylor in *The Principles of Scientific Management,* factories reorganized work processes for greater efficiency, using time-motion studies to maximize (and standardize) workers' movements. Taylorization of the workplace was linked strongly to "social efficiency" models of teaching all subjects (and students) at the K–12 levels, as discussed by Herbert M. Kliebard in *The Struggle for the American Curriculum, 1893–1958.* He observes the links between Taylorization of the workplace and of curricula: "Once the standardization of the techniques of production were achieved, the task of bringing the average worker up to the required level of work could be accomplished" (95). Schooling, too, could be Taylorized to prepare workers efficiently (albeit at individuals' discursive experiential expense). Composition instruction achieved this not only through current-traditional epistemology that divorced instruction from composers' genuine concerns (and that rendered writers and future workers more easily quantifiable via a theory of graphic display) but also through generic writing assignments and conventions that dramatically limited first-person discourse (which, once again, would have been unthinkable in a department of rhetoric). Finally, composition courses in this age were invariably structured around *books,* which, although on the one hand opened new horizons for readers, on the other limited those horizons in their own way through the codex culture they carried with them (Lanham), a culture that values literacy over orality and that has in fact imposed literate interpretive lenses on preliterate cultural phenomena.

This dramatic reduction in the dimensions that any discursive "I" might assume in writing courses dovetailed with shifts in business restructuring occurring at the same time. Following JoAnne Yates, Russell observes:

> In the late nineteenth and early twentieth centuries, American business reorganized human relationships through the new movement toward systematic management, a movement that depended upon impersonal written communication to subordinate the individual to a rationalized system. (103)

The impersonal written communication needed for the rationalization of management systems was effectively assured by the ideological form that composition instruction had taken, to be reinforced through the formalist theories underpinning textual interpretations of belletristic texts (and compositions about them) by midcentury, which will be taken up in chapter 2. For the moment, this brief history of composition serves to underscore the economic and ideological reasons for its modes in the modernist era.

That era was one of unprecedented U.S. economic prosperity, made possible not only by the Taylorization of workplaces and systematic management but also by the development of high-volume production in the industrial sector by the nation's core corporations. Says Robert Reich: "By the 1950s, the well-being of individual citizens, the prosperity of the nation, and the success of the nation's core corporations seemed inextricably connected" (43). The structure of these corporations at the core of the high-volume economy was one of absolute control: "Organizational charts graphically mapped out internal hierarchies, starting with a large box at the top containing the chief executive officer, and proceeding downward through levels of ever smaller and more abundant boxes" (51). Literacy demands of most workers were principally those of interpreting executive orders correctly and implementing them efficiently within the hierarchy. Says Yates: "Impersonal policies, procedures, processes, and orders flowed down the hierarchy; information to serve as the basis for analysis flowed up the hierarchy" (20). Expertise in writing required primarily a mastery in generating and interpreting impersonal written communication to the ends of executive efficiency, and perhaps because the middle class perceived its interests as so closely intertwined with those of big business, impetus for reconceptualizing college writing instruction for greater individual actualization was hardly forthcoming from the workplace experience. Thus macroeconomic organization of subjectivities joined that of curricular philosophy and institutional competition among disciplines to assure that composition instruction would replicate status quo discursive experience.

By the time the research agenda in composition had shifted, with many other fields, to theories of practice exploring interplays of structure and agency, the nation's economy had effectively shifted from high-volume production to high-value production. In the high-value enterprise, says Reich, "profits derive not from scale and volume but from continuous discovery of new linkages between solutions and needs" (85). Workers' literacies in such an economy, clearly, must go beyond the functionary practices of yore. The forms that workplace literacies will take remain to be seen, but even in this initial phase of reconsidering composition research and instruction, prior research in the field speaks to macroeconomic realities. Writing, as Janet Emig demonstrated in 1977, is more than a neutral medium of communication for preestablished knowledge. It is a mode of learning, which, when properly conceptualized and contextualized in local workplace cultures, can contribute to discoveries of new linkages between solutions and needs, at the very least.

Such a rethinking of writing's potential within organizational life is suggested by Shoshana Zuboff's work, in which she analyzes the shift from high-volume production (in what she calls the "automated" age) to high-value production (in the "informated" age). Predicting new shapes for organizations and new dissemination of information and authority within them, she says that "when work becomes synonymous with responsiveness to data, it engenders inquiry and dialogue, thus opening the way for workers to envision new possibilities and fresh alternatives to the reigning definitions of process, product, and organization" (302). "To put it simply," she says, "learning is the new form of labor" (395).

What, though, will writers learn through workplace writing? What should be their topics of inquiry and their modes of composition in conducting it? What forms might curricula take to prepare them for such inquiry? Because writing is not only a mode of learning but is in fact the means by which realities become socially constructed—by which local cultures create realities with effects far beyond their borders and reproduce the local realities of their organizations—writers must at the very least hone their skills in perceiving the ways and means of this social construction via language. And because writers not only compose but are composed by the discourses of the workplace, recent composition tenets tell us, they must hone skills in perceiving the mechanisms, dynamics, and effects of such composition. In the twenty-first century, learning about, during, and through workplace writing must embrace the interplay of organizational structures and agencies among them in the ongoing composition of writers' lived realities and the realities that they write/create.

This book supports such work. As the title suggests, part of this project borrows from recent ethnographic theory that explores the implications of the interpretive turn in the analysis of local cultures. The Cultures of Professional Writing course attempted to enact fieldwork methodologies linked to this new analysis, in this case on the part of practicing (or aspiring) professional writers and editors, who represent a class of professionals regularly tasked with composing as their central workplace duty. As mentioned in the preface, during seven consecutive springs, a total of eighty-four writers enrolled in an MA program in professional writing and editing conducted ethnographic analyses of workplace cultures in their organizational and discursive dimensions. While participating in course work, they also agreed to serve as my research subjects under the university's sponsored programs of research, following the guidelines of the Belmont Report. Our course thus became the site of "informed intersubjective research" (McBeth), in which all class discussions and individual conferences were audiotaped and all writings were photocopied or electronically stored. Students in the class had the option of not participating in my research (only one student chose this option), and grades were based solely on material production and regular, engaged participation, so that course participants would not feel coerced either to participate in research or to conform to a particular stance in their writing. (To see the current syllabus, go to http://mason.gmu.edu/~jhenry/512syl.htm.)

The course design was inspired by Lee Odell and Dixie Goswami's *Writing in Nonacademic Settings,* the groundbreaking text presenting studies of writing in workplace cultures by various academic researchers (mostly from rhetoric and composition). This text set the stage for a number of ethnographic studies of workplace writing, leading Carl Herndl in 1993 to voice this caveat: "This research lends itself to a mode of reporting that reproduces the dominant discourse of its research site and spends relatively little energy analyzing the modes and possibilities for dissent, resistance, and revision" (349). From the first Cultures of Professional Writing class meeting in 1993, I have emphasized the value of dissent, resistance, and critique to writers studying their careers, since such critique could afford them insights that would strengthen their writing prowess. As it turned out, of the eighty-four participants in this research, sixty-five chose to study their own places of work, and they required no prompting to mount critiques.

My research design was inspired initially by Dixie Goswami and Peter Stillman's *Reclaiming the Classroom: Teacher Research as an Agency for Change,* in which they present examples of classroom instructors conducting research collaboratively with their students to improve curricula and teaching practices. James Berlin has observed that "the teacher-as-researcher program in writing emphasizes the study of the unique language practices of students in their particular social setting" ("Teacher" 10), and I sought through my research design to focus students' attention on the unique language practices of their workplace social settings. Because the course's workshop format enabled frequent reporting by participants on these language practices, class sessions and research writing provided a forum for professional writers to share their own insights on workplace cultures with other professional writers.

In this respect, my students' ethnographic project differed significantly from that of contributors to *Writing Culture* and to the feminist volume *Women Writing Culture* that stands as a valuable epistemological update on the earlier work. Debts to each of these volumes will be repaid in later chapters; I mention them here to signal a significant difference in this book: unlike the academic ethnographer-theorists inspecting representative practices and addressing commentary on them to their peers in the academy, the researchers represented in this book were more concerned with inspecting the "instrumental" discourses of the workplaces in which they daily composed (and were composed) and in interpreting local cultures to inform their understandings of these compositions. Thus their aims were quite different, as were their audiences. I see their project as no less vital than that of their Ph.D. counterparts, even though their familiarity with ethnography and hence theoretical sophistication is less, because the researchers in this book have taken as their object of analysis a topic at the very heart of social constructionism itself: the composing through language practices of everyday realities. Professional writers daily compose and recompose the cultures of their workplaces however subtly through their discursive projects. Focusing on this aspect of composing through ethnographic analysis can illuminate the ways in which so-called instrumental discourses also constitute a cultural *poesis,* a "constant reconstitution of selves and others through specific exclusions, conventions, and discursive practices" (Clifford 24). That these researchers were often members of the cultures they researched also holds intriguing possibilities for intervention, which has been a key element of both applied anthropology and feminist practices for years. These possibilities are discussed at length in part three of the book.

Just as the title *Writing Workplace Cultures* signals this book's connections with ethnographic analysis, so does the subtitle *An Archaeology of Professional Writing* signal connections with Michel Foucault's work in *The Archaeology of Knowledge and the Discourse on Language.* He uses the term *archaeology* to indicate "a possible line of attack for the analysis of verbal performances" (206), these performances being construed not as utterances by individuals but as "discursive events." An endeavor in the history of ideas, his work entails a revision of historical interpretive approaches by revisiting certain sites of discourse (for example, that of mid-nineteenth-century medicine) to piece together the findings in that site, not so much in the interest of confirming hypotheses about a previous reality as to discern rules of practice underpinning it. Hence his choice of the extended metaphor of *archaeology*. My use of the term signals both Foucault's conceptual frames as they will inform some of my analysis of professional writing and the procedures through which this analysis is made possible.

Archaeological work is initially exploratory and then synthetic. In the exploratory phase, one slices through earth gingerly, methodically, alert for any colors or textures that contrast with the ground. When I worked as an archaeologist's assistant in the 1970s on a prehistoric site, we would skim off the soil, layer by layer, until a fleck of ivory or burnt sienna appeared. Then we would drop our shovels and take up dental picks, prying earth away from the color in the hope that more color would appear, producing a form. The ivory might be a tip of a finger or a hip or a knee, and our work consisted of uncovering the color in whatever direction it would take us, bones hardening in the air and leading us on eventually to expose the full body, which, depending upon how much the earth had shifted since burial, might lie at nearly any angle. In the case of burnt sienna, we would pick at it gently in the hope of retrieving a vessel fully intact, but such was rarely the case. Rather, we would salvage one shard here, another there, collecting as many as possible that seemed likely to belong to the same vessel, whereupon the synthetic work began: as logic and imagination suggested, we would piece together these shards to arrive at a representation of what might have been the earlier unity.

Foucault's archaeological work in the territory of discourses was similar in its procedures, though somewhat different in its aims. Philosopher Debra Bergoffen describes it as follows:

> I'm down there and I'm digging and I come upon these shards. I say: What do they make? How do these pieces fit together? How are they related to each other? What sorts of objects emerge when I put them together in certain ways? Shards is all we got. And shards, that's what Foucault is calling discourses. (in class, 5/1/96)

Part of Foucault's project was discerning the ways in which various discourses and practices surrounding them came together in discursive formations, offering positions to subjects who circulated in these formations and among these discourses. The work of this book rejoins his project and takes as its object of analysis not the historical uncovering of nineteenth-century discourses but rather the contemporary uncovering of twentieth- (and twenty-first-) century discourses in which professional writers (and others) are offered positions. Because writers are a class of professionals who regularly enact composition tenets as part of their primary work, this archaeology serves as a resource both for writers (and aspiring writers and writing managers) and for compositionists who want to reshape our field in light of these findings.

As I mentioned in the preface, this archaeology is aided by researchers' abstracts (appendix D) and by three large tables (appendixes A, B, and C). Using these tables along with the abstracts and index, readers can chart readings through the book according to their own interests or local circumstances by following a particular theme or researcher through each appearance and by comparing themes and researchers with others in a table or specific table cell. Though I draw syntheses and analyses for each table at various moments, part of the lure of an archaeological site is the similarities one perceives with shards in one's own dig.

Like an archaeological museum containing vessels from many sites, this book is dense with information, so that linear, word-by-word readings cannot correspond with any one reader's desires. Hence I have used numerous headings in part two, for example, which enable readers to glean a trend or pattern among research issues at a glance—then to consult the detailed bulleted lists as deemed pertinent. The tables may appear dense at first brush, but they gain dimension in tandem with my discussions and with the reading trajectories that readers bring to them and continue through them. (Readers who would like to ponder the shards of this archaeology in a hypertext excavation can do so at http://classweb.gmu.edu/classweb/jhenry/index.html.) In *Envisioning Information,* Edward R. Tufte observes that "high-density design also allows viewers to select, to narrate, to recast and personalize data for their own uses" (50), and my hope is that readers will indeed be able to do just that. When I began work on this project, I sought in my analysis to mount some "meta-ethnographic" commentary that would subsume course participants' work in encompassing narratives, but this attempt proved unfulfilling in its reductionism. Grappling with the politics and poetics of representation, concurring with Jean-François

Lyotard's strategy for countering master narratives through localized *petits recits*, I have come to agree with James E. Porter and Patricia Sullivan, who in their discussion of methodological interfaces in professional writing research, say: "The kind of theorizing we are advocating is postmodern in the sense that the maps we draw are not meta-maps, but rather heuristic ones" (319). I urge readers to view the many tables, researchers' abstracts, and indexes linking them as heuristic maps to aid them in charting their own projects, and I take satisfaction that these fragmented representations of my "research subjects" resist any totalizing accounts.

When I worked as a technical writer in the railroad industry, I not only began to realize how academic institutional structures and ideological practices had grossly undertheorized instrumental discourse, I also learned how valuable and complex the seemingly transparent concepts of readability and usability could be. I have tried to apply these concepts in this book, imagining my readers to be professional writers (or aspiring writers), workplace managers, writing teachers, curriculum designers, professional writing scholars, and compositionists, and assuming that many readers will fall into more than one of these categories. Readers at one extreme might deem this text too academically esoteric, at the other extreme too preoccupied with mundane discursive work. Yet these two extremes have every interest in conversing, and composition studies has every interest in making the conversation possible, as suggested by John Trimbur's account of postmodern composition: "By this postmodern version, composition studies situates itself in a nondisciplinary or postdisciplinary place where multiple, heterogeneous, and polyvalent discourses, projects, and interests intersect" (136). This book uses one archaeological dig to suggest some such intersections.

In terms of usability, I imagine readers not only reading but consulting this book, using it intermittently as a source for their own writing, course design, research, or debate. I imagine writers engaged in workplace composing—weighing the pulls of tradition and culture, disciplines and fields, the community, and their own values and experiences—and agreeing with James E. Porter that "every composing event is itself an ethical decision, not simply a presentation of an already preformed ethical position" ("Developing" 223). I imagine writers and scholars collaborating in critical literacy projects, exploring "how individuals are constituted as subjects outside educational institutions" (Anderson and Irvine 87) and working together "to address the relationship between literacy and empowerment in a given context" (91). I imagine readers in organizational cultures, concerned along with former labor secretary Robert Reich that the "sense of connectedness" between workers and national identity has disintegrated and convinced that one way to reshape this connectedness—in ways valuable not only to the nation but beyond it—is to examine the organizational and discursive structures and practices within local cultures that have perhaps contributed to this disintegration.

One central practice to explore is the structuring of authority. Zuboff depicts the ways in which authority moved out of workers' purviews with the shift to Tayloristic forms of work organization in this century. The parallel reduction of writers' authority to the essentially formal in composition theory and practice is too strong to ignore, and this book begins the work of reconstructing writers' discursive (and hopefully organizational) authority as a part of authorship. Here the notion of implied authorship proves invaluable, for within narratological theory every text has an *implied author,* defined by Gerald Prince as the "implicit image of an author in the text, taken to be standing behind the scenes and to be responsible for its design and for the values and cultural norms it adheres to" (*Dictionary of Narratology* 42). Writers in workplaces regularly compose these authors, and because they are part of a process that is responsible for values and cultural norms, they will need theoretical and methodological support in apprehending these cultural phenomena, and they will need epistemological support in lobbying for their rights in this authorship. As modes of composing change with the digitization of information and workplace restructuring in the twenty-first century, in fact, professional writers and students of writing could prove invaluable collaborators in rectifying misconceptions of what composition is. This book seeks to join the efforts of many compositionists and professional writing scholars over the past several years to achieve these ends.

PART ONE

Writers in Theories and Practices
(Mapping the Dig)

1 RESEARCHING THE DISCURSIVE SELF

In the *Archaeology,* the question "who is speaking?" actually
serves to underscore the multiplicity of social forces impinging
upon the self, forces that struggle against one another to enter
discourse through the "I." The subject always speaks from a
"discontinuity," from a point of intersection between divergent
interests, channels, and communities.

> —Kurt Spellmeyer, "Foucault and the Freshman Writer:
> Considering the Self in Discourse"

Anne: [To instructor] And the gap there between what you read
  and what you analyze, is making me as a writer very self-
  conscious as I write. And as I do this work.
Nidean: Are you self-conscious when you write anything? Or
  just . . .
Anne: Um—no—well, I'm taking a class in autobiography right
  now. And we share those pieces, and those are very personal
  pieces of writing. And those, I just let go and write. And if
  somebody doesn't like it, or doesn't understand it, I can sit
  there in the group and come back at him face to face—or
  her—anyway . . .
Branden: Um, could I just make a comment? Because I don't—I,
  I understand what you're saying [to Anne]—but I don't look
  at this like that. I, I thought this quote was really neat, in the
  Herndl article; he said that "Derrida is right when he says
  that the critical relationship that we establish with our own
  discourse is a measure of its quality and fecundity." I mean,
  that's—anyway—basically he's—what I'm trying to get out of
  this is just sort of develop this critical viewpoint of what I'm
  doing, and do the best possible thing that I can do.

> —discussion in class, 3/23/93

While composition was emerging as a field of research on writing processes in the 1970s and 1980s, continental theory was exerting enormous influence in American academe, in the humanities in general and in English in particular. Because much of this theory focused on discourse, discursive practices and traditions, discursive formations, and the construction of the subject therein, literature scholars were able to enhance interpretive frames brought to published texts. Many composition scholars found themselves positioned to use this theory in dynamic ways, given that their *primary material* was the writing of students, which made the authors of primary texts immediately available—often in researchers' own classrooms. Kurt Spellmeyer's use of Foucauldian theory to interpret freshman writing illustrates the parameters of this research: the "self" in discourse represents social forces that find their manifestations when one writes; the "I" is recognized as a subject of composition along with any claims that this "I" may predicate.

The potential of such research is enormous. After all, a theory of subjectivity as constructed in discourse links with diverse intellectual realms, including politics, psychology, and philosophy at the very least. In the realm of politics, for example, Althusser's concept of the subject as interpellated by ideological state apparatuses reminds us that our subjective identities are always shaped to a degree by the state and its institutions, including surrogate institutions from the religious to the educational that determine one subject's relationship to another. In the realm of psychology, Lacan's extensions of Freudian theory that posit a fundamental disunity in our psychologies, engendered in infancy upon first realization that the self is discrete from the mother (and coincident with language learning that permits acquiring the concepts of self and other), help explain at least part of the difficulty of representing oneself in writing—of finding adequate words upon each re-entry into discourse. In philosophy, Barthes's now-famous "death of the author" permitted a new approach to textual interpretation that sought out recurrent semantic codes in literary works and the cultural constructions imbuing each individual writer, and Foucault's essay

"What Is an Author?" inspected the subjectivity of authorship in the plane of sociological functions. Indeed, much of Foucault's work has enlarged the implications of social constructionism itself for understanding our daily subjectivities as lived among the myriad discourses with which we contend.

Compositionists, professional writing scholars and writers, and workplace writers and managers can benefit from such theory by focusing it on actual workplace writing experiences, academic writing experiences, and comparisons of the two. With respect to subjective identities as shaped by the state and surrogate institutions, for example, we might study the specific ways in which the structures and practices of our academic institutions shape writing subjects' relationships with other subjects, and how these relationships compare with those of the workplace. In what ways are writing subjects shaped as functionaries, and in what ways as collaborators or apprentices? Through what writing practices do we position subjects within institutions as coresearchers gleaning new linkages between problems and solutions? How can organizational structures and practices in academic and nonacademic settings be revised to promote productive and satisfying relationships among subjects (acknowledging that the political inflection of subjectivity is an ongoing discursive process) to the benefit of organizations and writers within them? Chapters 3, 4, and 5 offer shards that might serve academics and workplace discourse managers in imagining these revisions.

Psychological subjectivities as shaped through language practices have been addressed within many disciplines and from a variety of perspectives. However, such research to date has focused overwhelmingly on individual authorship, on manifestations of an essentialized and unified self, most often composed in an expressive mode. Much work lies ahead on gleaning the contours of discursive selves composed in organizational settings via collaborative authorship, reviewing these contours critically through varieties of theoretical lenses, and designing new frameworks for understanding the interplay among discursive selves and organizational practices, values and products. As Dorothy Winsor observes of workplace writing, "We must constitute ourselves in texts that we do not wholly control" (194). Such constitution elicits complex psychological processes on writers' parts, the study of which could yield greater value for writers and their workplace cultures. In chapter 2 appears a partial inventory of writers' subjectivities in psychological dimensions, and ensuing chapters demonstrate that even this partial inventory displays aspects of subjectivity that are dramatically truncated in most workplace writing. What steps might be taken by discourse managers in the workplace and professional writing scholars collaborating with them to enhance the structures and practices shaping psychological subjectivities of workplace writers? This question goes beyond the rhetorical, because "finding adequate words upon each reentry into discourse" can yield value for organizations and individual writers alike.

Researching the discursive self as shaped in academic and nonacademic cultures can thus prove valuable to writers, their audiences, their colleagues, and their managers—and to compositionists and professional writing scholars eager to understand better the practices and structures undergirding composition of the self within workplace discourses. One difficulty in accomplishing this research, however, is finding frameworks for interpretation that enable one to capture the often momentary, ambiguous, and even contradictory manifestations of subjectivity in the discourses encountered in academic and nonacademic settings.

In academic settings, part of this difficulty derives from the deficit models that have framed interpretations of student writing for so many years: because for decades academic essays have been approached as demonstrations of incomplete proficiency to be corrected, it proves difficult to discern in our readings a subjectivity beyond that of neophyte writer/learner. This difficulty has been compounded, ironically, by the strong expressivist strand in composition epistemology during the 1970s and 1980s that often harkened to essentialist concepts of identity, grounded ultimately in Freudian psychological theory positing a fundamentally unified self. Whereas such epistemology often helped teachers reengage students as writers within academic discourses from which they had become alienated, it simultaneously thwarted interpretations that would enable student writers to perceive the many subjectivities they assumed with each new essay, the many forces that struggle against one another to enter discourse through the "I."

In nonacademic settings, researching the discursive self has rarely been a project undertaken by organizations, despite the rapidly growing corpus of research by academics on workplace writing. This lack of initiative surely stems from broadly held views of so-called instrumental writing as "authorless"—and hence devoid of discursive selves. The topic of the discursive self, moreover, smacks of purely personal issues that most workplaces would pass over in favor of research on topics perceived as more pragmatic. Yet this book makes the case that research on the discursive self can yield applications in the workplace that, because of the theoretical richness underpinning them, could far outstrip applications focused solely on discursive products or processes with no eye to writers' lives. Practicing writers, managers, and writing scholars must collaborate on this research to uncover more archaeological shards for our inspection. In the pages that follow, I outline some approaches for pondering these shards grounded in narratology.

Reading Writers Narratologically

Narratology, the theory of narrative, concerns itself first and foremost with narrative structures and elements essential to telling a story. Principal among these elements are the narrator, the "speaker" inscribed in the text, and the narratee, the "listener" in the story (see Prince, "Introduction to the Study of the Narratee," for a fuller discussion of the characteristics of the narratee). Whether overt or effaced, these narrators and narratees are the lifeblood of most narratives: the narrator recounts events to her or his narratee while we readers observe from outside the world in the text.

Of course, narration takes many forms, narrators and narratees in some cases barely discernible, yet narratologists have identified a number of textual indicators of speakers' and listeners' presence in addition to the more obvious personal pronouns such as "I" and "you" (Piwowarczyk; Prince, "Introduction," *Dictionary*). These indicators allow us to trace the word-by-word emergence of the one who enunciates thoughts and the one who attends to them in the world of the text.

At a more macroscopic level, and as an extension of the symmetrical relationship between narrator and narratee, narratologists speak of an "implied author" and an "implied reader" for every text. Defined as the "implicit image of an author in the text, taken to be standing behind the scenes and to be responsible for its design and for the values and cultural norms it adheres to" (Prince, *Dictionary* 42), the implied author in a sense represents a text's *engagement* with the "real world" in which it circulates.

I use the expression "real world" to echo narratologists' designation of yet two more entities in this theoretically symmetrical relationship, the "real author" and "real reader." Exterior to the text, the real author is the flesh-and-blood writer who has generated the narrator(s), narratee(s), and the narrative structures through which they relate. The "real reader," by the same token, is any one of us who brings his or her eyes to the text. Figure 1, taken from *Story and Discourse* by Seymour Chatman, illustrates the entities I've described.

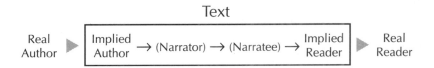

Fig. 1. A Narratological Framework for Reading Writers. Reprinted from Seymour Chatman, *Story and Discourse: Narrative Structure in Fiction and Film.* Copyright © 1978 by Cornell University. Used by permission of the publisher, Cornell University Press.

Using this narratological framework to analyze nonfiction texts yields valuable insight on discursively manifested selves. By demarcating the real author and that author's textual productions, we can separate momentarily textual representations of the writer from the biological writer, trace the complexities of textual "selves" in the forms of narrators, narratees, and narrative structures, then read these selves as they compose an implied author, responsible for the text and for the values and cultural norms it adheres to. The following section illustrates such analysis, which begins by identifying narrators and narratees in a given text.

Narratological Readings of Classroom Texts

In the excerpt from class discussion that appears in the opening of this chapter, three "real authors" have voiced utterances that constitute texts. The opening comment of Anne reveals two narrators, an "I" "as a writer," and an "I" who "do[es] this [intellectual] work." In the light of Spellmeyer's comments on the self in discourse, we can say that these two different appearances of an "I" represent moments when different social forces enter into discourse, in this case constituting an "intersection" among (at least) the interests of writing and the interests of conducting the academic work of ethnographic analysis.

The "you" of Nidean's reply seems to designate as narratee Anne's "writer" narrator. The interrogative construction signals this narratee once again, and depending upon one's interpretation of this mini speech act when tone and inflection are taken into account, this question establishes a narrator who might represent interests of collaboration (helping us all negotiate the issue of my analysis and render it fruitful) and of critique (pointing out to Anne that all "writing" demands self-consciousness).

Within the larger context of the course, Anne's comment to me was motivated by an earlier instance in which I had misinterpreted a narrator she had posited in a progress report. In pointing out my error to me, she had said that she was correcting me not just because I might come up with a faulty analysis of her as a writer but also because she knew that this analysis might be published and reach a wider audience, resulting in a misrepresentation to the community of composition scholars. Hence this "I" also speaks for that community.

Anne's response to Nidean reveals yet other issues concerning the self in discourse that were under negotiation in this scene. The student narrator that appears ("I'm taking a class") functions to pit one form of writing offered in our curriculum ("autobiography") against the form offered in this course, ethnography. (Invisible to other members of the class was a narrative begun when Anne previously took a pro-seminar in composition studies with me, in which she championed an expressivist approach to instruction and I a more social-epistemic approach. Less invisible, perhaps, are other narratives implied by the fact that autobiography as a course offering in English is more "established," as is the professor who teaches it in our department.) Anne's "student" narrator is joined by the "writer" narrator once again, marked by jargon ("pieces") and an "I" who summons a liberatory narrative ("I just let go and write"). A narrative of publicly defending a position ends her comment ("I . . . can come back at him face to face"), serving to point out an important facet of these course participants' subjectivities—as subjects of analysis—and to remind us all of the complexities of occupying the positions of analyst and analyzed in this forum.

Branden's intervention speaks to these positions. Like Anne, she posits a "student" narrator ("could I just make a comment?"), situating this narrator as a supportive peer ("I understand what you're saying") yet locating this narrator as a utilitarian reader who plumbs course texts to develop her writerly self: "what I'm trying to get out of this is just sort of develop this critical viewpoint." As she grapples to articulate this last position, the starts and stops marked by dashes in the transcription could be seen as graphic demonstration of the struggle among social forces to enter discourse.

At the "real author" level as I've framed it here, this scene shows issues of "selves and others" being negotiated with respect to the institutional subjectivities of instructor and student and to the research subjectivities of analyst and analyzed. At the textual level, other selves and others find manifestation, with different narrators providing sites for social forces to enter discourse, representing the interests of class participants, collaborators, peers, and writers. As concerns the interests of writers, they enter discourse here as multifaceted: as self-conscious work, as liberatory experience, as critical reflection.

As a "text," this excerpt from a class discussion in 1993 illustrates the complex subjectivities that surface and recede in a brief five-minute classroom exchange. The written texts that paralleled such exchanges, because they were focused on discursive practices in workplace cultures, provided similarly rich manifestations of subjectivity. Working with these student-practitioner-researchers each year, I composed analyses of subjectivities that we reviewed together as part of our informed intersubjective research. Thus the course entailed researching the discursive self as part and parcel of academic assignments focused on writing in workplace cultures, an endeavor that enriched this one-semester academic experience. To render this research valuable to writers and scholars exterior to the course, I will first review rationales for research on nonacademic writing then link these rationales to that of an archaeology in the following section.

Exploring Discursive Selves Beyond Academic Borders

Just as classroom studies of writers' discursive subjectivities are often hampered by the flat source medium of the academic essay, so are studies of writing in the workplace limited by their motivation: most often they are conducted exclusively to utilitarian ends, owing to funding, and focus not on writers so much as the writing. Such research thus ignores discursive subjectivities because they are deemed irrelevant. James E. Porter and Patricia Sullivan note this lacuna in workplace research, all the while suggesting links with classroom research:

> Workplace research too often assumes that knowledge about the workplace should feed classroom practice, but not vice versa. The classroom perhaps is the best site for effecting fundamental changes in the nature of workplace literacy; it certainly provides an opportunity for experimentation, for testing new possibilities (whereas workplace action can be constrained by "the way things have always been done"). (315)

The goals of research as framed in the Cultures of Professional Writing course are first to capture "the way things have always been done" in a given local culture and then to reflect critically upon these local practices and imagine possible alternatives, including alternative discursive formations and attendant subject positions.

As course instructor and researcher drawing upon course participants' primary research, I have sketched the methodologies for elaborating our informed intersubjective research along lines similar to those suggested by Gesa E. Kirsch and Joy S. Ritchie in "Beyond the Personal: Theorizing a Politics of Location in Composition Research." They suggest that "research participants must be invited to articulate research questions, to speak for themselves" (13). and each term, course participants did indeed elaborate their own research questions once we had framed the research through reviews of workplace ethnographies and an introduction to ethnographic fieldwork methods. This position on methodologies resonates not only with recent trends in composition but also with research principles grounded in feminism. Drawing on Sandra Harding's groundbreaking work on feminist theory and social science methodology ("Introduction: Is There a Feminist Method?"), Kirsch calls attention to the *purpose* of the researcher's questions: "they must be *grounded* in the subject's experience and be relevant to the subject" ("Methodological Pluralism" 256). Discerning more fully writers' subjectivities among workplace discourses seeks to heed this purpose.

Questions and issues raised through such research have varied dramatically and provocatively, both in researchers' chosen topics and themes to pursue and in their authorship in doing so. As to the latter, our classroom meld of research/writing workshop allowed us to address other issues of research principles raised by undertaking such work, in particular with regard to the entry into ethnographic discourse by course participants as primary researchers. As outlined in the introduction, ethnographers have embraced recent epistemological issues in authorship and the politics of representation with wonderful insight in recent years, leading to textual representations of cultures grounded in rigorous fieldwork methodology all the while situating the "I" who narrates these representations of "self" and "other." The vital questions that many ethnographic researcher-theorists have asked themselves revolve around their representative practices in the roles of scholars producing and reproducing academic fields. The questions that researchers have raised in the Cultures of Professional Writing course are no less vital, yet they are formulated in a different rhetorical arena: addressing their accounts to fellow writers, possibly to workplace managers, and through me to composition scholars and researchers in professional writing, course participants have struggled with composing an "I" (and its surrogates) that sways these audiences. Hence the intellectual realm of ethnography joins those of politics, psychology, and philosophy invoked earlier to theorize discursive subjectivities, with this theorizing linked solidly to pragmatics. Ruth Behar, addressing the plotting of ethnographic narratives as part of her introduction to *Women Writing Culture,* observes: "How we plot ourselves into our fictions has everything to do with how we plot ourselves into our lives" (15). Two central goals of exploring discursive subjectivities beyond the academy through the informed intersubjective research of our course and this book have been to equip professional writers with an array of ideas on how to plot themselves into their future work lives and to equip writing teachers with ideas for alternative plots in the classroom. Such ideas will hopefully spring from the archaeological displays and analyses in the following chapters.

As a writing teacher, I was prompted by my intersubjective research with course participants in 1993 and 1994 to revisit the opening chapters of *The Archaeology of Knowledge,* in which Foucault explores the construction of subject positions in nineteenth-century medical discourse. In the spring of 1995, I included this text in our course readings, and I prompted course participants to consider the subject positions of professional writers in twenty-first-century discourse as they engaged with Foucault's analysis. We discussed the text in class with the help of philosopher Debra Bergoffen, who extended her metaphor of uncovering shards during archaeological work, cited in the introduction, to say the following:

> There's no singular subject. There are subjective positions within particular discourses. I've got surfaces on which these discourses appear. And I want to know the rules by which these discourses operate. If I figure out these rules, I will discover how objects are composed . . . . I get an object by putting the shards together; I don't get an object by digging deeper. I don't look for intentions . . . I look for regularities, I look for rules. . . .
>
> When you do that you're going to discover, not that these unities never existed, but that they came into existence according to certain rules of discourse. It's not a question of "are these unities true or false?" Foucault says, let's see what practices produced those unities; let's see whether they're the only unities that get produced by these practices. Maybe if

we take a good look at the practices, we ll discover other kinds of unities. (in class, 5/1/96)

In Cultures of Professional Writing, course participants take stock
of the kinds of discourses at work in their research sites, conducting
primary archaeological work on the forms of discourse in which writers work, the ways and moments in which particular discourses manifest themselves, the ways in which certain discourses easily dovetail
with some while resisting connections with others, and the like. One
of our goals is to imagine alternative unities that might take form when
discursive formations and practices are exposed through this archaeological undertaking. This book seeks to support researchers and writers at other sites by displaying the shards collected over seven years of
research, in the hope that these shards can be compared to those of
other digs and that alternative unities can take form in other settings.
To support such comparisons, I extend the narratological readings of
student writers above to demonstrate readings that trace discursive
contours of subjectivity, as discourses shape writers' schooling, professional writing backgrounds, organizational sites of work, and workplace cultures. Because shards of Branden's discursive subjectivity have
already been introduced, I will trace her appearances throughout the
book as an illustration.

Branden's abstract, "Discursive Elitism in a Government Travel
Agency" (see appendix D), opens with a narrator identified as a "participant observer," thus introducing the social force of fieldwork methodology as part of the social sciences into discourse. This social force
is strongly bolstered by references to the "local culture," a "principal
informant," and the explicit naming of a scholar in organizational
psychology, Edgar H. Schein ("Organizational Culture"). The narrator is also a text analyst, thus introducing social forces emanating from
discourse studies generally and English studies in particular. These two
social forces—a tradition of research on social practices and structures
and a tradition of text analysis grounded in discourse studies—begin
to sketch a discursive formation in which certain objects of analysis
fall within the limits of valid study while others do not. This is no small
fact: discursive scenes from classrooms to workplaces regularly designate valid topics, and part of archaeological work entails making explicit the terms of validation. The "self" in this abstract finds its position among discourses validated by our course work and which might
not be validated by research "sponsored" (Brandt) by other institu-

tions. The implied author that emerges in the abstract has gleaned some organizational maneuvering via textual practices that she might not have gleaned outside this particular discursive formation—no trivial matter when we consider that the "real" Branden leaves the classroom with knowledge thus constructed.

Other shards represent aspects of Branden's discursive subjectivity via the tables in appendixes A, B, and C. Appendix A shows researchers' professional writing backgrounds, representing Branden as a freelance, self-employed writer. Such a writing "self" is exceptional in this data set, and scanning the table prompts one to consider discursive formations from a slightly different angle: the discourse of professional writing forms what Foucault would call "various situations that the subject can occupy" (*Archaeology* 53), in this case remunerative situations in which discursive range and scope vary significantly. The discursive work of a freelancer and the ways in which this work shapes subjectivity by virtue of the relations it establishes and prolongs with other workplace groups, for example, differs from that of journalists, of technical writers, of teachers, and so on.

Appendix B displays key points taken from Branden's written representation of herself as a writer. Here we might understand "formation" in the sense of schooling (the double entendre in French supports such a reading even though Foucault does not mention it) and note that scholastic experience shaped Branden's vision of what constitutes "writing" with a bias toward the literary tradition. Chapter 2 discusses the ways in which an "author function" has served to establish realms of discursive exclusivity as writers enter discourse, and Branden's equation of writing with Shakespeare signals such a function at work. Through publication under her name (a cultural *sine qua non* for assuming the mantle of "writer," many researchers report), she enters such a realm, albeit at a lesser status, and so manifests a self shaped in part by the forces of the publishing industry and the relations among writers and readers it establishes. The discursive self in this table also signals the interests of the market in shaping professional writing subjectivity.

Appendix C lists all researchers by the nature of the organization they studied. The categories I've derived to accommodate all sites of study prompt musings on subjectivity. In his analysis of the evolution of nineteenth-century medical discourse, Foucault speaks of describing the different kinds of institutional sites from which subjects speak and from which a discourse derives its source and points of application (51). Just as a subject's purview in a hospital (and its discourses) might differ from that in a clinic (and its discourses), so do subjects of discourse in twentieth-century professional writing discourse find their purviews shaped in different ways depending upon the nature of the organization. A writer in a private business is positioned vis-à-vis other subjects in very different ways from a writer in a government agency, for example, and the discursive selves that will take form in these scenes will differ dramatically.

Within each category of sites, too, the terms of subjectivity for writing selves differ significantly according to writers' work and positions as observed. Among the researchers who studied government agencies and institutions, we glimpse Branden observing policy and planning writing in a part of the Department of Commerce, suggesting subjectivities for writers that are quite directly shaped by the state. Against the background information of her abstract, we can imagine the organizational scope of writers being shaped by discursive subject positions that are inscribed in a weekly report that "allowed certain players to hold other members to projected roles in the organization, all the while elaborating their own." In government accounting, one's organizational roles as documented in reports can sometimes have the weight of terms writ in stone.

Branden's appearance in chapter 4 sheds light on an aspect of writers' subjectivities in organizations as inflected by document processes. The lists of skills, status, roles, and the like came from the full ethnographies and class discussions. In the section devoted to the dynamics of collective procedures and writing, we see Branden's abstract supplemented by the observation that an organizational player was able to gain personal credit for collective production through the process of document routing. The observation calls attention to the fact that document processing, seemingly benign in any flow chart, serves as a mechanism for presenting a self in different ways depending upon organizational position. Readers interested in this phenomenon might also consult Ana's account to glean ways in which the contours of document processing might offer slightly different subject positions depending upon the nature of the institutional site.

Chapter 5 presents discursive features of organizational authorship, with a particular slant. The first three sections approach discourse in a modernist mode, whereas the following three sections use a more postmodern approach. I explain this construction in chapter 5; for purposes here, one notes that Branden, while studying a document that in a modernist mode constitutes a policy statement (section 1), also observed organizational maneuvering (section 6) as an effect of discourse that posits subject positions strongly along government bureaucratic lines, as discussed above. As with the lists in chapter 4, one can glean more on this phenomenon of discursive subjectivity by going to abstracts of researchers observing similar features (Ana and Mandy).

As we trace the representations of any of the eighty-four researchers through these pages, pondering narrators, implied authors, documented discourses, and subjects' positions in them, we can use them to great advantage by pondering Foucault's celebrated questions: "What are the modes of existence of this discourse? Where has it been, how can it circulate, and who can appropriate it for himself? What are the places in it where there is room for possible subjects? Who can assume these various subject positions?" ("What Is an Author?" 120).

Though these questions were used by Foucault to conclude his essay postulating ways in which an author "function" had taken form in literary discourse, the same questions speak compellingly to professional writers, discourse managers, researchers, and compositionists as we research discursive selves. The term "author" might hinder, because the belletristic tradition uses this term solely for the literary author. But as Roger Chartier points out, earlier ages prioritized uses of "author" differently: in seventeenth-century France, for example, the term "author" was used more often to designate one engaged in discourses of practical affairs than literary affairs (40). The history of U.S. composition instruction as sketched in the introduction works against us here, since most composing has been taught under paradigms of belletristic authorship. Yet archaeological inquiry resists understandings limited exclusively to recent pasts and pushes us to imagine other unities.

So, too, does recent composition theory aimed at exploring the discursive self, as sketched in the introduction. Lester Faigley's prompt to explore agency as constructed from multiple subject positions can be considered while pondering the many workplace subject positions represented in the following chapters in specific organizational contexts. Likewise, we can respond to Susan Miller's suggestion that we seek to disclose connections between specific local and textual superstructures (and that we highlight how writing situations construct their participant writers before, during, and after they undertake a piece of writing) by considering the shards of this archaeology and matching them with shards from other sites. To aid us all in such explorations of agency among institutional structures and practices, the next chapter completes part one of this book by sketching a profile of the eighty-four professional writers and aspiring professional writers whose research and researching selves define the terrain of this archaeological undertaking.

2 WHAT IS A WRITER?

A few years ago I would not have defined myself as a writer, and today I still don't use the term "writer" if asked what I do for a living. I usually reply, "I'm in public relations." Then, if asked what I do on a daily basis, I respond, "I do a lot of writing." Still, I hesitate to categorize myself as a writer. . . . I think my hesitation comes from my immediate perception of what someone is when she does define herself as a writer. My first thought is that the person must write literature or poetry for a living. The rest of us are journalists, or public relations professionals, or proposal managers, but not writers.

—Ann, self-assessment as a writer

How, under what conditions, and in what forms can something like a subject appear in the order of discourse? What place can it occupy in each type of discourse, what functions can it assume, and by obeying what rules? In short, it is a matter of depriving the subject (or its substitute) of its role as originator, and of analyzing the subject as a variable and complex function of discourse.

—Michel Foucault, "What Is an Author?"

As noted in chapter 1, Foucault's project in "What Is an Author?" was to trace ways in which fetishisms of literary authorship worked to maintain systems of hierarchy that admitted certain subjects while excluding others. In proposing an "author function" as an object of study in place of flesh-and-blood authors, he sought to prompt discursive inquiry into the ways in which the *concept* of authorship operated systemically in cultural constructions of knowledge. As a title, historically, the term "author" identified a set of discursive subjects distinct from "writer" and marked by cultural features such as publication. Discussing figures of the author in seventeenth-century France, Roger Chartier observes that "the term 'author' presupposed printed circulation of works and, in return, recourse to the press distinguished the 'author' from the 'writer'" (40).

In her essay "writing and Writing," Sharon Crowley traces ways in which current-traditional composition pedagogy has effected similar systemic distinctions among subjects:

> There's writing, which is the simple ordering and recording of thoughts or information and which can be done as easily by a secretary or a committee or a machine or a technical writer, since its author-ity is not relevant to its status as text; and there's Writing, what Authors (and authors) do. (97)

Crowley uses capitalization to signal levels of exclusivity in sketching the ways in which current-traditional epistemology works to maintain exclusion, positioning the student writer's work outside the realm of the real: "Each such [writing] effort is expendable, marking, as it does, only a stage in a learner's/writer's progress toward 'real' writing" (94). The subject position offered by such epistemology to student writers is thus always one that replicates distinctions based on cultural practices of publication, which date, as Chartier's research demonstrates, to at least the seventeenth century and an era when the modes of discursive production and consumption were radically different from those of today. Because writers such as Ann have been disciplined by such discursive epistemology, it's easy to understand their inclination to disqualify themselves as writers, even if they spend the majority of their active lives writing. Crowley's ironic equation of secretaries (a culturally gendered position), committees, machines, and technical writers (her ordering heightens the irony) signals several of the features marking professional writing at the end of the twentieth century, which will be explored from various angles in this book to characterize the authorship of professional writers.

I have chosen Ann's comments as an epigraph because they reflect a strongly recurrent phenomenon in the researchers' written and oral self-representations as writers all seven years: more often than not, these professional writers and aspiring professional writers would not claim the title "writer." Whereas current-traditional epistemology helps explain this phenomenon, so does a consideration of other epistemologies that have figured in these researchers' educations. Their ages varied from mid-twenties to mid-forties, meaning that the English classes in which they received composition instruction (at both secondary and postsecondary levels) would have been strongly shaped by New Critical understandings of texts in force since at least the early 1960s and still strong today. Like all theoretical movements, New Criticism has advantages and disadvantages, yet with regard to its effects on studying writers' understandings of their own subjectivities established through and elaborated within discursive work, the disadvantages weigh heavily. By eliminating the (published) writer's intentions and the reader's affect from the domain of "objective" criticism, New Critical thought frames discursive products as nearly autonomous objects. That the instances of an "I" entering discourse via student writing in such a theoretical arena would be dramatically limited goes without saying; and it seems quite plausible that a secondary effect would be a systematic, subtle suppression of one's affect as a legitimate and important concern upon entry into discourse as a writer.

Thus professional writers often deny themselves their titles as a result of several forces in English disciplining, making them a professional class marked by remarkable self-effacement—particularly with respect to the other professional classes with which they daily interact. This self-denial is compounded by strictly formalist understandings of writing that circulate widely among those other professionals: in written self-analyses and in class discussions, the metaphor of a "talking handbook" has recurred when professional writers described their colleagues' manifested understandings of their expertise. Given the likelihood that most of these colleagues endured Composition 101 in a current-traditional model that emphasizes primarily formal characteristics (which Sharon Crowley characterizes as driven by a "theory of graphic display," *Composition* 97), this interpretation of professional writers' subjectivity is perfectly understandable. As a professional class, then, writers find their discursive subjectivities constructed in dramatically reductive manners from a number of cultural quarters. Part of the project in this book is to begin reshaping the terms defining this class by taking stock of its own "author functions" and the cultural processes related to those functions.

As a professional category, "professional writer" is somewhat diffuse, owing to the varieties of writing that might be performed and the wide range of workplaces that serve as sites for writing. (Bureau of Labor statistics group writers with "artists, entertainers, and athletes" and provide categorical breakdowns only for "authors," "technical writers," "editors and reporters," and "public relations specialists" [table 11].) Barbara Couture speaks in terms of "career writers," intimating occupational longevity and limiting her set to those who write on technical and "professional" subjects: "Technical/professional writing is that variety of writing in the workplace that is constrained by the occupational responsibilities of *career writers,* a term I shall use to refer to those professionals in organizations who write on technical/professional subjects for a living" (26).

Couture's definition allows her to contrast professional writing with other kinds of writing prevalent in workplaces—in her study, with engineering writing and administrative writing. She further contrasts professional writing to these two by pointing out that "technical/professional writing has been defined as a rhetorical category by career writers' perspectives on effective communication and by rhetoricians' perspectives on the role of the technical/professional writer in organizational contexts" (26).

This positing of technical writing and professional writing as synonymous is driven not only by Couture's particular data set but also by the evolution of professional writing as a topic of instruction and research in academic settings. Sullivan and Porter describe a "curricular geography," in which "professional writing" has traditionally found itself in a parallel slot with "technical writing" and "business writing," all three of which are usually positioned in English departments as an "adjunct or service" to "English [as] Literature" (see figure 2). Sullivan and Porter propose a new geography that establishes professional writing as a major and recognizes it as a research field, forecasting, perhaps, directions in curriculum and research to come that can indeed begin to characterize professional writing more fully in terms of its local and larger cultural functions. Their proposal, grounded in a review of curricular history, resonates with observations from the workplace: Kathleen Gregory, following the work of Van Maanen and Barley, has described "occupational communities" that crosscut organizations in Silicon Valley, and as the field of communications coevolves with technology, occupational communities of writers are certain to grow. (One could argue that the Society for Technical Communication constitutes one such community, its membership 23,000 strong.) The interests that unite writers as a professional class are developed in part three, drawing on the profiles and desires as documented in this chapter.

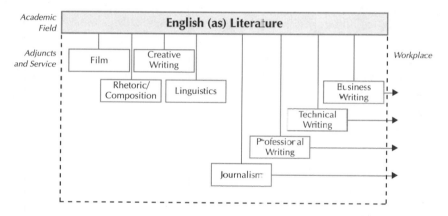

Fig. 2. Sullivan and Porter's Curricular Geography. From Patricia A. Sullivan and James E. Porter, "Remapping Curricular Geography: Professional Writing in/and English." *Journal of Business and Technical Communication* 7 (1993), p. 393, copyright © 1993 by Sage Publications, Inc. Reprinted by permission of Sage Publications, Inc.

Were we to expand Couture's definition of professional writing to begin to embrace the work of professional writers in adequate detail, we would probably want to include some reference to the handling of digitized information in the form of text and graphics, given the degree to which professional writers now handle document design and Web design. We would certainly emphasize that most often these writers work in collaboration with other writers and specialists from other fields, managing the plural authorship of singular texts in the capacities of drafter, editor, associate editor, technical writer, and the like. In practice, rarely do professional writers live exclusively the subject position of textual originator, thus providing a concrete example of a Foucauldian tenet aimed at exploring authorship in the cultural plane. Professional writers in practice live subject positions multiply configured by organizational and discursive structures, and this archaeology attempts to map some of them by cataloguing data on eighty-four such writers' backgrounds and workplace experiences.

This chapter initiates some cataloguing by drawing upon appendix B, in which topics in written self-assessments are summarized. In the second class meeting of our course each year, researchers submitted prose analyses of themselves as writers, based on a model for planning professional trajectories that was provided by the university's career services office in the first class meeting. Under headings derived from topics and commentary in these analyses, I draw some syntheses. These syntheses are offered to complement readers' encounters with individual researchers as they trace them across various chapters and to point out trends and patterns that mark this class of professional. Thus some initial profiles of professional writers take form, serving as a springboard, hopefully, for all readers desiring to grasp in greater complexity what a professional writer might be.

Profiles of Professional Writers

Appendix A displays the backgrounds of the eighty-four researchers, 81 percent of whom were women, who took part in this project. As a glance reveals, the majority of them had experience primarily with organizational publications, most often in the capacity of editor, copy editor, or editorial assistant in the publication of annual reports, brochures, newsletters, magazines, and the like. Other backgrounds figuring heavily across this set of researchers include technical writing/editing and analysis/correspondence. The technical writers and editors had worked in contexts from small entrepreneurial businesses to midsize software or engineering firms (in which they found themselves working in technical writing teams) to large contracting corporations with the government. The analysis and correspondence writers often had experience in composing (singly and collectively) reports and letters for both internal and external audiences, several of them in very large corporate settings. Other workplace discursive experiences that these researchers brought to this project included public relations/policy writing, research writing, journalism, graphic design, and teaching. That thirteen of the researchers held experience in this last field owes in part to the fact that our MA program offers a track in the teaching of writing and literature, and several students from that track had taken Cultures of Professional Writing as an elective. Yet as discussions throughout the book display, I hope, teaching and professional writing overlap theoretically and pragmatically in many ways, most of which remain untapped in contemporary inquiries into each. Finally, it is noteworthy that only two of these eighty-four researchers had no prior experience in professional writing, and only two more had experience solely as self-employed freelancers, which means that the large majority of researchers represented in this book were already familiar with professional writing in organizational settings.

As a set, these writers' experiences also reflect George Mason University's geographic location. Just fifteen miles from Washington, D.C., the university offers the only MA program in professional writing and editing in the area. Thus many people who have gained professional writing experience in the governmental, para-governmental, and lobbying organizations that abound come to the program in Professional Writing and Editing to update knowledge and skills to enhance their current organizational status or to move to a better job. Many, too, work in the burgeoning beltway private sector producing publications for private and public audiences alike. The analyses of themselves as writers used for the following profiles touched upon literally hundreds of aspects of writing, and finding appropriate categories for classifying shards from these analyses has been no easy task. Indeed, in archaeological work, classification is a much more complex task than it might seem, as Ken Dark explains:

> Take, for example, a piece of pottery: is it the dimensions (or some of them), or the fabric . . . which we consider worthy of classification? Do we consider the surface treatment of the inside or the outside of the pot? How much variation is significant? Do we assign importance to the weight of the pottery sherd, where it was found, its colours, its possible function, or the way it has broken? The choice between these options is not obvious. . . . (78)

The parallels between traditional archaeological fieldwork and discursive archaeology in the realm of professional writing are compelling: among the many "shards" turned up through research on and by professional writers, which categories prove the most fruitful in yielding knowledge on writers and their subjectivities as a professional class? In this chapter and the chapters to follow, I have derived categories with an eye to specific users of this book, whom I envision to be practicing writers, workplace managers, academics teaching and conducting research in professional writing, and other scholars interested in the domain of professional writing as it might inform theory and teaching in discourse studies. The categories for mounting an initial profile that address all of these users and which emerge convincingly from the commentaries on writing backgrounds by the researchers in this project are the following: Learning to Write, Conceptualizing the Self in Writing, and Professional Writing Experiences.

Learning to Write

Current-traditional composition epistemology and New Critical literary theory as sketched theoretically above have joined other forces to shape these writers' discursive understandings and experiences as they report them. Students admitted to the MA program in Professional Writing and Editing in which this research took place possess undergraduate degrees in English, for the most part. This bias is due largely to admission procedures that screen applicants with an eye to the graduate courses in literature that must be taken as part of the degree; students with no backgrounds in literature, it is feared, will have a difficult time performing in these courses and so few are admitted. Thus as a "data set" the self-assessments as writers reflect a strong literary disciplining which, when effected through curricular forms common to most undergraduate departments of English, in turn reflects a construction of instrumental writing as peripheral, less complex than writing in the belletristic tradition, as noted in Sullivan and Porter's discussion of curricular geography. Yet a glance at appendix B reveals that constructions of writing as an essentially individual endeavor, prizing fiction and poetry as more interesting or more venerated, begin before undergraduate work or even scholastic experience. Such views of writing derive no doubt from the many and varied cultural representations of writing that begin in early childhood, to be reinforced through schooling practices. As mentioned in chapter 1, Foucault's frequent allusions to "discursive formations" prove provocative in this sense, in that "formations" can designate both the networked practices produced by specific institutional sites of discourse and the schooling of any writer operating among various discursive formations. The double entendre provokes the simultaneous consideration of cultural constructions of writing and individual articulations to these constructions that no postmodern understandings of discursive work can do without. The syntheses that follow are offered to prompt such consideration.

Writing "talent" often manifests early in life. Nancy dated her writing debut to age six, and Nyck "dreamed of writing since fourth grade." Many other researchers cited similar early signs (Alice, Brenda, Daisy, Gary, George, Grace, Gwen, Itsy, Janice, Megan, Tom). Stories of childhood story writing are so prevalent, in fact, that people who were attracted to writing after childhood may even refer to themselves as "late bloomers" (Norma). And even as researchers noted influences from the immediate environment (Red noted that his mother was a painter), the sense of a calling lent by such constructions of writing led one to claim a "natural affinity for language" (Hart), and another to fear, albeit tongue-in-cheek, that "the writing gene had passed me by" (Jan).

Initial forays into writing are often in the realm of fiction. Nancy's oeuvre at age six was a novel (*The Big Dog*), Brenda penned a "mystery novel," Megan a "creative writing book" in fifth grade. Janice wrote of "sitting on the floor around my father's desk, pretending to write stories while he worked on his column." Clearly, the storytelling impulse is strongly culturally bound with writing.

Writing skills develop over time. Emma noted shifts over time from "notecards and outlines" to "writer-based" writing, to "audience-based," mirroring some shifts in composition theory and pedagogy in the last two decades. Cass pinpointed key moments in development throughout her life, and Mandy traced her learning even into the present. Gwen cited learning on the job, Kyle still intends to "practice to perfection," Heather is "just starting out as a writer," and Anita considers herself a "writer-in-progress."

Schooling in writing included rewards, nurturing, exposure to varieties of genres. Megan won her fifth grade creative writing contest, and has her name "engraved on a plaque that I assume still hangs over the doorway of a bright yellow classroom at James Buchanan Elementary School." George remembered winning a high school essay contest, and Bernie's high school experience offered him writing as an "expressive outlet." Cass "excelled in research papers in high school," and Albert developed in high school AP English, later to be encouraged by a college English professor. Kirsten noted college instruction by a professional magazine writer. Many researchers cited forays into poetry, journal writing, humor writing, and letter writing alongside other academic writing (Alice, Brenda, Grace, Gwen, Helen, Karla, Kyle, May, Phoebe, Starla).

Learning writing is often autodidactic. Even as these researchers acknowledged the many school influences in their writing, they also occasionally raised the issue of autodidacticism when learning to write. Rachel noted early employment and teaching herself to write in different styles, and numerous researchers mentioned struggling alone with finding the right words. Comments such as these surely derive not only from the primary construction of writing in our culture as essentially individual but also from the commonplace that good writing can't be taught—only learned. In some cases (Gwen, Tess, Maggie), it derives as well from the reality of having to learn constantly to perform duties as professional writers and editors—a topic to be rejoined below and in later chapters.

Undeniably, we begin learning to write from the earliest ventures into discourse, even before learning forms of any kind—even before learning, one might argue, the very rudiments of inscription, so strong is the promise of discursive engagement. As one learns to write in U.S. culture, we glean from the syntheses above, not only does the sway of narrative loom powerful but also schooling practices emphasize, structure, and reward *only* individual achievement in discursive work. Thus both broad cultural forces and schooling emphasize individual talent in the singular authorship mode of fiction, reinforcing an understanding of the writer as independent and solitary in production, an understanding deconstructed by Linda Brodkey in "Modernism and the Scene(s) of Writing." In professional writing perhaps more so than any other form, such an understanding of writing is not only theoretically counterproductive but pragmatically impossible: professional writers write in contexts, and recent theory and research aimed at classroom practice (Lunsford and Ede, *Singular Texts/Plural Authors*; Forman; Lay and Karis; Reagan et al.; Selber et al.; Dias et al.) underscore the need for teachers to offer students new scenes for conceptualizing their writing selves. As we ponder the profiles of professional writing and workplace authorship in its cultural dimensions, it behooves us to consider how these childhood experiences fundamentally shape one's understanding of discursive selves—and to consider those early discursive experiences that later become lost or transformed.

Conceptualizing the Self in Writing

Early learning, schooling, and the discursive experiences that ensue produce an array of conceptualizations of the self in writing and as a writer, as suggested by the self-assessment topics in appendix B. Syntheses across them highlight some of these conceptualizations.

The writer at times becomes a medium. Closely related to the theme of autodidacticism is the narrative of writer as medium. Leigh wrote of a story "flowing out of me naturally," Alice noted that "interest allows immersion" in a topic, and Lois likens the writer to a "reverse prism," speaking of "stories demanding to be told."

Writing is often equated with literary authorship or publication under one's name. Branden "equated writing with Shakespeare" early in her life, and Mandy is "not a writer yet" because she is unpublished. Hart constructed her idealized writerly self as an amalgamation of three renowned writers in fiction and nonfiction. These researchers' thoughts echo those of Ann cited in the chapter's epigraph, a strong cultural commonplace in the United States.

Writing is an encounter with the world. Writing may constitute an exploration of this world (Jillian), permitting the writer to learn about it (Gloria, Gwen, Holly, Lisa, Tess) and to enjoy it (Brenda, Daisy, Sarah, Tess). Close observation and analysis may be a part of this encounter (Janice), as may be interviewing other people (Adam, Jackie, Kirsten, Maggie). It may be perceived as both an art (Chet, Red, Rex) and a science—as in problem solving or puzzle solving (Brenda, Corinne, Ellie, Joe).

Writing is protean in terms of difficulty and engagement. Writing is hard work at times (Emma, Hart, Norma), easy at others (Lee), humdrum at still others (Brenda). It requires discipline (Gary, Sue) and practice (Adam, Kyle), and one must be "methodical and precise" (Gary).

Writing exposes oneself. Inevitably exposing one's self to assessment by and response from others (Brenda, Daisy, Sue, Tom), enduring their scrutiny (Ann) and editing (Starla), writing requires coming to terms with vulnerability (Tom).

Writing is linked to feelings. Writing can serve as a refuge (Hart) and can be employed to examine feelings (Lee), invariably eliciting them: writing is playful (Lee), painful (Kelly, Tess), fun (Anita, Kirsten, Kyle), therapeutic (Janice, Nyck, Phoebe, Red, Sue), even cathartic (Leigh).

Writing represents a livelihood. Even though only Joanne, Rachel, and Ravi developed this topic in their self-assessments, the topic surfaced frequently in class discussions.

Writing elicits emotional reactions. It provides satisfaction (Ann, Daisy, Karla), a sense of purpose, responsibility and pride (Ann, Ginger, Gloria) or of "occupational pleasure" (George), involving creativity (Ann, Liz)—even passion (Chet)—and at times engendering frustration (Ann) or stress (Norma). Writing can render one "prone to agonizing" (Adam, Adria) or moody (Sue), making it difficult, to "convey emotion" (Corinne); or, alternatively, one can attain "an emotional high from crafting words" (Elaine) or maybe even a "thrill" (Mack).

Writing is at times highly "personal" (as opposed to public/professional). Many researchers deemed it pertinent to represent their writerly selves as at least bivalent between the personal and the professional, including in the former category writing such as personal correspondence, journal entries, and poetry addressed to friends. Jen cited the former as the "most clear" and Ann actually included "proposals for nonprofits" among the personal, since they afford her satisfaction through volunteering. Jeff idealized his writerly self as a "male Erma Bombeck," and Ray fictionalized his future self as "writing independently on the beach in Honolulu, Hawaii." Ray's comment serves to pinpoint the element of escapism that imbues many of these researchers' comments on their writerly selves (and that reflects a common cultural experience of *readerly* experiences of authorship), and at the same time limns a leitmotif among professional writers: for many, their ultimate aim is to write a novel and publish it.

This last opposition of categories, the personal and the professional, is significant in a variety of ways. It is strongly recurrent. Among those students who did not employ it in their written self-assessments, the professional/personal binary almost inevitably surfaced in class discussions at some point during the course. In part yet another facet of the narrative of individual talent so frequent in these researcher's comments on early discursive experience, this opposition of categories also underscores the degree to which writing—as engagement with language and discourse—is so often integral to knowledge that one builds in several discursive domains simultaneously. Yet as later depictions of workplace writing experiences will show, writers are frequently positioned both organizationally and conceptually in ways that dramatically limit the kinds of knowledge they might pursue, thus leaving much of the potential of workplace discursive work untapped. As noted in the introduction, organizational researcher Shoshana Zuboff claims that in informated workplaces, learning is the new form of labor. Janet Emig's demonstration that writing constitutes a unique mode of learning, when teamed with studies of writing in its heuristic dimensions (e.g., Young et al.), underscores the degree to which the early-twentieth-century shift in both the academy and the workplace toward undue focus on production at the expense of inquiry has undermined writing labor's potential. Yet the following section reveals aspects of discursive formations that, even as they are heavily configured by production rationales, nonetheless hold potential for rectifying this philosophical wrong turn.

Professional Writing Experiences

That so many professional writers summoned distinctions between professional and personal writing stems without doubt from many influences, yet the earlier depictions of learning to write make it clear that broad and deep discursive formations support a primary identification with writing as singular activity. As the syntheses below demonstrate, the workplace almost inevitably presents formations that frame writing as just the opposite—as collective work requiring skills and knowledge in extratextual domains.

Bringing rhetorical skills and knowledge to other people's texts. Professional writers edit others' work (Andrew, Chet, Corinne, Diane, Ella, Ginger, Grace, Holly, Jackie, Jeff, Kyle, Leigh, Maggie, Mary, Phoebe, Ravi) and find solutions to problems in the writing of others (Jillian), at times conceiving of their own work as "translating" the thoughts of others (Brenda) or even as a "soupmaker" (Anita).

Managing projects from beginning to finish; multitasking; meeting deadlines. Writers manage documents (Cass, Jeff) and give them order (Sarah), effecting results (Diane), putting together "creative products or volumes" (Jackie), and overseeing projects from start to finish (Brenda). They handle a variety of tasks and projects simultaneously (Gloria, Helen, Kelly, Phoebe, Sarah, Tess), at times in large volume (Kelly), and use many skills in doing so (Gwen, Leathe, Phoebe), all the while meeting deadlines (Brenda, Daisy, Holly, Jeff, Mack, Nyck).

Exercising various skills to complete writing projects. They must be thorough (Gwen) and often must develop and exercise research skills (Brenda, Cass, Gloria, Gwen, Kirsten) and interviewing skills, drawing particularly on skills endemic to journalism (Adam, Brenda, Carolyn, Daisy, Jackie, Kelly, Maggie, Marla, May, Nidean). They collaborate (Carolyn, Corinne, Ginger, Joanne). They may have to learn new skills on their own as they go (Maggie). In recent years, writers have developed skills at integrating images and text (Adria, Ella, Jane, Joanne, Mary).

Exercising diplomacy. As they negotiate with content specialists, they at times take the position of a "diplomat" (Joe); such a position requires exhibiting patience and understanding (Gwen).

Gleaning and achieving utilitarian ends through writing. Depending upon the local culture, writers might gain some organizational autonomy through self-motivation and discipline (Gloria), and they might use writing to innovate and experiment (Gloria). They may "generate enthusiasm and public interest in an organization" (Kirsten), or they may even see themselves as "in charge of the public image" (Albert).

Teaching. Mack wrote that he enjoyed "telling stories to teach and delight," signaling the didactic element that often figures in professional writing. Lee, a full-time teacher and writing center director, tapped her perspective to enumerate a number of functions that writing serves: to learn, to explain, to aid reading, to provide information, and to explore. Her comments reflect some of the insights to be taken by professional writing theory and practice from composition, and Kelly cites teaching composition explicitly as a part of her formative experience leading to professional writing. That several of the researchers in this book held backgrounds in teaching owes in part to the fact that they were completing degrees in the teaching of writing and literature. Yet just as the researchers cited above illustrate conceptual movements from composition to workplace writing, so do other researchers forecast movements in the opposite direction: Bernie, Cass, Daisy, Ella, and Lisa, all currently professional writers, hope one day to teach. New unities that might be composed from shards from these two fields are explored in part three.

Changing careers. As writers seek to become teachers and teachers seek to become writers, several of the other researchers in this volume aim to change careers. Andrew and Lois enrolled in the MA program to resituate writing as they resituated their careers. Jackie, though certain she'd remain in "communications," would like to explore different "arenas," such as "technical writing, publishing, teaching, and advertising copywriting"; Sarah was considering embarking on a freelance career. Tess wrote of "finding her professional culture" in which she could best exercise her writing. Though it is to be expected that participants in any degree program often envision a new career, in this case the large percentage proves telling of the profession: post-Fordist "flexibility" in labor expends those workers whose skills are *apparently* the least difficult to replace. Ana's abstract is illustrative in this respect.)

What Will Writers Be?

In the introduction I briefly traced the sea change in theoretical movements and practices addressing "subjectivity" within the academy over the last three decades of the century. This change was paralleled by technological changes that reshaped the very conceptualization of writing—from activities associated mostly with printed text and its distribution to those associated with "volatile and interactive electronic text[s]" (Lanham 11). As recently as 1993, when Challie undertook her analysis of e-mail as an index of organizational climate, "writing" was still seen in our culture largely as the final printed matter that computers helped produce. Thus this archaeology reflects a particularly transitional period in U.S. cultural understandings of what writing is and what a writer does.

Given this shift, if we review the profiles of writers as represented in this chapter and imagine their counterparts of the future, we will no doubt see dramatic differences in their "formations" as writers. From earliest ages, their forays into writing will be computer-mediated, marked not only by the conceptual tools and pragmatic support that computers offer but also by the networking among writers (and readers) and the intertextuality that computers render complex and tantalizing. The cultural power of narrative that captures would-be writers will be funneled through new channels in addition to those of yore, and the learning of writing will be enhanced exponentially by extracurricular forces and presences. (Scholastic preparation will differ dramatically, too, if the forecasts of researchers in Garay and Bernhardt's *Expanding Literacies* are even remotely on target.)

The self as conceptualized in writing and as shaped through discursive forces will be subject to digitized influences. Intimate feelings, noted by researchers in this archaeology as often formed and reformed through entries into discourse, will in the future be shaped through discursive entry that can interconnect with other selves and other feelings instantly and across continents. The emotional reactions bound up in writing and the exposure that one senses through writing will be shaped and sensed quite differently. The notions of "private" writing and "public/professional" writing will most certainly change, and though digitized information and its flows will channel most of these changes, discourse will remain at the core of what is happening, regardless of the channels.

The collective work that researchers in this volume describe as the *sine qua non* of professional writing will undoubtedly develop in many, many ways. Here the sea change in national economic reorientation from high-volume to high-value still awaits widespread workplace reorganization. (Sarmiento, quoted in Hull, claims that 95 percent of U.S. companies still organize the workplace along Taylorist principles [14], and his claim is echoed by the findings of researchers in this archaeology.) The continuation of Taylorism in workplace cultures undercuts the organization's potential on a number of fronts, as noted by Johndan Johnson-Eilola:

> Taylorism, however, always falls short of its goal of completely specifying and optimizing activities. Unlike easily reproducible mechanical parts of identical properties, people bring with them a broad range of abilities, attitudes, behaviors, and social relationships that resist integration into the machine. (*Nostalgic Angels* 228)

Johnson-Eilola's metaphor of the machine was chosen not only to characterize workplace structures but also to remind us that the computer's current and future omnipresence in those structures requires compositionists and their allies finally to investigate and teach writing with heightened reflexivity as concerns subjectivities produced through machine-mediated composition.

To help professional writers resist integration into the machine—or rather, to reconfigure the status and purview of professional writers in organizations which will be compelled to change structures (and hence metaphors)—we can take steps, theoretically and pragmatically, to support the professional "class-in-formation," as John Frow would term it, of writers. Frow's term will be developed in chapter 5; I use it here to stress that because professional writers daily enact—and indeed, embody—composition tenets in organizational sites, it behooves compositionists in particular to inspect the process of formation of this class more closely. By 2006, according to the Bureau of Labor, 347,000 people will be employed as professional writers (table 2), and between 51 percent and 66 percent of them will be women, depending upon the category of professional writer (table 11). These people will represent composition tenets as we elaborate them and as we define them as inextricably related to social movements such as feminism and others.

As part of their self-assessments summarized in appendix B and frequently in class discussions, researchers in this volume mentioned skills and goals in the domain of the social. Gwen's comment that she "seeks a contribution to society" is illustrative. Yet currently these writers' possibilities for realizing this goal through professional writing proves limited, in part because reigning epistemologies of composition have colluded with Taylorized organizational structures to deny professional writers a say in the social ends of organizational authorship. I use the term "authorship" both to return to Foucault's questions about the legitimization of particular subjects' purviews within various institutionalized discourses and to recall the ways in which the "author function" has systematically established realms of discursive exclusivity, placing professional writing at the lower reaches of these realms. I recall, too, the narratological framework from the previous chapter that reminds us that every text carries an implied author responsible for the cultural norms and values undergirding it, another realm of authorship to which professional writers contribute yet from which they are usually excluded at the level of executive decisions.

Andrea Lunsford adds another important issue as we ponder the notion of "authorship" and the ways in which it has shaped our understandings of writers. She traces ways in which the theoretical critique of the sovereign author which opened the doors for imagining new modes of composing has been dramatically countered in the digital age by the appropriation of "authorship" (and the rights to ownership) by the corporate world ("Rhetoric"). In the interest of controlling (and selling) access to information and knowledge under the aegis of "intellectual property," corporate legal teams answer the question "What Is an Author?" with a resounding "us." Because composition tenets and practices during the twentieth century paved the way for sundering writing from writers and their desires, values, and goals, the fruits of such authorship customarily belong to those at the top of Taylorized hierarchies or to those for whom they serve as agents. So does the power to decide about writing's effects in local cultures and our larger culture.

Lunsford argues for advancing rhetorical theory and practice that promotes "alternative forms of agency and ways of owning that would shift the focus from owning to owning up; from rights and entitlements to responsibilities (the ability to respond) and answerability; from a sense of self as radically individual to the self always in relation" (535). To enact such rhetorical theory and practice, she continues, "Scholars of rhetoric and composition need to identify, theorize, and begin systematically practicing and teaching alternative forms of subjectivity and alternative modes of ownership" (541). Using shards from archaeologies such as this, we can begin constructing theories that will not only restore writers' rightful places in alternative modes of ownership but also investigate subjectivity based on empirical findings in workplace cultures. Part two provides lengthy documentation to such ends.

PART TWO

Research on Discursive Work in
Organizational Settings (Uncovering Shards)

3 IN FIELDWORKPLACES: RESEARCHERS' SITES OF STUDY

The foremost prospects and possibilities of auto-ethnography in anthropology at this time lie in the following: (1) the substantive and heuristic values of its diverse concepts and theories; (2) the ethical and moral issues it perpetually confronts with respect to the use of human subjects as sources of data; (3) the voices from within—the internal political affirmation of cultural diversity and autonomy for sometimes neglected populations and peoples; and (4) its potential advisory capabilities in programs of change or development.

—David Hayano, "Auto-Ethnography:
Paradigms, Problems, and Prospects"

Sometimes the starting point is the thing you're most drawn to, or [chuckling] the thing you're most repelled by [bringing laughter from the class] . . . the section of your work that you wonder about.

—Professor Margaret "Peggy" Yocom, in class, 2/15/94

When David Hayano sketched the possibilities for autoethnography in 1979, he was addressing an audience composed primarily of anthropologists. His goal, in part, was to dispel lingering positivist presumptions in anthropological thinking, which held that any member of a culture was unable to mount an "objective" account of that culture's norms, values, ways of knowing, and the like, because that culture member could not avoid being "subjective." Hayano traced the first appearance of the term "autoethnography" to a seminar in 1966 during a discussion of Jomo Kenyatta's 1938 study of his native Kikuyu people. In denying scholarly status to Kenyatta's account, positivism had joined forces with the Eurocentrism that imbued much of the early work in anthropology, which is particularly ironic in light of anthropology's methodologies aimed at surmounting ethnocentrism.

I was led to research autoethnography because of the fieldwork conducted by the researchers in this book. In 1993 I anticipated that researchers would study workplace cultures foreign to them (and so had prepared readings and prompted guest lecturers to address key issues in representations of the Other), but most researchers, that year and in the years since, chose to study their own cultures (77 percent). Their decisions were driven by pragmatism, since fieldwork requires so much time on site, yet by a stronger motive still: the desire to investigate some aspect of their writing work lives that they were most intrigued by—or most repelled by—to invoke folklorist Margaret Yocom's prompt on research beginnings. And in the current theoretical scene that has replaced positivism's supposed "objectivity" with a "positioned subjectivity" on the part of the researcher, autoethnographic projects remain as ripe with potential as they appeared to David Hayano over two decades ago.

In the realm of applied research, autoethnographic accounts of workplace writing hold advisory capabilities for programs of change or development, as will be seen throughout this book. Organizations can draw on the analyses of professional writers that identify overlaps, confluences, and barriers between writing processes and local cultural processes, as can academic writing programs that prepare writers for these jobs. These academic programs can likewise up the ante: the "substantive and heuristic values of [autoethnography's] diverse concepts and theories" can invigorate academic programs by identifying an array of cultural issues relevant to composition's epistemologies, issues that under the current-traditional paradigm are considered exterior to composing processes. Those same cultural processes and writing processes, together with their overlaps and barriers, become compelling sites of inquiry for compositionists and composers investigating the formation of the subject via discursive processes. When we take not only these processes but also the many shards turned up through archaeological work as our material for synthesis and analysis, we can enhance composition's terrain—plotted impressively in recent years as concerns race, gender, and ethnicity in subject formation—to include empirical data on professional class formation via discursive work.

In doing so, we might build upon the work in ethnic and national identity formation associated with autoethnography as it has been popularized in the discipline of English. Many readers are familiar with Mary Louise Pratt's 1991 essay "Arts of the Contact Zone," in which she used the term "autoethnography" to indicate "a text in which people undertake to describe themselves in ways that engage with representations others have made of them" (35), and in which she traced a seventeenth-century Peruvian's response to imperialist Spanish representations of native South Americans. In the case of workplace ethnographies and the composition inquiries to be sparked by them, the autoethnographies in this project describe writers in ways that engage with given representations of writing as sets of essentially formal operations and of writers as discursive functionaries. Such representations are diametrically opposed to the rich views of writing represented in the previous chapter, and one question that should compel all compositionists is that of the cultural processes and common understandings that make for such reductionist representations. Surely part of our task is to equip learning writers to do battle with these representations, at the very least, and in better-case scenarios to dismantle the epistemologies undergirding them in our academic programs and curricula.

Less familiar than Pratt's account of autoethnography among those in the discipline of English is that of Françoise Lionnet, who used the term "autoethnography" to describe Zora Neale Hurston's autobiography *Dust Tracks on the Road,* because this text defined, by Lionnet's accounting, Hurston's "subjective ethnicity" (383). Hurston was a colorful figure, accomplished in both anthropological research (she studied under Franz Boas) and fiction (*Their Eyes Were Watching God,* first published in 1937, was reprinted in 1987 and now figures on countless literature reading lists), who often melded these two discursive traditions in her writing, and who, in bell hooks's estimation "broke new ground by pushing anthropological work across boundaries, giving it a place in mass culture, taking it back to the same space from which African-American folklore had emerged" (143).

Against the profiles of writers in chapter 2, Hurston's writerly identity proves tantalizing. Like Hurston, many of these professional writers are engaged in writing fiction or creative nonfiction, impelled by the strong bonds between writing and narrative that our larger culture promotes, and like Hurston, many of them are equally driven by a desire to intervene in social spheres via the instrument of their writing. Unlike Hurston, their research in this project has to do less with "subjective ethnicity" and more with something akin to "subjective work identity," if we take the term "subjective" not as the opposite of "objective" but rather as an update on this obfuscatory term. In the pages that follow are shards on workplace writing identities, establishing an initial inventory of writing practices and writers' positions in organizations. As we ponder these shards, we can begin to see the value of construing work sites as fieldwork sites and writers as producers of knowledge on the imbrication of writing processes and cultural processes.

This initial inventory is based on appendix C, "Writers' Work and Positions by Nature of Organization," which displays sites of research in four categories: private businesses and corporations, government agencies and institutions, professional associations and societies, and educational and nonprofit institutions. As an inventory of sites, this chapter thus provides baseline data on the array of professional writing positions that these particular researchers depicted in their analyses. In many cases, writers' positions in and of themselves were not the foci for researchers' ethnographies; rather, other topics and themes became foci, with writers' specific tasks and organizational positions situated as part of the workplace within which local cultural processes took form. This inventory alone might serve professional writers and scholars of workplace writing as they reflect on their own circumstances against the array provided here and any individual examples that might resonate with personal experience. Shorthand entries such as "writing" or "editing" collapse a host of skills and knowledges, as is demonstrated in chapters 4 and 5. Yet even these shorthand entries imply larger complexities as one scans each table from site to site and imagines the contrasts in discursive work as a function of audiences, purposes, and nature of the tasks. The subject position of "reporter" contrasts dramatically with that of "indexer," for example, as we imagine the discourses encountered in these respective jobs, colleagues from other professional groups with whom writers interact, and the nature of final discursive products coming from each organization.

If we consider each table for "programs of development," to invoke Hayano, these programs conceptualized at least in part to support writers in enhancing their subjective work identities as composition tenets and practices suggest, a number of reflexive practices that writers might tactically employ emerge. I have suggested a few such practices with each table by grouping certain researchers under umbrella tactics that their work suggests, presented in bullet form. Then drawing on composition tenets and practices, I have suggested some preliminary implications for future work, coded by an arrow, like this: →. Readers will no doubt discern a number of implications beyond mine; I offer them to sketch the kind of synthesizing across sites that archaeological work of this kind can promote. In many cases, the syntheses that I offer with each table anticipate discussion to come in later chapters.

Finally, the chapter concludes with reflections over all four tables, noting links between certain aspects of writers' work and organizational positions across different kinds of organizations, qualifying my own categories as the tables can be read not only with but against one another, and once again sketching topics that will be treated more fully later. In the spirit of this text conceived as an archaeology and as heeding postmodern tenets in its enactments of intersubjective research, the inventory of sites that follows is offered in the hope that it will provide readers with ideas for local applications in the classroom or the workplace, that it will prompt readers to construct readings of specific researchers on their own through the abstracts and other tables, and that through this baseline data on discursive practices and formations it will suggest possibilities for further collaboration among academics and practicing writers.

Writers' Work and Positions in Private Businesses and Corporations

Discussion of this first category of organization profits from distinguishing between small businesses and those of medium or large size. Researchers analyzing organizations of fifteen persons or less, for example, often found writers filling a "jack-of-all-trades" role as they managed document drafting, cycling, review, and publication. Yet from even the nine sites in this category, we can glean a number of discursive endeavors, inflected not only by the size of the organization but by the nature of the organization's business and the other writing professionals at work in them. Such was the case with Nancy and Ellie, as they followed the evolution of a proposal to a school district to build an addition to an existing secondary school. As a counterexample, Lois, who focused on 3-D and virtual representation in a local unit of ten in an organization of 300,000, observed high specialization in the writers' work and interpersonal dynamics shaded less by workplace intimacy and more by the interplay between organizational position and professional personas. As one scans the table, an impressive array of writing projects and subtasks takes form, their complexities faintly discernible when writers' organizational positions along with those of other professional groups are imagined.

From this initial inventory of writers' work and positions in small and large businesses, aided by researchers' abstracts, we can imagine tactics that writers and scholars of professional writing might consider further to enhance writers' subjective work identities, as follows:

Independents and Small Organizations (less than fifteen people)

- Tracking protean job duties and expectations (Ann, Nancy and Ellie)
  → *formulating log and journal entries, other self-documentation*
- Monitoring interplay between official organization position and local cultural position (Ann, Nancy and Ellie)
  → *framing journal entries; undertaking studies in organizational studies and social psychology*
- Teaching (Ann, Janice, Nidean, Sarah)
  → *teaching as an outside consultant to the organization or as a language expert teaching other culture members*
- Learning various skills in the full cycle of writing and publications processes (Ann, Chet, Mack, Nancy and Ellie, Nidean)
  → *learning to learn; conceptualizing performance as a function of other players' positions within and with respect to local culture (e.g., as when functioning as a liaison to the exterior, representing clients to a public or representing the organization to clients)*

- Finding a niche as an independent (Mack, Sarah)
  → *developing knowledge in a specialty field and remaining current; developing a clientele and maintaining or expanding it; developing skill at long-distance interaction with the local culture through points of contact*

Larger Organizations (fifteen or more people)

- Scrutinizing writing duties in the context of the larger organization (Adam, Adria, Carolyn, Lois, Mary, May, Meg, Nyck, Ravi, Starla)
  → *expanding job duties in tandem with organization dynamics*
- Juxtaposing 3-D and virtual representation (Adria, Albert, Lois)
  → *judging when and how to muster virtual representation; monitoring the interplay between face-to-face interaction and written interaction*
- Calculating self-representation as a function of both organization position and players (Leathe, Lois, May, Starla)
  → *learning the personalities of organization players; learning the local norms governing self-representation up and down the organization*
- Studying and learning organization subcultures (Adria, Carolyn, Jeff, Joanne, Joe, Lisa, May, Rex, Tess)
  → *approaching other divisions of the organization as cultures to be learned in order to coordinate work and teaching; contextualizing writing and editing teams within the larger organization*
- Developing skill in one aspect of writing and publications processes as configured by local culture (Elaine, Ella, Ginger, Jen, Jeff, Joe, Lisa, Nyck, May, Red, Rex, Starla)
  → *revisiting writing tasks that are already familiar (such as abstracting) as the demands of local organizations reconfigure them*
- Reflecting on the local organization (and division) in the national context (Adria, Carolyn, Joanne, Joe, Jeff, Leathe, Lois, Meg, Ravi, Red, Starla, Tess)
  → *knowing the history of a field of writing such as journalism within an industry such as the newspaper industry; or of an organizational entity such as communications divisions*
- Anticipating turnover (Adria, Holly, Tess)
  → *studying broad cultural trends in the workforce; preparing for new writing exigencies in the workplace of the future*
- Employing World Wide Web rhetorics (Adria, Gary, Meg)
  → *learning Web composing and linking as discursive formations and practices extending across cultures and grounded in business rhetorics*

Because the preliminary tactics as I've sketched them above are grounded in composition tenets and practices, the use of journals and logs is summoned several times. This practice in composition classrooms, usually configured as providing writers an expressive venue alongside transactional compositions, in this context holds new potential—as a tool to monitor individual parts in collective and cultural action. This potential will be borne out in later chapters and discussions of researchers' foci on self-documentation.

The suggestions for additional studies are directed towards students preparing for careers as writers, for career writers undertaking further studies, and for curriculum designers. Similarly, the observations on teaching remind us that this oft-overlooked skill is frequently employed by writers in organizational settings—from formal instruction to brief interactions over texts. One implication is that writers who have formal experience as teachers might rethink this experience in terms of professional skills and qualifications; another is that students and instructors might configure student class presentations with this future workplace subjectivity in mind. "Learning to learn" and "conceptualizing performance with respect to other players" likewise evoke course design and classroom activities, and are included here to reflect current workplace realities and anticipate realities to come in the context of the national economy, a theme rejoined in later chapters.

Developing knowledge in a specialty field speaks to active writers and students and represents another twist on writing across the curriculum, all the while reminding us that writing instruction divorced from writers' field interests might fall short of its empowering potential. Developing skill in long-distance interaction with workplace cultures anticipates writers' positions to come and emphasizes the need to develop organizational acuity as well as rhetorical and technological acuity. This organizational acuity should include the scrutiny of writers' duties in the context of the larger organization, to eschew the subject position of passive agent and to aid in conceptualizing not only writing but writing *positions* as process, too. By so doing, writers who learn the norms governing representation up and down the organization may be more politically astute in manifesting their ideological positions on organizational products and claiming their share of authority in organizational life. Representation of writers within the organization (a topic developed in chapter 7) will take many forms in the future, virtuality among these forms, which prompts writers and scholars alike to take electronic media not only as tool but also as material for inquiry in our writing instruction.

Finally, the suggestion that writers strive to locate their local organization in its umbrella national industry and to learn the histories behind this industry and/or specific organizational divisions (such as communications) is offered to bolster writers both ideologically and materially. Knowing the larger context enables writers to position themselves and fellow workers on fundamental workplace issues (as demonstrated in chapters 4 and 5), and studying the national economy and trends can help professional writers anticipate new directions for work in a high-turnover field. I have listed only three researchers as those whose work suggests this category of high turnover, but the work histories of professional writers confirm serial employment as the trend. Holly and Tess are listed because both of these researchers lost their jobs during the course of their research, driving home the reality of writers as replaceable laborers for all members of the class.

Writers' Work and Positions in Government Agencies and Institutions

Two of the most frequently cited elements of writers' work in government agencies and institutions are collaborating to produce collective reports and composing in elaborate review processes across divisions and up the hierarchy. Branden observed elaborate review and cycling of documents in the Department of Commerce as various writers collaborated to produce final reports, as did Liz in the World Bank. Other researchers noted some of the particularities in managing such composing across divisions (Gloria focused on input from several divisions in composing a letter from the Library of Congress to a citizen) and up the hierarchy (George investigated writing and reading as part of the military's "chop chain" review).

Writers in the government need knowledge of government structures and the dynamics that figure as part of them: the writers in Cass's study needed to know as much about the intricacies of government contracting as they did about the subject of the contract. For writers linked with the military (as many government writers are, directly or indirectly), familiarity with and understanding of military procedures and mind-set also seems a valuable skill, as does an understanding of political rhetoric. Amid these understandings and knowledge must figure acuity in envisioning the public as audience quite often, discerning the forms that discourse will take as it moves through many layers towards ultimate end users.

Perhaps more so than in the private sector, the work of writers and editors in government positions entails coordinating composing between headquarters and field offices. Similarly, the writing of policy and procedures proves more prevalent in writers' work, at least in this data set. Researchers identified two kinds of writers' work that surely recur in other kinds of organizations: writing in the mundane forms to sustain daily office functioning (Gwen spoke of purchase orders and administrative renewals) and composing on the World Wide Web.

Some syntheses across these sites and some preliminary tactics for other writers and scholars based on these positions and writers' work are the following:

- Collaborating to produce collective reports (Anita, Branden, Liz)
  → *tracking contributions of others and of oneself; learning collaborative production skills such as group maintenance*
- Composing in elaborate review processes across divisions and up and down the hierarchy (Ana, Branden, Cass, George, Gloria, Jane, Kali, Liz, Rachel)
  → *tracking contributions; learning local chains of command and persons occupying positions; incorporating reader-response theory into composing processes for writers in the chain*
- Contending with political discourse (Kolar, Leigh)
  → *studying political discourse rhetorically for the ways in which it positions senders and receivers of messages; studying this rhetoric against backdrop of specific organizational cultures*
- Envisioning the public as audience (Branden, Gloria, Jane, Ray)
  → *charting the routing of documents as they move from inception to ultimate readers; reading documents for the politics that shaped them, perhaps by tracing successive drafts; informing conceptualization of this kind of composing through research in technical writing on user advocacy*
- Coordinating composing between centers of power and the periphery (Helen, Sue)
  → *studying the flow of information between headquarters and field offices for the ways in which it reproduces and changes local culture*
- Composing and being subject to policy-and-procedures writing (Brenda, Ray)
  → *studying policy-and-procedures writing as a genre, not only learning forms and conventions but also discerning cultural norms and values*
- Composing writing that sustains office functioning (Gwen)
  → *developing organizational knowledge through the cultural spot-analysis that these tasks permit*
- Employing World Wide Web rhetorics (Albert)
  → *learning Web composing and connecting as discursive formations and practices extending across cultures*

Several of the preliminary implications listed above with each point resonate with implications drawn for writers currently working or envisioning work in private businesses and corporations. Tracking contributions by oneself and others to collectively authored reports clearly dovetails with the suggestion made in the previous section for tracking protean job duties through journals or logs. Learning local chains of command not just from the perspective of position in these chains but also from the perspective of these chains as displaying aspects of organizational culture can enable writers to improve their writing and perhaps improve the local culture: the suggestion to incorporate reader response theory into composing and review processes comes from George's own suggestions in his study of ghostwriting in the military (discussed at length in our coauthored essay "Workplace Ghostwriting").

Writers who envision government writing positions surely will want to study political discourse, to render themselves more astute when composing within this discourse, whether to realize personal goals within the organization (as in the cases of cabinet speechwriters in Leigh's study) or to take stock of their own reluctance to justify dubious composing practices by final results (as in Kolar's study of Senate press office writers fabricating letters from constituents). Similarly, these writers will want to study composing for an audience that is often the public, distanced from composers through layers and levels of collective authorship. This is no small topic, requiring background reading in case studies or archival work in specific organizations that traces the evolution of documents as shaped by political forces. To inform this topic has come recent theory and research on writers as end-user advocates (Sullivan and Porter; Slack, Miller, and Doak).

As coordinators of composing between headquarters and field offices, writers and editors might want to note that their work serves not only document production but also cultural production and reproduction, a topic rejoined in chapters 5 and 8. Similarly, writers in organizations are always implicated by policies and procedures that discursively define aspects of the local culture and subjectivities within it, suggesting that writers envisioning work in any organization study this genre at some point.

Finally, like many other classes of professionals, writers may perform a number of mundane writing tasks to serve office functioning. In such organizational positions, writers might use these tasks to inform themselves more fully on structures and players in the local organizational culture. Web composing, too, will probably eventually fall into the category of mundane tasks, yet writers and aspiring writers now will do well to study the rhetorics of the Web as they evolve, affecting not only individual writers and their local culture but subjectivities wrought by our larger culture, too.

Writers' Work and Positions in Professional Associations and Societies

Writers and editors in associations and societies are invariably located in communications divisions or media relations departments, which underscores parallels with writers in the organizations previously reviewed. In contrast to writers in such divisions and departments in the private sector and in many government positions, though, writers' work lives in associations generally seem more constrained. Because the *raison d'être* of these organizations is narrowly configured (they exist solely to inform their constituents and to lobby Congress) and because frequently the decision-making staff in these organizations are comprised of people with experience in the specific industry, writers and editors are usually occupied with coordinating and manipulating other people's texts. Writers have few occasions to initiate and actualize projects of their own (Jackie and Kyle being the exceptions in this data set), and writing cultures often position their discourse workers as functionaries at the association's service (a topic addressed in chapters 4 and 5). This said, a synthesis of positions and writers' work with implications for other writers and scholars is as follows:

- Editing and composing monthly informational updates and topical articles (in the genres of newsletter or association magazine) for a clearly defined audience (Bernie, Brenda, Heather, Itsy, Jackie, Jan, Karla, Kirsten, Kyle, Lena, Mandy)
  → *developing research skills on specific industry topics and monitoring broader cultural events for their implications; learning publishing within monthly deadlines*
- Editing brochures and books marketed to constituents (Diane) or the public (Corinne)
  → *honing editing skills in a narrowly defined niche by interpreting editorial decisions in light of past publications and current membership demographics; embodying a personage or cultural values in public relations materials*
- Reviewing, selecting, and editing contributions from constituents for publication in association magazine (Bernie, Brenda, Kirsten, Kyle, Lena)

→ *studying the industry and the constituency to discern most important topics and treatment of them; elaborating organizational purview somewhat through these skills*

- Working in a communications division in an organization whose sole function is to lobby Congress (Bernie, Jan)
  → *honing skills in editing, studying the history of the industry, learning as many skills as possible*
- Doing the graphics work for association publications (Challie)
  → *learning desktop publishing in as many platforms as possible; studying the interrelationships between text and visuals*
- Using e-mail to coordinate projects (Challie, Jackie, Kirsten)
  → *developing judgment in e-mail use; reading e-mail not only as informational but also as a reflection of the culture*

Perhaps because researchers in the Cultures of Professional Writing course have cast their own employment with associations as short-term, many of the implications drawn above suggest using the organizational position to develop as much transportable skill and knowledge as possible. To that end writers might seize the opportunities presented by the organization and educate themselves in publishing along monthly deadlines. Similarly, even if writers and editors do not envision long-term work with the same industry, they might want to develop research skills on industry topics that would transfer. Work on book projects produced by an association would present a similar opportunity and from a perspective that many publishers do not enjoy: a ready-made market with demographic information on that market easily at hand.

As for coordinating submissions from constituents for publication in the organization magazine, similar implications have been drawn: by studying the industry and constituency to discern most topical issues, editors develop a skill they can take elsewhere. This position of coordinating manuscripts from the field clearly parallels that held by Helen and discussed in the previous section. Just as Helen might construe editing as producing and reproducing culture, so might editors so engaged in associations, even though their say in this shaping probably is less.

Challie stands as a bit of an anomaly in this data set, since she worked as graphics expert in her association rather than as writer or editor. Yet when her position is considered alongside earlier implications for writers to accumulate diverse skills in organizational authorship, it encourages the learning of desktop publishing in many platforms and studying document design theory and research particularly for the insights on relationships between text and images. (Challie's focus in her research was on e-mail as an index of local culture and is discussed at greater length in chapter 5. Using e-mail to coordinate projects, now a workplace commonplace, was only beginning to take hold in 1993. Its currency today reflects just one rapid transformation of writing processes as imbricated with cultural processes.).

As final exceptions that perhaps confirm the rule, the work of Jackie and Kyle as editors for association magazines was by their accounts challenging and provocative. Kyle's was filled with opportunities to initiate and carry through his own projects, including composing imaginative and entertaining articles on industry issues. He admitted in individual conference that part of his creativity came from using an otherwise chaotic local culture with high turnover to stoke his creativity, as discussed in chapter 5. Jackie addressed in her ethnography the tugs she felt from her training as a journalist as she edited an association magazine and weighed content for its newsworthiness as compared with promotional discourse. Such tugs between various discursive traditions and writers' organizational mandates are addressed at greater length in chapters 4 and 5.

Writers' Work and Positions in Educational and Nonprofit Institutions

In a sense, this category of sites draws together the most heterogenous writing activities: teachers currently working in classrooms or writing centers, writing with and to students, to parents, and to administration; administrators writing both to represent their unit up the hierarchy and to collaborate in governance within the hierarchy; professional writers engaged in representing the institution to various audiences, through a variety of publications; writing scholars corresponding with one another in a virtual culture; and staff engaged in the daily running of support offices in an educational institution or a nonprofit institution. In the case of teachers, this research offered the occasion to step back from their day-to-day work with students and inspect their writing and other aspects of communication within local cultures whose primary mission is education. Other researchers looked at subcultures such as a publications office or university relations department that bear close resemblance to writing cultures in the private domain. Teachers' ethnographies spark us to renew our understandings of educators' work as it represents another form of "professional writing," and researchers in publications offices and the like prompt us to consider subtle differences in writers' work and positions in these locations compared with work in the private sphere. A synthesis of positions and work across all sites, with implications for tactics, yields the following:

- Representing the organization to former members and prospective members (Hart, Kelly), or to members and nonmembers (Alice, Andrew, Emma, Kelly, Lara, Marla, Megan)
  → *developing skills in interpreting demographics as part of audience considerations; developing skills at appealing to multiple audiences simultaneously; using serially multiple audiences to inform reflexivity*
- Documenting and representing a unit's work to vie for money and support for development (Lee, Megan)
  → *developing acuity simultaneously in local organizational politics and in national theoretical and pragmatic trends; representing work up the hierarchy; studying the "genres" of solicitation and acknowledgment*
- Communicating with extraorganizational educators in a virtual culture (Jillian)
  → *infusing local cultural knowledge with knowledge culled from a national and virtual culture*
- Administering governance of the organization (Tom)
  → *managing representations and documentation across the culture and up and down cultural hierarchies*
- Composing writing that sustains office and organization functioning (Emma, Phoebe)
  → *developing organizational knowledge through the cultural spot-analysis that these tasks permit*
- Teaching writing (Alice, Anne, Julie, Kate, Marla)
  → *discerning parallels between teaching formally as an occupation and teaching informally as a professional writer; alternatively, for teachers, devising shifts in practices when one's work is construed as professional writing*

Like writers in associations and societies, writers in these educational and nonprofit institutions who represent the institutions to various audiences need to develop skills at interpreting demographics to appeal to multiple audiences, simultaneously or serially. One imagines course design in classroom contexts that incorporates composing exercises attempting such audience appeals. professional writers might review their own portfolios with this aspect in mind as it constitutes a valuable yet easily overlooked skill. (During her research, Megan conducted archival research on rhetoricians' analyses of "vague discourse.") For practicing teachers, the appeals that they make serially to their students, students' parents, and administration might be used as source in sketching some discursive features of the local culture, to be used for renewal and development, culturally and individually.

Perhaps more so than their counterparts in the three kinds of sites mentioned earlier, educators vying for funds and support in their organizations often have little experience or guidance in accomplishing this task within their local cultures. Developing acuity in local organizational politics clearly is required, and keeping abreast of national trends provides warranting for projects. (Dialogue with extraorganizational educators via virtual culture appears a powerful and promising practice to aid such work.) Like their counterparts in the other kinds of sites, writers in these educational and nonprofit settings also engage regularly in the mundane writing of office management, but unlike their counterparts these writers may engage in governance of the organization. In this data set only one researcher (Tom) studied this aspect of writers' work, in his case tracing the subtle shifts in the wording of a memo composed by the college senate president when addressed up or across the hierarchy. Tom (like his classmate Phoebe who focused on writers' memos in a nonprofit) was surprised at the lack of experience evidenced in the memos he studied, which will probably resonate with college educators who must learn administrative and hierarchical writing on the job with no prior training. One might review curricula in rhetoric and composition, and other fields, with this in mind.

Finally, construing educators' writing to students, colleagues, parents, and other audiences as forms of professional writing suggests once again the potential that lies in formally articulating hidden skills and knowledge that teachers as writers bring to bear on writing projects; professional writers in other spheres might study teachers' writing for local applications. For teachers who envision a lifelong career in the profession, reconsidering one's work as professional writing can perhaps lend new perspective on one's individual practice as circumscribed by the local culture of the school.

Writers' Work, Fieldwork, and Subjective Work Identities: Syntheses from Shards

This inventory of writers' work and positions in eighty-three organizations enables some preliminary syntheses across the data set. For professional writers, writing projects are almost always collaborative, engaging coworkers from other professional classes, entailing multiple reviews, and often targeting multiple (and sequential) audiences (which might include themselves as citizens), fraught with second-guessing on issues of organizational representation above and beyond a document's ostensible "content," requiring interpretations of organizational cultures to the ends of adequately and appropriately delivering discursive products. On the job, writers may find themselves the lone "writer" in the organization, they may work in teams of like-minded writers and editors, they may find themselves in organizations as populous as big cities, or they may figure as communications emissaries to other divisions, which are inevitably shaded by an organization's history and an industry's history. Their work may be highly constrained in its representational dimensions; in many cases this work could constitute an ongoing portfolio of discursive skills and knowledge that are subject to updating in a high-turnover profession that requires ever-increasing knowledge of software platforms and digital rhetorics connected with writers' work. Unlike their colleagues from other professions, though, writers enter the workforce with precious little preparation for such arenas and few tactics for defending and enhancing their professional status in manners similar to other professions. And as long as popular conceptions of writing as purely formal and writers as discursive functionaries who do not contribute to the content of an organization's deliverables prevail, writers' lots are not likely to change.

One way to envision change, to reconfigure popular understanding of writing in ways commensurate with recent theories of discourse and subject formation, to unleash the potential of writing for organizations, their constituents, and their audiences, is to conceptualize *all* discursive work sites as potential fieldworkplaces. To deconstruct reductionist understandings of writing wrought by composition's past epistemologies, we can begin with the simple precept that because writing constitutes as well as reflects realities, writers' work must entail reflexivity on the whys and wherefores of such constitution—as we talk about writers' work and as we teach writers even the rudiments.

As we draw on scholarly fields and disciplines to aid us in reconfiguring misunderstandings of writing, ethnography is undeniably a primary source, as is folklore. Particularly promising in folklore is its long-standing object of study—the lore of folks—which in subjective work identities always figures strongly. Indeed, so much academic research on organizational culture seeks to render visible the invisible knowledges that circulate informally among workers. Also promising is folklore's embracing of reflexivity in fieldwork methodology: Professor Yocom's comment in the chapter epigraph might at first blush appear whimsical, yet she pits her felt sense of attractive or repelling phenomena against rigorous fieldwork methodology in order to produce knowledge of those phenomena which holds sway in both social science circles and in English circles. Like Zora Neale Hurston, she melds discursive practices from these two fields to produce representations adequate to her site, her respondents, her self, and her professional discipline of folklore. Not only does such an approach, through its open acknowledgment of the researcher's inevitable part in research, reinforce the principle of positioned subjectivity as a methodological touchstone, it also frees one to address conditions of work that might not have appeared valid topics within a positivist framing of research and writing.

The professional writers represented in this book take to folklore's questions and methods quite easily, and many who have read Hurston's fiction, moreover, are delighted to encounter her in another discursive realm. Ultimately, this resonance may presage more than individual empowerment, if indeed writers and their academic collaborators can begin construing writing workplaces as fieldworkplaces. For even as the reflexivity learned and exercised as part of such fieldwork may inform programs of change and development, so this reflexivity may lead further, to broader questions of subjective work identity. Writing on the future of folklore and the questions remaining for this field to confront, Barbara Kirshenblatt-Gimblett says, "what colonialism is to the history of anthropology, nationalism is to the study of folklore" (143). Because professional writers are a class of workers made possible by specific composition epistemologies that dovetailed with national economic formation, as argued in the introduction and chapter 2, these writers (and scholars in their fields) may ultimately have to confront the ways in which the writing of workplace cultures continues to sustain forms of nationalism that in an ever-shrinking digitized world prove counterproductive. But that confrontation will lie somewhere down the road, once writers have been empowered as a professional class by virtue of their understandings of cultural production via writing in organizational sites.

In the meantime, a formidable task lies before writers and scholars learning from their work: to bring academic understandings of subjectivity and lived workplace realities together for a greater understanding of subjective work identities. Says Patti Lather: "a discursive focus on networks of practices which constitute subjects in shifting, multiple, contradicting sites constructs a more complex understanding of identity and citizenship" (42). The shifting and multiple sites that constitute writing subjects in workplace cultures can speak volumes about writerly identities and writers' purviews as citizens within organizational contexts. The next chapter presents shards in this sector of the dig.

4 ORGANIZATIONAL FEATURES OF WORKPLACE WRITING CULTURES

Although we might want to be cautious in recognizing it as such, the corporation, certainly the organization, has become the major arena for public life for the individual in modern Western civilization.

—Mary Beth Debs, "Corporate Authority"

It is remarkable how little most of us understand the relationship between power, knowledge, and organizations. It is time that we give up the faith that the goal of communication is always clarity and brevity. In practice, the politics of organizations and organizational politics have as their goals limiting, obscuring, or hiding information.

—Jennifer Daryl Slack, David James Miller, and Jeffrey Doak, "The Technical Communicator as Author"

Thus we all seem like fish swimming in a corporate sea full of bits and pieces of jumbled information floating all around us. But the actual snagging of those snippets of information is not easy and frequently involves asking a lot of questions and attempting to make deductions based on observations.

—Starla, final ethnography

Mary Beth Debs's 1993 caution in recognizing organizations as the major arena for public life for the individual seems increasingly unneeded with each passing year, as technological processes accelerate cultural processes in ways that bypass collective public scrutiny of years past (Virilio) and as student subjectivities, formerly lived prior to and fairly discrete from work lives, become increasingly protracted and integrated into the requirements for workplace performance at functionary and even middle-management echelons. Because workers must augment the qualifications bestowed by earlier schooling—whether at the high school, baccalaureate, or even postgraduate levels—those at the lower levels of organizational charts find less and less time for the public lives associated with earlier models of citizenry, even as many of the organizations employing them exercise more and more influence on the polity's leisure and civic purview through the lobbying that drives political policy. This situation argues from yet another perspective for the value of autoethnographic work in writers' workplace cultures, since such work might support collective action within the organization or at the very least render individual writers more conscious of their real purview (as contrasted with that indicated on an organization chart) in these major arenas for public life.

The comments of scholars Slack, Miller, and Doak echo inquiry from many sectors of the humanities aimed implicitly at enriching the analysis of work-life subjectivities, in their case by a focus on authorship in the cultural and sociological planes and on so-called instrumental discourse as it constitutes local realities, which are otherwise inflected by power and knowledge articulated to diverse agendas and agents. To explore the workings of these agendas and agents in organizational arenas, the *petits recits* such as Starla provides prove valuable as empirical records against which to balance claims from theoretical realms and to imagine strategies in the light of them. Strategies for writing scholars and practicing writers collaborating with them are developed fully in part three; in this chapter they remain purposely inchoate so that readers might ponder the shards herein according to their own theoretical bents and pragmatic needs.

At the same time, the chapter builds on the archaeological inventory of writers' positions and work provided in chapter 3: the "given" nature of workplace writing cultures provided by the earlier inventory are in this chapter problematized by analyzing the imbrication of organizational processes and writing processes. The bases for this analysis are the themes and topics explored by researchers in their workplace writing ethnographies. For most of these researchers, this occasion to document and analyze their workplace cultures—armed with the methodological tools to mount such an analysis and a forum of like-minded practicing writers—was a novel experience that provided them with the first occasion to take stock of the organizational structures and processes among which they worked. The themes and topics they explored were many, as indicated in appendix B and implied in the abstracts in appendix D. In this chapter I have drawn on the full ethnographies and class discussions of them to mount a database of organizational features explored by researchers. This database is represented by lists in each of the following sections, which group themes and topics under umbrella headings. Classifying researchers' work has been an arduous task, since their analyses invariably developed topics and themes in varying degrees and with frequent navigating between organizational issues and discursive issues. I have tried to be faithful to what seemed to be researchers' primary intentions, based not only on their written ethnographies but also on class discussions and individual conferences. In some cases these intentions seemed to be several and hence certain researchers appear in more than one category.

From the perspective of readers' usability, I see this multiple categorization as a boon, since it offers additional shards of researchers' work in this collective dig, allowing a fuller representation of each researcher to take form for readers and, hopefully, prompting more connections with other local cultures. Connections between empirical data and theory, and among writing cultures, can equip practicing writers and collaborating scholars with the grounding for something akin to "cognitive mapping" as suggested by Fredric Jameson, in which a subject's specific local, historic, and economic circumstances are linked to more global professional class structures in which he or she is implicated (415–16), thus offsetting the limited capacities for effecting change grounded *only* in the *petits recits*. From the organizational features explored in this chapter, we can begin mapping at the very least some recurrent dynamics between individual writers and organizations, dynamics of collective procedures and writing, and writers' practices with respect to organizational goals. To aid this mapping, I have summarized trends and patterns for each of the following sections. In the conclusion to the chapter, these trends and patterns are synthesized for the inquiries they suggest and for development in later chapters.

Dynamics Between the Individual and the Organization

This category arose because many researchers crafted ethnographies around their own work or another individual's work they observed against the backdrop of organizational structures or practices. Ethnographies of this kind tended to focus on writers themselves in a local cultural context as opposed to those analyses that focused on whole document processes or broader cultural dynamics and the ways that discursive work interrelated with these dynamics or with ultimate organizational goals. The fact that several researchers appear in more than one category underscores the ways in which their development of a particular topic would introduce new themes, which in turn might suggest a new topic, etc. Readers may want to consult this section in tandem with chapter 3, "In Fieldworkplaces," since many of the organizational positions and work of writers represented there connect explicitly with this section. As is immediately clear upon scanning the table, moreover, this section has implications for writers' expertise in organizational authorship, suggesting curriculum design and course work in preparation for it; these implications are addressed in part three.

Writers' Skills

As all professional writers know, the skills they put to use in their daily discursive work often far outstrip their representation in job titles. Perhaps because researching professional writing as part and parcel of a local culture prompts a complex understanding of individual talents such as "skills," topics and themes in researchers' ethnographies revealed a number of aspects of writing skills that illustrate facets of day-to-day workplace subjectivities, as illustrated by the following list:

Writers' Skills	Researcher
captioning	Rex
coding entries	Norma
composing vague discourse	Megan
constructing and maintaining World Wide Web pages	Adria, Albert, Gary, Leathe, Meg
converting data to narrative	Leathe, Nancy and Ellie
developing professionally through tasks	Adria, Gloria, Joanne, Red
designing documents	Adria, Nidean
editing engineers' proposals	Jeff
enforcing formats and standards	Kirsten, Sue
fabricating letters	Kolar
finding and sustaining a niche as freelancer	Sarah
framing questions to authors as editor	Helen, Kyle
gaining clients	Janice, Ravi, Sarah
learning organization history . . . as manuscript coordinator	Grace
. . . as organization history writer	Elaine
mastering jargon ("Bankese")	Liz
mining metaphors	Leigh
self-documenting	Gwen, Meg, Ray
teaching writing as writing center tutor	Kate
using organization culture to stoke creativity	Kyle

Leigh developed a theme of "mining metaphors" when she shadowed a cabinet speechwriter drawing metaphors systematically from the current secretary's past, from the administration's positions on relevant issues, and from popular discourse, then assembling these metaphors within conventions appropriate to the occasion of the speech. Megan analyzed the parameters of "vague discourse" in memoranda of agreement between a university foundation and its donors as these agreements enabled the disbursing of funds with a flexibility deemed appropriate by both parties. Gloria's theme of professional development noted how librarian researchers often used assignments to broaden their expertise, providing the individual with varied work and the organization with ever-developing employees, thus tracing a provocative interplay between local culture and culture members' subjectivities within the larger topic of representing the library through correspondence. Both Helen and Kyle sketched themes of organizational culture influencing the ways that editors framed their discussions with authors, and Grace similarly recognized the organizational culture's history holding import for her discussions with authors as manuscript coordinator. Kyle spoke of using the at-times-chaotic local culture to his own ends to stoke playfulness and creativity.

If these and the other entries in this table are synthesized to draw observations on recurrent subjectivities lived by writers while honing skills in organizational authorship, one recognizes (at least) the following issues:

- When converting data to narrative and when narrating in other specialized writing tasks such as captioning, letter writing, and the like, writers compose implied authors who embody cultural norms and values, with these writers' subjectivities bound up in these norms and values as they compose.
- Working with other people's metaphors and with multiple contingencies in producing writing in a specialized genre (such as a speech) may require a suspension of personal values in the service of the organization.
- Contrary to stock admonitions in prescriptive composition tenets, writers at times must compose vague discourse to render their documents most effective.
- Self-documentation is a writing skill to be developed like others. Integrating it into other writing projects can help writers develop acuity in this form of self-representation; using self-documentation enables one to track development and acquisition of new skills and knowledge within any given culture.
- Editing can be construed as cultural renewal and/or reproduction, a practice with more far-reaching implications than generally acknowledged.
- Just as the organization employs writers, so may writers employ the organizational culture, if they are astute in positioning themselves mentally and psychologically with respect to the culture.

Writers' Status

Issues of status that arose in some ethnographies had solely to do with contractual circumstances; for example, a speechwriter working for the government having civil servant status, or government workers occupying grade levels concordant with qualifications and reflected in salaries. Other issues of status had less to do with terms of contract and more to do with the organization's mission and *raison d'être,* reflected in structures and chains of command that position writers as discursive functionaries, as in the case of the association writers discussed in chapter 3. Yet even though such status is determined primarily by the principal function of the organization, it calls attention nonetheless to the conceptualization of writers' expertise as having to do solely with form, a trend recurrent across the following observations on organizational status:

Writers' Status	Researcher
apprentice	Ann
civil servant	Leigh
functionary	Diane, Jan, Karla, Mandy
effective status less than official organization status	May
employee for management	Jan, Red
ghost	George Kolar, Leigh
nebulous organization status	Anita, Heather, Nyck
second-class organization member	Ana, Bernie, Rachel
status shaded by government grade levels	Gwen, Jane, Liz
status time-limited unless move to management	Lena
support staff	Carolyn, Ella, Ginger, Jeff, Liz
tenuous status, depending upon contracts	Ana, Kali

This epistemological link becomes more evident when the theme of status is raised by a writer or editor in an organization other than a trade association, as in the case of Jeff, a technical editor in an environmental engineering firm. This theme of status has clear implications for reconfiguring writing curricula and making explicit to writers the theory underpinning reconfigurations, and is developed in chapter 8.

A third theme of status has implications for writers' own direct interventions on behalf of themselves in the workplace: the theme of official organizational status. May developed this theme by noting her effective status as inferior to organization chart status; Anita discussed her civil status as a contractor to a government entity; Heather and Nyck developed the theme in discussions of various writers' nebulous status altogether within the organization. In May's case, her research led to a resolve to be more savvy in future job interviews and to attempt to make her organization purview an explicit part of the contract. In Nyck's case it led to his drafting several job descriptions that were adopted by his organization. In Heather's case, she found employment in another organization.

In recent years researchers have also focused on the increasingly tenuous status of writers in organizations. Ana noted that her tenuous status hinged on her position as a technical writer (which, she noted ironically, entailed learning the technologies and needs of clients) while middle managers (who did not learn technologies and needs) were more secure. Kali sketched a Kafkaesque scenario of hirings and firings as a function of labyrinthine accounting practices in government contracts (which is developed in chapter 8's discussion of interventions) and Lena noted that in the organization she studied, writers could not be promoted above a certain level unless they moved into management positions.

A synthesis of the themes of status developed in researchers' ethnographies yields at least the following observations on writers' subjectivities:

- The functionary status is clearly unrewarding—writers might think of it as temporary, using the job to learn as many skills and gain as much knowledge as possible in order to move to a better culture. Alternatively, writers might request special training sponsored by the organization to keep publications, processes, and products current while enhancing writers' skills.
- Discrepancy between official organization status and real purview, or nebulous organization status altogether, ultimately undercuts organization projects. Writers and their collaborators should work to demonstrate this to organizational superiors so as to negotiate guarantees of solid authority and attendant remuneration.
- Writers' tenuous status within organizations is only becoming increasingly tenuous as post-Fordist tenets of "flexibility" take hold in organizational management. Writers and their collaborators will need clout to counter this trend, as discussed in part three.

Writers' Roles

Writers' roles in organizational authorship ranged from the apparently idiosyncratic to roles that would seem to obtain more systematically in workplace cultures, as shown in the following list:

Writers' Roles	Researcher
daughter in family	Nancy and Ellie
talking handbook	Adria, Joe, Ravi
team members	Chet, Ella, Jackie, Jeff, Joanne, Joe, Kelly, Kirsten, Leathe, Mary
tutee	Ann
idea generator	Leigh
information gatherers	Daisy, Nyck, Red
liaison to exterior	Starla
roles self-elaborated through review process	Brenda
translator	Leathe

Ann found herself frequently cast in the role of "tutee" in the four-person PR firm where she worked. Ellie's role as "daughter" in her five-person firm is similarly incidental, though one suspects that in small businesses a certain family dynamic may subtly shape lived subjectivities. As a counterexample to these two, Brenda observed editors elaborating organizational roles for themselves via the review process. Other roles, as in the case of Adria, Joe, and Ravi, who occasionally occupied the role of talking handbook to their coworkers, are clearly linked with limiting conceptions of writing and writers.

The role of "idea generator," a theme in Leigh's ethnography of speechwriters, identifies a workplace subjectivity that employs certain writing processes frequently associated with the planning stages and lodging these processes in explicit and multiple sources determined by the organization. The role of team member signals subjectivity within small groups (as in the writing and editing teams of which Chet, Ella, Jackie, Jeff, Joanne, Joe, Kelly, Kirsten, and Mary were a part) while alerting us to the ways in which team-member roles are likewise mitigated by the team's life in the larger local culture (as Kelly depicted it in her study of the shift to team projects in a publications office). Finally, the roles of "information gatherer" and "liaison to the exterior" call attention to a subjectivity that is simultaneously inward- and outward-looking with respect to the local culture, positioning the professional writer and work at a nexus with extracultural values and norms. (Scholarship on professional writers' user-advocacy role pertinent to this role is developed in part three.)

A synthesis yields the following:

- Even though certain roles for writers in organizations may emerge as incidental (e.g., as tutee, or as daughter), writers might be vigilant for the ways in which these roles inflect roles as writers: discerning inflections may allow writers to understand those parts of learning that are context-dependent and more in the service of the organization than the writer, or to keep incidental roles such as family member from overly influencing professional roles such as technical writer.
- Writers might attend to organizational processes (such as document review) that allow them to elaborate certain of their own roles.
- The subjectivity of "talking handbook" is likely to endure as long as do archaic conceptualizations of writing as purely formal;

collaboration between academics and practicing writers can help change these conceptualizations.

• Roles such as "idea generator" suggest a revisiting of cognitive process models to situate activities such as brainstorming and nutshelling not only as they spark initial ideas for writing but also as they can help *locate* these ideas within the local culture, as part of organizational projects and in the embodiment of the culture through written documents.

• The shapes and roles of teams in organizations are certain to diversify in the future, as teams take form temporarily around specific projects and as members of teams such as editing teams assume the role of envoy to subject-matter teams. Writers and curriculum designers should account for these various forms of subjectivity in writing research.

• Writers' roles as links to the exterior underscore yet again the need for writers and for writing curricula to emphasize study of larger cultural processes.

Dynamics of Collective Procedures and Writing

In contrast to the themes that focused on an individual writer's skills, roles, or status within the organizational culture are those themes that focused more on collective procedures per se, as these procedures became manifest in document processing, as procedures were inflected by subcultural dynamics, and as procedures worked to stabilize or in some cases change local cultural practices. Here again, researchers often appear in more than one category due to the number of different themes and topics broached within any given ethnography.

Document Processes

A flowchart of document processes tracing organizational publications as they move from inception through review and to final publication might document standard routing, but it could never document the intricacies of the publication's interrelationship with organizational players and policies along the way, as the themes and topics developed by researchers in this section make clear. Those themes and topics developing the intricacies of document processes are united in the following list:

Document Processing	Researcher
chain of writing and editing	Daisy, Red
"chop chain" review	George
cycles and boilerplating in proposals	Nancy and Ellie
deadlines!	Chet, Daisy, Jane, Kelly, Kyle, Leigh, Maggie, Mary, Red
decisions and authority in newsletter publication	Holly
editorial board intervention in newsletter publication	Karla
information flow vs. document process flow	Carolyn, Starla
managing documentation	Adria, Ella, Joanne
manuscript review entirely on Post-its	Brenda
personal credit for collective production	Ana, Branden
production teams in publications office	Kelly
review and dissemination system	Jackie, Kirsten, Sue
speech writing as "idea factory"	Leigh
turnaround between editors and authors	Grace, Helen, Jackie, Kyle, Lena, Maggie, Sarah
waste in review and publication processes	Mandy

In small niche organizations, document processes may become highly repetitive, perhaps inuring writers to wrinkles and possibilities for innovation or even to the covert roles that they play in authorship— as Nancy and Ellie concluded when they recognized Ellie's role in revising boilerplate used in proposals. In larger organizations, the disparity between real information flow and the information necessary to assure efficient and effective document flow may at times be enormous —as Starla discovered when she tracked a press release through its many revisions and keyed each revision to critical information from specific organizational players. Document processes are ultimately bound up in complex collective procedures, which can obscure agency and dampen individual credit, and which can be used by organizational players for personal benefit: Ana noted a middle manager's insistence on being included in a review process to which he could add nothing yet from which he could garner budgeting; Branden observed a government writer co-opting credit for ideas of collective origin; Mandy observed managers attempting to push through unauthorized publications to further their careers; Holly observed occasional mayhem in publication production spawned in part by players' organizational battles and in part by high turnover that yielded hazy organizational memory.

This category underscores the interplay between organizational knowledge (and memory) and the document publications (and processes supporting them) that often represent the organization to the exterior or to its culture members. In some cultures document production includes strong surveillance of representations, as in the high-security cultures of the military (part of Sue's job consisted of combing each document leaving her division) or high-control cultures such as associations (class participants with experience in newsletter publication were amazed to learn from Karla that an *editorial board* at her trade association held meetings for each issue). This surveillance may be teamed with disciplining culture members, as George maintained upon investigating his cowriters' attitudes as inflected by the chop-chain military document review, where superiors up the hierarchy "chop" material from the original prose. In any case, publication processes frequently cut across divisions, implicating at the very least players within operations divisions and communications divisions, which might include a subdivision dealing with graphics and publications platforms. These processes are frequently hierarchical, too, whence surveillance (and whence, as George's research demonstrates, ultimate prose forms at times rife with bureaucratese that no individual writer would have used).

These hierarchical and cross-divisional processes that represent the culture to its members and to outsiders may be repetitive and fairly standardized in routing across organizational structures, yet as processes bound up in organizational dynamics influenced by players in various positions, they offer occasions for reshaping parts of these collective procedures. When Brenda tracked editors' reviews of articles submitted to the publications division of the association where she worked, she discovered neither standard forms for evaluation nor ongoing cataloguing of this work. She also witnessed three editors subtly crafting their own roles through these document processes (e.g., as gatekeeper or content specialist) through their reviews of submissions. Kelly actually encountered a near absence of standardization of procedures when the publications office she studied shifted to a "team-approach" to project management that had individual players forming new teams for nearly every new project.

Finally, document processes may be dependent upon nonorganizational players, as demonstrated by themes of editors' collaboration with nonstaff contributors (Grace, Helen, Jackie, Kyle, Lena) and by themes of reporters' coverage of events and solicitation of information from witnesses (Daisy, Red). Observations on writers' workplace subjectivities drawn across this category yield the following:

- Writers are often involved in document routing and publication processes that are repetitive, possibly inuring them to new wrinkles suggested by a particular project or to new conceptualizations of their jobs if the process is viewed macroscopically, as part of the organization culture.
- Perhaps because of their frequent secondary status within organizations and certainly because they often are located outside inner circles of information and knowledge in organizations, writers may encounter disparities between the information they receive and the information necessary for efficient and effective document processing.
- Involved in review and publications processes that are often hierarchical, writers may be subject to disciplining through these processes. Writing in some cultures is subject to high surveillance and writers to a panopticon subjectivity. Within such cultural processes, writers may contribute to collective authorship that falls short in its prose of their individual standards.
- As individuals contributing to collective authorship, writers mesh individuality with collective representation, yielding a subjectivity shaped by collaboration yet driven by necessity to document personal input. Under such conditions, they may shape their subjectivities through articulating roles in the organization to roles in document processes; similarly, writers may shape organizational procedures somewhat by bringing skills in organizational analysis to daily activities such as document processing.
- As members of teams in the organization's collective authorship, writers may find themselves living subjectivities that frequently shift as a function of new team formation and new close collaborators.
- Writers' workplace subjectivities are shaped not only by the local culture but also by links to outside cultures, through collaborators or interviewees on writing projects.

Subcultural Dynamics

This category grew from the number of studies that raised themes of smaller cultures within the larger organizational culture and dynamics among them that at times interconnected with writing processes and products. In many cases, the theme emerged from a researcher's taking stock of how a unit seemed to hold norms and values divergent from those encountered in other units, prompting closer inspection of these norms and values and inviting analysis that interpreted behavior as neither idiosyncratic nor wholly individual. Unlike many themes that contained occasional glimpses out at the world beyond the culture of the local organization, these themes produced close inspection of worlds within the organization, leading class discussions and researchers' development of themes to harken to theoretical notions such as the "discourse community." In several cases, such theoretical framing enabled researchers to confront stereotypes held within their own unit about coworkers in other units with different educational and professional training and values. Though I have used the shorthand *vs.* in the list that follows to mark the subcultures that researchers identified through their topics and themes, the dynamics of these subcultures in these ethnographies were not necessarily oppositional; indeed, in a few cases subcultures were perceivable only when framing analysis in terms of different classes of professionals engaged in the same project.

Subcultural Dynamics	Researcher
academic, professional, and government subcultures in a society	Grace
administration vs. teachers in schools	Emma, Lara, Marla
agendas of different divisions and public relations writing	May
engineers vs. writers and editors	Jeff
communications office's status in larger university organization	Hart
coordination between different divisions . . . in correspondence writing	Gloria, Jane
. . . in magazine writing	Kirsten
flouting nine-to-five conventions	Ravi
MFA writers vs. composition and rhetoric writers in an English department	Kate
management of worker affect by director of another division	Cass
management vs. writer and editor employees	Diane, Red, Rex
new contracts reshaping teams, work, and cycling	Ana, Elaine, Joanne, Kali, Kelly, Leathe, Mary
organization division parallels with gender	Lisa, Rachel
professional staff vs. . . . . support staff	Ella, Ginger, Liz
. . . volunteers	Jackie
top-down and bottom-up cultural dynamics	Lois
veterans vs. novices	Rex
writers' culture in an oral organization culture	Ray, Tess

Jeff was one researcher who was able to reverse commonly held stereotypes within his unit about engineers' purported poor writing abilities as allegedly evidenced by their overnominalization. He interviewed several engineers and discovered that certain phrases perceived by technical editors as confusing noun strings (he cited in his final ethnography the phrase, "the raw influent soluble phosphorous concentration") were perceived by engineers as common shorthand. When editors unstrung these nouns, engineers perceived them to be undermining their authority, since other engineers reading the text might read this alternative wording as denoting a lack of familiarity with common phrasing and hence, perhaps, a lack of experience in the profession. Other researchers identified similar dynamics between organizational divisions and sought to account for these dynamics by characterizing ways of knowing and making sense within a division's culture: Hart sketched such characteristics of a communications office in a larger university culture, as did Tess of the communications division within the travel agency where she worked. In Tess's case, she was able to couple this observation of her communications division as a subculture with the observation that many of the ways of knowing within it derived from experience as writers, which at times fell at odds with a largely "oral" corporate culture. Ray identified a similar opposition, in his case noting that much of the knowledge in his police department was communicated orally, at times positioning him as a writer as an outsider. Rex's study traced similar outsider/insider dynamics based on one's time in the local culture.

Other researchers addressed dynamics that took form when writing crossed subcultural divisions (and hence different ways of knowing locally) or when the local divisional culture was inflected by issues such as gender (as in Lisa's study of writing in a bank cited earlier). In some cases, subcultural dynamics were observed not along any organizational divisional lines per se, but as a function of either "top-down" or "bottom-up" norms and values. As might be expected, the top-down cultural dynamics often were engendered by management, and the bottom-up dynamics by employees, which included writers in most settings. The most striking example of organizational dynamics that underscored the ways in which a local culture can upset long-standing traditions in a profession and remind writers that they ultimately occupy inferior organizational status came perhaps from Red's study: the new owners of the regional newspaper where he worked as reporter overturned the age-old subjectivity of journalists as self-managers of their on-scene time when they installed time clocks and punch cards to monitor journalists' time away from their desks.

A synthesis of subjectivities across these themes of subcultural dynamics yields the following:

- Writers are frequently located in writing and editing teams, communications divisions, or publications offices within the larger organizational culture, producing a subjectivity that will encounter other subjectivities shaped by their respective organizational positioning. Organizational authorship entails managing these diverse subjectivities wrought by subcultural dynamics.
- As professionals who bring a way of knowing grounded in writing practices to a workplace culture, writers will encounter ways of knowing grounded in other kinds of discourse communities and discursive practices. Organizational authorship takes form among these many ways of knowing.
- Writers new to a culture may encounter subcultures established at least in part by length of time in the organization, producing a subjectivity not only as novice but also as outsider to traditions and practices established over time. Writing to meet one's goals may mean monitoring one's socialization into such subcultures as they shape writing practices.
- Writers may encounter subcultural dynamics emanating from below, beside, or above them in the organizational hierarchy and thus be obliged to align themselves explicitly or implicitly, permanently or momentarily, with these dynamics.
- Most often writers as a class of professionals figure as employees within the organizational hierarchy, located below executive management.

Cultural Stabilization and Change

The topics of cultural stabilization and change usually emerged toward semester's end, once researchers had developed other themes or explored other topics and were able to step back and consider implications for the broader local culture. The list below presents shards on cultural stabilization and change, in several cases as researchers pinpointed specific roles played by writing practices as part of such stabilization and change.

Stabilization/Change	Researcher
alienation stemming from organization restructuring	Adam, Heather
change in culture membership necessitates change in writing procedures and purview	Janice
change in culture through reorganization into publication teams	Kelly
change in on-line culture membership over time	Jillian
changing school culture through changes in students' research writing topics	Alice
stated change in management theory resulting in no real change in practices	Jan
high turnover and therefore no institutional memory	Adria, Holly
remodeling culture through formalization of policy	Andrew
stabilizing culture through . . . continuous quality improvement and e-mail	Challie
. . . socialization	Kolar
. . . written formalization	Jackie, Nyck
writers' knowledge protection during downsizing	Ana

Nyck hypothesized that formal written job descriptions might stabilize job duties in a culture often characterized as disjointed, plagued by high turnover and vague responsibilities. Similarly, Andrew forecast a stabilizing of some cultural practices through the writing of formal procedures at the campus police force he was studying. Challie's data-rich study of e-mail messages within the association where she worked as graphic designer prompted her to classify these messages by type and then use these types to gauge the organization's "continuous quality improvement," reasoning that the frequency of clearly misaddressed messages and misunderstood uses for e-mail indicated a failure in training to maintain this quality improvement. Her study concluded with suggestions that would bolster this training and, presumably, stabilize some cultural practices.

Kolar's study of socialization into the practice of fabricating letters in a senator's press office reminds us of the strength of socialization into locally stabilized writing practices when a culture is undergirded by powerful discourses, a topic rejoined in chapter 5. Jan studied a similarly top-down culture, an industry association, as it attempted a cultural shift to "issues management." When Jan traced writing practices and decision making as a function of this purported shift, however, she found no change.

Other researchers touched upon themes of stabilization and change by observing the changes in cultural membership over time as it influenced writing practices (as in Jillian's study of on-line discussions at Megabyte University), of high turnover yielding no institutional memory (as in Adria's study of high-tech contracting), of changes in local cultural organization as it affected writing practices (as in Kelly's study of a publications office's shift to project teams), and changes in writing practices consciously enacted in the hopes of changing organizational culture (as in Alice's study of her own fourth grade classroom, in which she substituted for the conventional lessons in research writing her own project locating research topics in students' home and ethnic cultures).

A synthesis yields the following:

- Writers' work within larger organizational structures and dynamics may make them agents of stabilization of the culture, including many of the culture's norms and values; alternatively, writers' work within these structures and dynamics may make them agents of change. In the latter case, the scope of agency probably will depend upon the coincidence between the proposed changes and the organization's goals and underlying discourses.
- Writers in organizations driven by powerful discourses and aims will most likely be subjected to strong (even if subtle) socialization into the culture's norms and values.
- Many cultures change over time with changes in membership and with perceptions of organizational mission; writers' subjectivities will shift with these changes, at times dramatically through organizational restructuring.

Organizational Goals

Of all the researchers represented in this book, Lee alone developed organizational goals as her central theme. She did so because she was intent upon using this research to garner funding and institutional support for her writing center, which she had until then run on a shoestring budget with an all-volunteer staff. Ultimately she was forced to confront the disheartening realization that norms and values in the broader community college culture were such that support probably would not come. Though disheartening, this realization granted her enhanced perspective on the culture's valuing of her own writing as a teaching professional, later prompting her to resign. Other researchers investigated organizational goals in varying degrees as their explorations of other topics and themes implicated the goals of the organization.

Organizational Goals	Researcher
assuring reelection	Kolar
assuring that the Web site is visited	Gary
gaining and fulfilling contracts	Ana, Janice, Kali, Ravi
garnering and disbursing funds	Megan
lobbying	Bernie, Jan
maintaining membership	Nidean
perpetuating image	Corinne
preparing boys for college entrance	Anne
procuring and maintaining clients	Ella, Ginger
site for writing instruction vs. . . .	Lee
computer lab	
. . . graduate student support	Kate

Megan's study of the vague discourse necessary to memoranda of understanding between donors and a university foundation enabled her to link this discursive phenomenon explicitly with organizational goals, since without such discourse the organization would be dramatically hampered in meeting its goals. Similarly, Gary's simple observation that the organization he studied could not exist if its Web site were not frequented enabled him to analyze stylistic changes to Web copy accordingly, as a function at least in part of number of hits. Studies in recent years by Ana, Janice, Kali, and Ravi have likewise placed organizational goals squarely among those themes and topics developed in analysis.

Other researchers touched upon organizational goals more tangentially: Nidean in her observation of the goal of maintaining membership as shaping local language practices; Anne in her realization that the strong organizational goal of preparing boys for college through conventional argumentative writing sabotaged her own efforts to instruct the boys in expressive journal writing; Jan, Bernie, Ella, Ginger, and Kolar in their acknowledgment of intractable organizational goals shaping cultural practice; and Kate in her implicit challenge to the local organizational goal of providing support for MFA graduate students by trading stipends for work in the writing center, while graduate students concentrating in the teaching of writing and literature were rarely offered such positions.

Important aspects of writers' organizational subjectivities are highlighted by the theme of organizational goals:

- Individual writers in organizations most likely stand very little chance of realizing personal goals in or through their writing if these goals stand at loggerheads with larger organizational goals. Though this observation may seem a truism, in this context it calls attention to a subjectivity with little clout if not acting in chorus with a professional class or classes (including, perhaps, allied scholars).
- In some organizational contexts, organizational goals and organizational authorship are nearly synonymous, so much does the organization exist through and by virtue of its representation to a specific clientele through specific documents. In the case of World Wide Web representations, author-audience dynamics are already shifting out of the slow feedback loops of the past.

From Organization Charts to Discursive Digs: Imagining New Unities in Subjective Work Lives

A review of organizational features developed as topics and themes in researchers' ethnographic analyses underscores the degree to which professional writers find themselves in the paradoxical position of being charged with producing discursive representations while excluded from inner circles of information and knowledge that could inform those representations. In the dynamics that often obtain between individuals and local organizations, writers' second-class, support-staff, functionary status inevitably undercuts their effectiveness as well as the organization's potential. Starla's comment in the chapter epigraph came in the midst of a fifty-page ethnography documenting a local culture in which players at upper echelons hoarded information to leverage on their own behalf, a workplace dynamic noted in other forms by several other researchers in this chapter. Clearly, such a zero-sum ideology works against writers and the organizations that employ them, yet this ideology endures, subtly interlocked with composition epistemologies positing form as separate from content and writing as a mode for communicating predetermined thoughts rather than for exploring and instantiating reality.

To imagine new unities, writers and writing scholars will need to devise inquiries in classrooms and in workplaces that take phenomena such as "role" and resituate them with respect to ongoing social constructions of realities via discursive acts and events. To do so, writers will need to elaborate new approaches and skills in monitoring their writing practices and the interplay between these practices and local cultures' norms and values. Writers' "skills," configured through popular understandings of composition grounded in current-traditional epistemology, will require renovation in the light of social constructionist theory and postmodern understandings of the ways in which discourses shape subjective work lives.

Equipped with such understandings of writing in organizational settings, writers may be able to mine document processes for their full potential, gleaning value where before no unities beyond mundane production appeared. Writers may be able to perceive subcultural dynamics in great complexity and to embrace these dynamics for their full potential, too, bringing their knowledge of discursive processes to bear on organizational processes in which such dynamics can offer springboards for enhanced understandings of knowledge emanating from various discourse communities. Writers may be able to identify and problematize their roles as agents of organizational stabilization and change, along with the norms and values therein reified through discursive practices. (Susan Katz's exploration of document review develops this potential.) Ultimately, writers may be able to assume greater say in organizational goals by virtue of their power to realize through their discursive work some unities of value that lie beyond the grasp of other professional classes. In *Information Ecology,* Thomas Davenport, who specializes in "re-engineering" organizations claims that information technology is relatively unimportant in harnessing the value inherent in information; writers, through their knowledge of information processes as imbricated with organizational processes, can harness value in ways that information technology only makes possible.

As organizations increasingly become the major arenas for individuals' public lives, writers, through their skills and knowledge of language theories and practices, can become vital agents in assuring that these arenas assure viable lives, public and private, for all who live the effects of organizational authorship. The reflexive practices suggested in chapter 3 can aid them in achieving this goal, as can their "voices from within" various organizations, to invoke once again the potential of autoethnography as seen by David Hayano. Speaking from within organizations, equipped with knowledge and theories developed in tandem with collaborators from the academy, writers as discourse specialists engaged in new modes of composing can sketch new unities for themselves and for us all via organizational authorship. Researchers in this volume have already tread upon this ground, uncovering shards that match organizational structures and practices with discursive features in local cultures, in the process identifying phenomena that can enable us all to engage in some cognitive mapping to the end of new unities. The next chapter presents their foray into this territory.

5   DISCURSIVE FEATURES OF WORKPLACE WRITING CULTURES

Postmodern rhetoric would begin by assuming that all discourses warrant variable subject positions ranging from mostly satisfying to mostly unsatisfying for those individuals named by them. Each institutionalized discourse privileges some people and not others by generating uneven and unequal subject positions as various as stereotypes and agents.

> —Linda Brodkey, "On the Subjects of Class and Gender in 'The Literacy Letters'"

Mandy: I wanted to know how much of your stuff—how much needs to be revealed in our ethnography—I'm doing my ethnography in my work setting, which is a[n] association with no blacks in upper management. Blacks are only in lower positions, as a secretary, or they work in the mail room. That's across the gamut. And I want to know how important that is in my ethnography. Do I need to reveal that? Because in my mind I'm always conscious of that, especially in my interactions with my bosses, who are all except for one— one's a white female, the rest are all white males—I'm conscious of their interpretation of me as a black female. Does that need to come across in my ethnography? . . . I mean, it's part of me, and I think it's important. But I'm afraid if I put that in my ethnography, it might go off on a different tangent and that might not be what the ethnography is supposed to be about.

JH: A different tangent from what?

Mandy: From—Because we're doing an ethnography of writing. It might go off into a different um—

JH: But wasn't Peggy Yocom's ethnography about herself some?

> —discussion in class, 3/9/93

To speak of the discursive features of workplace cultures is to embrace an array of understandings of the term "discourse." One use of the term refers to any linguistic unit beyond the sentence; that is, a paragraph or series of paragraphs forming a unit, or "full text" (Kinneavy 4). Another usage refers to language use as determined by the conventions of a particular community or socialized group, often referred to as a "discourse community" in composition literature. Finally, poststructural and postmodern theories of discourse would define it as a way of thinking (and knowing and talking) about the world, inherently ideological and positing language not as a vehicle to describe a preexisting reality but as the material out of which thought and reality are constructed.

With postmodern theories of discourse come postmodern rhetorics that assume that all discourses warrant variable subject positions and that these subject positions vary dramatically, at times, in terms of the purview and agency they grant their occupants (Brodkey, "On the Subjects"). Of course, subjectivities become "articulated" (see Hall) to various ideologies and to authority differently in different local circumstances. Hence the value in the *petits recits* coming from professional writers' autoethnographic analyses, since these stories enable us to see the actual assignment of subject positions through discourses at work in local cultures, to witness the imbrication of discourses and subjective work lives, and in some cases to imagine alternative unities made possible by changing the configurations of discursive environments.

Such was the case with Mandy as she struggled with her autoethnographic authorship, evidenced in the excerpt from class discussion used as chapter epigraph. We had been reading many of the "first-generation" workplace ethnographies conducted by academic researchers who did not belong to the workplace cultures under study and who focused on such discursive issues as overnominalization or inappropriate narration (see, for example, Brown and Herndl) in "nonacademic" writing. In part because these researchers were nonmembers of the culture under study and in part because they were proceeding under research paradigms that minimalized the researcher's presence in accounts, issues such as the kind raised by Mandy rarely emerged, and when they did, the treatment of them could be no more than cursory. Mandy sought on the one hand to emulate these earlier ethnographies in their fieldwork rigor and theoretical sophistication, yet at the same time she wanted to analyze issues ever present in her subjective work life as a writer. Bolstered by our classroom discussions of current social science tenets of positioned subjectivity and of recent methodologies from ethnography and folklore, autoethnography among them, Mandy was able to limn some of the institutionalized discourses and the privileges they bestowed and withheld at her organization.

In her ethnography, we see a culture highly inflected by racism and sexism in its staffing policy, as indicated in Mandy's above comment. White executives in this association occupy powerful subject positions that enable acts as repugnant as a public upbraiding of the all-black staff in the mail room. As Mandy collected other data for her autoethnography, she saw the discourses of sexism and racism working in other ways: along with the range of subject positions made possible by these discourses came a range of informational subterfuges. Middle managers, who knew that the flow of information between document production teams and the executives above them was less than salubrious, attempted to exploit this cultural feature to their own ends, in one case ending in a mass publication halted in midproduction when the subterfuge was discovered. Otherwise stated, "discourse" as understood in the postmodern sense had fractured the unities of discourse most valued by workplace management: brochures and proposals that usually serve strong instrumental ends, or discourses in the modernist sense.

Mandy's research thus demonstrates the power both of the genre of autoethnography and of understanding discourse simultaneously in modern and postmodern terms as we attempt to map discursive features of workplace cultures. This genre enables inspecting writers' subjective work lives for their quality, and readers will note that Mandy also appears as a shard in the section on discourse effects, documenting the frustration that can infiltrate writer psychology under such circumstances. And a simultaneous focus on kinds of writing, underlying discourses, and effects of discourse enables an analysis of the ways in which the capacity of the organization is hampered by counterproductive underlying discourses (as documented under "knowledge and behavior" as "producing waste").

The eighty-four researchers represented in this volume harkened to all three understandings of discourse listed above, to judge by class discussions and ethnographies in draft and final forms. To classify the shards turned up by such work, I have chosen the umbrella categories of discourse forms and discourse effects. The broad category of discourse forms includes shards that derive from each of the three definitions of discourse outlined above. For example, kinds of writing and organizational products include shards suggesting the modernist definition of "full text," for the most part. The category of multiple discourses hinges strongly on the second definition that invokes notions of "discourse community." The category of underlying discourses is strongly bound to postmodern definitions of discourse, as are the categories of knowledge and behavior and writer psychology listed under discourse effects. As Mandy's appearance in three different sections of this chapter demonstrates, researchers often fall into several categories simultaneously, enabling us to glean cultural complexities in discursive forms previously viewed as flat and mundane under composition's formalist epistemologies or the liberal humanist epistemologies with which they have so often been allied.

As in the previous chapter, I have commented on selected shards within each table to hint at complexities beyond these telegraphic representations, based on researchers' full ethnographies and class discussions. I have also drawn syntheses across each table, to support discussions in the conclusion and in part three, and to aid readings across each table that connect with other locales, other small stories, and with other mappings-in-process that can render small stories big.

Discourse Forms

Though as noted above the "forms" represented in the first four sections below vary dramatically in nature—from mundane, tangible artifacts to the more intangible ways of knowing and thinking—this umbrella category serves to partition these discursive features as produced (or reproduced) by a culture from the repercussions of production (and reproduction), which are presented in the two concluding sections. The discussions of selected shards and syntheses across subtables aim in part at broadening composition theory's repertoires and understandings of "form."

Kinds of Writing

Like Mandy, researchers each year found themselves accumulating a mass of data with many intriguing insights on local cultural practices, yet they were often unsure about the ways to link these insights to discursive practices. Many researchers resolved this issue by selecting a specific kind of writing that touched various organizational players or that stood as a significant organizational publication and then systematically studying its links to other cultural practices and ways of knowing. These kinds of writing, listed below, do not include the many other kinds of writing that were mentioned incidentally as researchers explored other topics and themes.

Kinds of Writing	Researcher
academic	Alice, Anne, Kate, Lee
books	Diane, Maggie
brochures	Nidean
captions	Rex
correspondence	Ella, Emma, Gloria, Jane, Janice, Lisa, Megan, Phoebe, Rachel
editorial review	Brenda
editorials	Jen
e-mail	Amy, Challie, Ella, Jillian
job descriptions	Nyck
magazines	Helen, Jackie, Kirsten, Kyle, Lena
memos	Jan, Jihad, Lois, Megan, Tom
mission statements	Lara, Megan
news	Daisy, Red
newsletters	Holly, Itsy, Jane, Karla, Leathe, Meg
organizational analyses	Mary
organizational histories	Elaine
patient logs	Norma
personal 'zines	Mack
policy	Branden, Ray .
press releases	Ann, Corinne, Kolar, Starla
proposals	Jeff, Leathe, Nancy and Ellie, Ravi
public relations	Hart, May
reports	Anita, Jane, Julie, Leathe, Meg, Rachel
self-documentation	Gwen, Meg
society journal articles	Grace
solicitations, acknowledgments	Megan
speeches	Leigh
technical documentation	Adria, Ana, Carolyn, Jeff, Joanne, Joe, Kali
World Wide Web pages	Adria, Albert, Gary, Jackie, Leathe, Meg

So it was that Nidean's research on a fitness consultancy's language practices aimed at developing and sustaining membership included a discussion grounded in the graphics and editing principles of the company's sales brochure which identified this brochure as one cultural artifact among others contributing to a serious, "no-frills" depiction of body sculpting. Inspections of mundane writing such as correspondence led researchers to perceive among standard formats some extensions of the local culture's values, as in Lisa's analysis of writing styles across divisions that reflected not only traditional values upheld by these divisions within the banking industry but also local values that had taken form along gender lines. In Gloria's case, she traced the emergence of an implied author in letters sent out by the Library of Congress to a citizen, this author embodying conflicting messages owing not so much to divisional values as to the dynamics of composition across divisions. Other researchers were able to see quotidian writing through new eyes: the style of illustration captions as subtly shaped not by knowledge of reading practices but by socialization into conventions among veteran writers (Rex); the writing of policy as a redefinition of cultural practice, overturning values clung to by some members with romantic fervor and hence positioning the policy writer (Ray) as countercultural; composing World Wide Web pages as a complex management of representations of team members based on their own on-line representations to the technical writer (Albert), reflecting a local culture often grounded more in virtual interactions than in face-to-face ones.

In even the most purportedly banal kind of writing in organizational settings—the memo—we see a complex interweaving of discursive forms and cultural practices. Jan noted the use of memos as organizational smokescreens enabling business as usual while ostensibly changing; Jihad, the inept use of memos by lower-rung employees; Lois, the attempt by top management to shape virtual cultures through blanket claims that employees at lower echelons interpreted skeptically; Megan, the complex understandings that underpin vague discourse in memos of understanding; and Tom, the institutional leverage attempted through subtle changes in tone when memos went up the hierarchy.

These kinds of writing encountered in the workplace suggest the following observations on writers' subjectivities as related to them:

- The multiple subject positions implicated in many kinds of writing in the workplace may include any of the following (and more): organization members who contribute directly or indirectly to documents, funding organizations or clients that may have commissioned the organization, other members of the organization who may be affected by the document (including prospective members, too), addressees of documents leaving the organization, the constituents, extraorganizational writers, end-users of a document, people who are the topic of writing, and in many cases the general public. Because agency takes form among these many subject positions, professional writers require structures and practices to monitor and assess this agency.

• Because discourses such as instrumental discourse govern much workplace writing, this form of writing requires reflexive analysis, to determine not only forms of agency but also eventual acts to which compositions may be linked.

Organizational Products

This category took form because a few researchers focused on specific documents that were quite literally part of the organization's end product, as in Jen's study of the editorials in the job announcement newsletter produced at the small private organization where she worked as editorial assistant. Kinds of writing in this category are quite similar to those in the previous category, with the exception that they target end readers more immediately in many cases. (Including Joe in this category is a bit of a stretch, in that he studied the style manual produced for internal consumption; all the same, the manual did represent an end product discrete from organizational writing supporting other end products.)

Organizational Products	Researcher
association newsletter	Jackie, Karla
corporate histories	Elaine
correspondence about research	Gloria
editorial pages of job announcement newsletter	Jen
letters soliciting funds for educational development	Megan
magazine	Helen, Kyle, Lena
press releases	Ann
publicity brochures	Corinne
reference books and brochures	Adam, Chet, Maggie
software	Gary
software documentation	Carolyn
style manual	Joe
recruitment brochure/alumni magazine	Hart
World Wide Web page	Gary, Leathe

Because these discursive products often play vital roles in an organization's solvency, which often depends upon consumer satisfaction with the product, these artifacts can perhaps indicate new directions to be taken in conceptualizing end-user roles in organizational authorship. Gary's research on Web page revisions undertaken as a result of user feedback and number of hits, mentioned earlier, augurs such reconceptualization. Those publications circulating in relatively closed circuits, such as association newsletters, augur similar reconceptualizations, as Jackie's tracing of input from member-contributors via e-mail attests.

In another vein, Joe's research raised issues of misrepresentation of a class of workers through an official organization publication, and Helen's research on an organization's editing processes raised issues of reproduction of local cultural values through the discursive work of the organization's magazine. Such issues suggest two more observations on writers' workplace subjectivities:

- Writers often have little say in an organization's end products, yet studying these products in concert with local and larger cultural processes may hold potential for exploring new author-reader dynamics in composition.
- Organizational products at times misrepresent writers as a class of professionals, particularly when those products are generated without due input from writers.

Multiple Discourses

This category parallels that of subcultural dynamics discussed in the previous chapter as part of the organizational features explored by researchers. But whereas explorations of subcultural dynamics tended to identify subgroups prior to (and in many cases independently of) identification of specific discourses that shaped their ways of knowing, explorations of multiple discourses usually began with the identification of a kind of discourse in texts or utterances, then the characterization of this discourse and its operations within the local culture. These multiple discourses are represented in the following list.

Multiple Discourses	Researcher
"artistic" discourse/business discourse	Phoebe
engineers' discourse/editors' discourse	Jackie, Jeff
"feminine" discourse/business discourse	Jen
legal discourse/plain English	Ginger
medical discourse/lay discourse	Norma
official organizational discourse/ workers' discourse	Diane, Lois

oral discourse/written discourse	Ray, Tess
promotional discourse/news discourse	Jackie
scholarly discourse/business discourse	Elaine
school discourse/home discourse	Alice
school discourse/work discourse	Julie
writers' discourse/writing teachers' discourse	Kate

As illustration, Jen identified in the editorial pages of a job announcements newsletter what she characterized as a "feminine" discourse in its nurturing and supportive qualities, balancing, in her view, the cut-and-dried quality of the announcements, which she referred to as a "business discourse." Phoebe similarly identified a discourse of artists that imbued the business writing at the nonprofit organization where she worked, marked by excess verbiage and embellished (and inexact) prose accounts of organization events in official memos to file and sent up the hierarchy. Taking stock of such discourses and the ways they interrelate with local cultural practices, even if the terms of analysis remain inchoate, can enable writers to reexamine their own terms of membership and positions with respect to an organization's undertakings, as it did in the cases of both Jen and Phoebe.

Exploring multiple discourses can also enable writers to revise their understandings of their jobs and to perform them with greater satisfaction and insight, as in the case of Jeff's explorations of engineers' discourse as edited by technical writers discussed above. Jackie similarly found herself assessing her newsletter's content as driven by both a "news" discourse (drawing on her background as a journalist) and by a "promotional" discourse, which she perceived as less substantive. These explorations can provide writers with another means of interpreting official organizational discourse and spontaneous reactions to it from the ranks as it has implications for their own work and as it sketches contours of a workplace culture. Such was the case for both Lois and Diane. Lois solicited her colleagues' responses to a memo from the CEO and interpreted these responses as a measure of how workers positioned themselves vis-à-vis the positioning of readers implied by the memo. Against daily displays of inattention by management to work in the publications division, Diane interpreted the various seminars and workshops conducted by outside animators to the goal of quality improvement as a subterfuge intended to placate workers. The ways in which multiple discourses work to position culture members will be rejoined in the next section on underlying discourses. Insights on writers' workplace subjectivities afforded by these and the previous observations are the following:

- Writers are likely to encounter multiple discourses as they mediate organizational authorship. These discourses may emanate from specific discourse communities (such as engineers) and even subcommunities (such as hydraulic engineers) or they may take form through local practice. As subjects among these discourses, writers require tools for interpreting them and crafting their consequent professional practice.
- Among the multiple discourses that professional writers will encounter in organizations most certainly will figure an official organizational discourse emanating from the upper hierarchy and various spontaneous discourses containing counterpositions; as subjects among these discourses, writers require tools for interpreting them and crafting their consequent professional practice.

Underlying Discourses

The official organizational discourses noted by Lois and Diane were in their turn inflected by management discourse more generally, as articulated by organizational players whose job it was to manage other workers. Constantly under elaboration through the many institutions that are devoted to research and training in management (whether part of graduate study preparing workers for management positions or part of in-house training), with firm ties to other powerful discourses such as market discourse, management discourse will undoubtedly continue to position professional writers as discourse workers in the foreseeable future. Writers' subjectivities will be shaped by the forms this discourse takes within local structures and dynamics, suggesting implications both for writers as they individually plot their career courses and for writing scholars and researchers in the fields of professional writing and composition. Through similar alliances, other discourses shape workplace cultures and hence the subjectivities of culture members. Some such discourses, turned up by researchers in the Cultures of Professional Writing course, appear below.

Underlying Discourses	Researcher
anti-school	Mack
education	Ann
egalitarian discourse	Amy
elitism	Branden, Mary
fund-raising	Megan
"ghosting" discourse	George, Leigh

lobbying and execution	Bernie, Jan, Karla, Kirsten, Mandy, Meg
history and tradition	Bernie
management	Cass, Diane, Lois
market discourse	Ara, Gary, Nidean, Ravi
military contracting discourse	Acria, Kali
military discourse	Arita, George, Sue
political discourse	Kclar
safety	Lena
sexism	Lisa, Rachel
sexism and racism	Ana, Mandy

Bernie noted discourses of history and tradition in the law profession association where he worked as an editor, permitting him enhanced understanding of his second-class organizational status, since the histories and traditions deemed prestigious in the field of writing are classically attached only to literature and poetry. Researchers Lisa, Rachel, and Ana each like Mandy identified ways in which a discourse of sexism curtailed the prowess of professional writers and hence the productivity of the organization. Amy noted an expressed discourse of egalitarianism at odds with enactments of decision making.

As we investigate the composition of subjectivities through discursive practices, we might also analyze the workings of discourses in organizational settings as they articulate with other discourses to produce specific subject positions, as in the alliances between management discourse and market discourse mentioned above. Ann's occasional subject position of "tutee" in the small public relations firm where she worked signals the presence of a specific kind of discourse of education in arms with market discourse and others. As writers and scholars of writing we might ask ourselves what other subject positions are likely to take form through these articulations, how we might interpret such positions, and what the implications are for writers, their organizational cultures, and subjects beyond these cultures.

Both George and Sue, as employees of the military, were ever aware of military discourse and the way it positions its subjects; in the case of this discourse in particular, its strong alliance with political discourse and its track record of supporting discourses such as sexism and heterosexism suggest workplace cultures in which writing takes place in less than salubrious conditions. Insights on such conditions as they affect writer psychology and culture members' knowledge and behavior will be treated below, in the discussion of discourse effects. For the present, implications across the category of underlying discourses for writers' subjectivities are the following:

- As discourse workers in organizations, writers are sure to encounter a discourse of management allied with other discourses and enacted in particular forms locally, along with the counterdiscourses these discourses will engender; writers will need analytical tools and training to apprehend the workings of these discourses so as to interpret their implications for themselves as culture members and for organizational authorship.
- In workplace cultures writers will find themselves subject to varieties of discourses that vary from locale to locale. They will need tools and training to discern these discourses, to know their histories in other environments, to understand how they articulate to other discourses locally, and to plan careers and to interpret these cultural phenomena in their implications for organizational authorship.

Discourse Effects

Just as the above discussion of discourse forms seeks to enhance understandings of these (seemingly neutral) forms as imbued with local cultural norms and values and contributing to a culture promoting specific kinds of subjectivities for its members, so does the discussion of discourse effects which follows attempt to enhance our understandings of the ways in which specific cultural configurations produce real effects that members experience. Early postmodern and poststructural theory construed the (textualized) subject as an effect of discourse. In the light of recent theoretical developments that admit individual agency through specific articulations among discourses effected in given cultural moments and scenes (see Stuart Hall's work, noted earlier), this section attempts to sketch effects of discourse upon subjects in workplace cultures under empirical study. First comes a summary of effects on a specific class of culture members: professional writers as they exercise their craft. Then come observations on the effects of discourse on the workplace culture as a whole, through a focus on behavior and ways of knowing.

Writer Psychology

When researchers focused on the effects of discourses in the local cultures they studied, they raised several themes having to do with perceived effects on the mind-sets that writers brought to their writing, as summarized in the following list.

Writer Psychology	Researcher
activity report ratcheting up expectations	Meg
attention to self-documentation . . . as protection	Ray
. . . for recompense	Meg
deadlines as prompt	Che , Daisy, Jane, Kelly, Kirsten, Kyle, Leigh, Maggie, Mary, Red
engagement based on whether writing is perceived as academic or nonacademic	Anne
freelancer autonomy/insecurity	Mack, Sarah
frustration	Carolyn, Diane, Elaine, Ella, Holly, Mandy, Rachel
low morale	Adam, Lisa, Sue
psychology tied to credentials	Nyck
resignation	Bern e
self-motivated standards	Kali
shift in psychology as a function of self-documentation	Gwen
split-subjectivity via virtuality	Adria, Albert
withdrawal of engagement	Ana, George, Heather, Jane

Through interviews with writers in the military chop chain, for example, George found that in some cases writers did not even attempt to visualize their ultimate audiences. When I asked him in conference why he thought that "Tom," one of his interviewees, adopted such an approach, he said:

> I think he's just been beaten to a pulp, and it doesn't do any good, so he's not going to do it anymore. He's gonna write it like he would write it if he were the boss, and if they want to change it—he knows they're going to change it—let 'em change it. (individual conference, 9/4/94)

Otherwise stated, a disciplining discourse that often dominated document review processes in this local culture had resulted in a withdrawal of full engagement by a writer in the writing project. Other researchers identified "low morale" among writers—as related to cultural processes that had writers believing that they were judged on factors other than their writing performance (Adam, Lisa) or that kept writers in the dark about decisions above them that would ultimately affect their working conditions (Sue). It would be difficult to isolate any one discourse producing such results, but in Lisa's case discourses of sexism and management discourse (at the very least) produced this effect, and in Sue's (who worked in a military office), discourses of sexism and authoritarianism. Undoubtedly, many other discourses were at work in these settings, some drawn from fairly generalized discourses and others unique to local settings; provocative for professional writers researching such cultures and for scholars collaborating with them is not only identifying these discourses but pondering the way they interact with one another to produce different ranges of possible subject positions for different culture members.

Taking stock of the ways that various discourses articulate can in some cases enable individual writers to effect shifts in their own writing psychology: when Gwen realized the degree to which a discourse of surveillance imbued even her casual and incidental discussions with her supervisor, she shifted her mental approach to logging her activities, reconceptualizing such record keeping as a kind of self-documentation that could one day serve to justify writing decisions. Ray similarly increased his memos to file once he realized that the discourse of orality underpinning his local culture had teamed with others to frame his policy writing as deriving from his own impetus rather than from institutional mandate.

One might dismiss elements of writer psychology as idiosyncratic and writers' objections to particular subjectivities as beyond their rights. But against these demonstrations of the interleaving of writer psychology and organizational structures and processes, it would seem more expedient for writers, scholars of professional writing, and workplace managers—if only in the name of organizational productivity during the national shift to a high-value economy—to seize upon such indices of a counterproductive culture and effect changes in local cultures that would prompt changes in such subjectivities. Ideas for such a project will be explored in part three, linking observations elsewhere on professional writers' subjectivities with the implications drawn here on the topic of writer psychology. Two key observations on the links between writer psychology and subjectivity as shaped by a workplace culture's discursive features are the following:

- By its nature, writing engages writers' affect; writer psychology is not merely individual but bound up in the various subject positions supported by the structures and dynamics of an organization. Writers can benefit from developing acuity in discerning the ways that individual psychology is shaped by psychologies engendered by the specifics of a local culture.

- Organizations can benefit by making positive and imaginative writer psychology a priority, producing cultural dynamics that support writers as they manage organizational authorship.

Cultural Knowledge and Behavior

In addition to exploring the effects of various discourses on writers as they performed their work, certain researchers observed more general effects of discourse on culture members' behavior and the knowledge that informed it. From socializing culture members to adopt local norms to disciplining long-standing culture members, different discourses positioned culture members in ways that prompted certain kinds of behavior. Similarly, the ready-made frames for interpreting reality provided by some discourses at times prompted misinterpretations and hence erroneous knowledge. Some of these effects are presented below.

Knowledge and Behavior	Researcher
adopting local norms	Kolar, Nidean
coping with stress	Ginger, Mary
demanding patience	Anita, Chet, Jane, Kyle, Lena, Maggie
disciplining	Ann, George
managing affect along with effect	Cass
mismanaging	Heather, Phoebe
positioning with respect to discourse of administration by culture members	Jihac, Marla
positioning writer as "shield" for higher-ups	Ray
producing alienation	Adam, Heather, Holly, Karla, Tess
producing waste	Mandy
prompting counterculture	Diane, Lois
prompting misinterpretations	Grace, Jeff
requiring diplomacy	Ella, Jackie, Jeff
undermining morale	Nyck, Sue
working the bureaucracy	Ana, Branden, Mandy, Meg

Researchers' themes tended to inspect some of the results of cultural knowledge and behavior wrought by specific discourses: the ways that various culture members might subtly position themselves with respect to administrative discourse (Marla, Jihad, for example, or the way in which a particular cultural member, in this case a writer, became positioned as a "shield" for an organizational superior through the confluence of various discourses (Ray).

Such observations transcend individual happenstance in organizational life, since they go beyond the anecdotal to identify systemic issues that ultimately affect organizational authorship. Researchers' treatments of these themes prompt the following observations on writers' workplace subjectivities:

- Writers not only work in discourse, they endure the effects of specific discourses in local cultures (along with other culture members) as these discourses shape knowledge and behavior.
- One of the effects of discourse in a culture is that it positions different culture members differently, in concert with organizational structures and dynamics, and, as indicated in the chapter epigraph, often limits a subject's scope and range of action.

Taking Inventory

As all archaeological work benefits from reflective inventories of shards, so this section of *Writing Workplace Cultures* concludes with reflections over the shards in this chapter and the two preceding it. This chapter aimed to match discursive features of workplace cultures to organizational structures and writers' positions and practices. The multiple classifications of researchers and their research into several lists can prompt us to imagine unities that might take form across these many situations where currently no unities exist and to place the realization of such unities on our agendas as practicing writers and/or collaborating scholars.

On this agenda would therefore figure the reconceptualizing of writers' skills, currently undertheorized as they contribute to organizational authorship and cultural reproduction. Similarly under-theorized are "mundane" forms of workplace writing, forms of instrumental discourse which, when studied empirically in local cultures, yield insight on the subject positions they create and implicate and on the realities they produce and reproduce. Scholars in professional writing can aid professional writers by reviewing professional writers' skills through the lenses of cultural theories to render the representations of these skills—in educational institutions and in the workplace—adequately complex. Scholars and professional writers can collaborate in researching mundane forms of workplace writing to render understandings of these forms similarly complex.

Also on this agenda are writers' current statuses in workplace cultures, wrought largely by the poor epistemological framing of discourse work that sends writers as professionals into workplace environments without the theoretical leverage necessary to argue and substantiate their contributions to the organizational mission and the local culture in the emerging high-value economy. To aid writers at least partly in rectifying low status, scholars can work to elaborate new and richer theories of authorship as informed by the collective authorships of workplace realities, focusing at the very least on the inadequacy of theorizing authorship as an individual phenomenon when organizational authorship is always collective. In this era of national cultural shift from an economy grounded in high-volume industries and the structures of authority they carried to high-value industries and the new structures of authority required for success, the links between authority and authorship should serve as topics not only for intellectual inquiry but also as vital research for development.

The agenda thus calls for reconfiguring much instruction in discourse theory for future and even current discourse workers. It also calls for instruction in other areas: writers will witness their organizational roles inflected by many other roles, and instruction in role theories could equip them to deal with this reality. Similarly, as culture members who encounter many discourses as they mediate organizational authorship, they will require instruction in theory and methodology that equips them to perceive and interpret these discourses, whether they come from specific "discourse communities" or emanate from other organizational entities. Professional writers of the future could also benefit from instruction in organizational theory, thus entering the workplace equipped with some of the same theoretical background of the people who will be managing them.

In these workplaces, writers will enjoy unique organizational positions, frequently glimpsing workplace subcultures as they mediate organizational authorship. Through the mode of learning that writing represents, they will be positioned intellectually to produce knowledge on the local culture that no other professional can produce. When this learning is informed not only by organizational theory and research methodology but also by discourse theory that elaborates on writing as inscription of local cultures, writers will be endowed with a reflexivity that can serve the individual and collectivities. As links to other cultures—through their occasional functions as liaisons, their experiences in other organizational cultures, and their membership in virtual communities of writers that will form and share knowledge—writers can one day convincingly claim their rights and responsibilities in organizational goals and end products.

At the top of our agenda should figure in bold letters the fact that discourse theories have advanced phenomenally in the last two decades while popular understandings of writing have remain largely unchanged. Practicing writers, as a class of professionals who regularly enact composition tenets, will be positioned strategically in the national economic shift from high-volume production to high-value production, and it behooves us all to equip these writers with understandings of recent discourse theory and to imagine along with them the implications. As information technology renders discourse work increasingly key to national economy and even to national identity, writers' potential to play a greater role in organizational authorship is likely to expand dramatically.

An agenda stemming from this preliminary archaeology thus has immediate implications for writers and scholars concerning at least three phenomena. First, the nature of writing instruction represented in the academy is only beginning to be dislodged from epistemologies grounded in formalism and liberal humanism. The gleanings presented in these three chapters make it possible to envision educational experiences in discourse work that represent this work in greater complexity and enable a greater number of students to engage in it productively and meaningfully. Second, our representation, teaching, and reflexive use of writing in the workplace could serve to augment popular notions of writers' expertise. And finally, interventions will change as scholars intervene in discursive subjectivities theoretically and practically through teaching, and as writers team with scholars to lay groundwork for interventions in organizational authorship theoretically and pragmatically. Part three undertakes exploration of these phenomena.

PART THREE

Implications and Applications
(Links to Other Shards, Other Sites)

6 REPRESENTING DISCURSIVE WORK IN THE ACADEMY

It is a question of the discursive *representation* of interests, of calculation and hypothesis. There is no class essence and there are no unified class actors, founded in the objectivity of a social interest; there are, however, processes of class formation, without absolute origin or telos, with definite discursive conditions, and played out through particular institutional forms and balances of power, through calculations and miscalculations, through desires, and fears, and fantasies.

—John Frow, *Cultural Studies and Cultural Value*

So, what questions does this [class discussion of flexible labor in a post-Fordist economy] raise for us as knowledge workers? As information workers?

—Professor Tom Moylan, in class, 4/4/95

The "It" in John Frow's comment above refers to class formation, a topic immanent to inquiries into workplace lives. Like many other cultural theorists, Frow observes the inadequacy of models of socioeconomic class grounded in traditional Marxism which posit class interests as objectively pre-given, determined exclusively by economic forces. He proposes a provocative interplay of economic, political, and ideological forces shaping the processes of class formation, and he points out in so doing that he understands "ideology" not in the archaic sense that allowed attribution of "false consciousness" to workers who were unable to discern their own best interests but rather in the sense of symbolic representations that we all make to ourselves daily. His focus on processes seems extremely valuable as composition scholars collaborate with students in exploring discursive subjectivities under the process paradigm, particularly in light of the speed with which workplace writing processes—and jobs—change in postmodern times. Equally valuable for such collaboration in exploring discursive construction of subjectivities beyond the academy is his attention to institutional forms as they shape (and are shaped by) discursive conditions. Particularly provocative in his formulation is the reference to desires, fears, and fantasies—for such affective elements, often excluded from high theory, speak to the heart of all writers' work.

Among the representations of themselves as writers in chapter 2, the researchers in this book frequently noted their affective selves: writing exposes oneself, writing is linked to feelings, writing elicits emotional reactions. The huge success of expressivist composition instruction in the 1980s and 1990s is owed, no doubt, to this aspect of writing, particularly since this style of instruction came in the wake of formalist hegemony in literary studies and concomitant current-traditional epistemology in composition, along with its institutional ghettoizing that granted so little focus to writerly affect and worldly aspirations in discursive engagement. Yet expressivism is decidedly modernist, positing the writing self as unified and essentialized, a "real author" intent upon tapping that innermost self and relaying it to paper as if unmediated. This epistemology, epitomized by approaches such as Peter Elbow's "Closing My Eyes As I Speak: An Argument for Ignoring Audience," appeals to the liberative elements of writing such as articulated by Anne in the epigraph to chapter 1. Expressivism's narrative of liberation is momentary and personal, cut off from the world of work, ignoring a host of issues offered by considering the relationality between selves and others in identity formation (undeniably one of the assets of postmodern thinking), and ultimately disempowering for writers because of its conceptualization of the writerly self in such narrow terms. At least part of the task of representing discursive work among ourselves as writers and scholars, with our colleagues, with coresearchers, and with students, has to do with revisiting the affective elements of discursive engagement and rethinking them w th respect to workplace selves and others. An equally important part of our task as compositionists is exploring the discursive representations of interests as they take form in organizational settings and as our epistemologies and practices compare with these interests.

In Frow's analysis, he speaks of interests as spanning three spheres: the ideological, the political, and that of production. Class relations form and reform across these spheres, producing ideological class relations, political class relations, and economic class relations. Frow is quick to point out that "all social relations are made up of elements that are *simultaneously* economic, political, and ideological" (107). Composition's postmodern focus on the "subject" as shaped by discursive forces blends easily with such a framework, if we recall the philosophical domains for exploring subjectivity as outlined in chapter 1, that is, the political, the psychological, and the social/cultural. The shards of part two, moreover, provide a basis for exploring the representations of writers' interests in the sphere of production, an element of composition that modernist epistemologies ignore almost entirely. In this sphere, writers' positions in the workplace are among the most tenuous (as illustrated by the frequent observations of high turnover in this archaeology), rendering Tom Moylan's question in the chapter epigraph all the more compelling: what questions does post-Fordist production raise for information workers and their collaborators in the academy?

In this chapter I explore some questions that we might raise and some steps we might take in academic settings to render composition's forms more adequate to postmodern professional writing realities. one that acknowledges the role of language and writing in all three of

Frow's spheres. I will begin by recalling differences between modernist and postmodernist understandings of discourse, and then I will sketch the implications of postmodern understandings for writing as imbricated with value and for writing as always tied to power. Against this backdrop, I then will present ideas for melding composition studies with discourse studies more generally. The chapter concludes with ideas for designing a discourse studies curriculum.

The Content(s) of Postmodern Composing

In *The Content of the Form,* historian Hayden White critiques discourse models that posit form and content as disparate, proposing in their stead a "performative" model of discourse:

> From the perspective provided by this model, a discourse is regarded as an apparatus for the production of meaning rather than as only a vehicle for the transmission of information about an extrinsic referent. Thus envisaged, the content of the discourse consists as much of its form as it does of whatever information might be extracted from a reading of it. (42)

White makes this claim in the context of a discussion of the "multi-layeredness" of discourse and its "consequent capacity to bear a wide variety of interpretations of its meaning" (42), a feature explored at length in chapter 7's discussion of writing's representations in the workplace. I mention it here not only to signal at least one model of discourse to be tapped in re-presenting discursive work in the academy but also to emphasize the value of historical perspective in conducting archaeological work on discursive processes. White's claim echoes that of D. F. McKenzie in his study of formal adjustments to plays in the eighteenth century (that is, numbering scenes, providing marginal indications for speakers, etc.) which had distinctive effects on the reception of the work (Chartier 10). "Forms effect meaning," McKenzie observes (Chartier 90), and with the radical transformations in media forms during this last decade, the roles and subjectivities of writers in effecting meanings through these media and among the many layers of discourse that exist in workplace cultures require an equally radical re-presentation.

As composition scholars tapping postmodern theory and other theories of subjectivity to aid us in our composer-centered field of inquiry, the discursive work of professional writers has strong implications. Empirical findings in the previous chapters support the theoretical contention that composers' subjectivities are shaped through the forms of workplace composing. Hence part of our task in re-presenting discursive work to students, professional writers, and colleagues alike must entail ongoing archaeologies, course design, curriculum design, and a rethinking of classroom methodologies that anticipate and problematize the discursive constructions of self that will be effected through workplace composing—that mode of composing most often employed during most people's writing lives. James Berlin states it this way: "If the perceiving subject, the object perceived, and the community of fellow investigators are all in large part the effects of linguistic practices, then every discipline must begin with a consideration of the shaping force of discourse in its activities" (*Rhetorics* 68). Whether or not other disciplines will eventually take up this task may well depend upon composition's capacity to demonstrate the value of such an undertaking.

Writing and Value

In *The Work of Nations,* cited briefly in the introduction, former labor secretary Robert Reich traces the evolution of U.S. economic development through its shift from the high-volume economy of the early twentieth century to the high-value economy at century's end. He sketches the kind of work and workers that this economy requires, arriving at three categories of service: routine production services, in-person services, and symbolic-analytic services (175–77). Professional writers fall into this last category, because "symbolic analysts solve, identify, and broker problems by manipulating symbols" (178). This work is key to the high-value economy, because the value produced through such work derives from "continuous discovery of new linkages between solutions and needs" (85). As symbolic-analytical work that bestows value, then, writing coexists with other kinds of work at the heart of this sector of the economy. Yet the potential of professional writing for infusing value remains underexploited for at least two reasons. The first is that popular conceptions of language and discourse as mere packaging for thought inhibits full exploitation of language practices. (Reich's own discussion of language use conveys this view). Attempts at measuring technical writers' "value added" to organizational products have begun to characterize ever so provisionally the role of language in *discovering* linkages between solutions and needs (Society for Technical Communication), yet even these attempts seem to harken to modernist models of discourse, for the most part. Still dramatically unexplored are the potentials of writing as a mode of learning and of discourse as an apparatus for the production of meaning—for enhancing all kinds of value throughout workplace cultures, in the economic domain and in others.

The second reason why professional writers' work remains underexploited in generating value is that organizational hierarchies remain largely pyramidal, in spite of the imperative in a high-value economy to flatten hierarchies and tap workers' potential more fully. Says Reich:

> The high-value enterprise . . . need not be organized like the old pyramids that characterized standardized production, with strong chief executives presiding over ever-widening layers of managers, atop an even larger group of hourly workers, all following standard operating procedures. In fact, the high-value enterprise *cannot* be organized in this way. (87)

Judging by the organization charts regularly presented in class by researchers in this book, organizational structures in most workplaces studied remain highly pyramidal, replicating archaic models. Though many of the organizations studied were not enterprises in the business sense, 40 percent of them were, and even among these 40 percent only two organizations—those studied by Leathe and Mary—professed a flattened hierarchy. A few of the smaller businesses might be perceived as "flat," but in most cases the shape derives from size rather than conscious configuring of organizational structures to tap workers' expertise to the fullest. Among the government agencies and trade associations, hierarchy is firmly entrenched and most likely will remain so *ad infinitum,* in spite of purported efforts to "reinvent" government.

These organization charts reflect Sarmiento's claim from chapter 2—that 95 percent of U.S. companies remain Taylorist in their organizational structures—which might be explained from several viewpoints: the size of the U.S. economy alone permits such organizational inertia; high-value products in some cases may be produced adequately through high-volume structures; patriarchal ideology pervades organizations to such a degree that movements to improve meet numerous obstacles; and so on. Yet certainly some organizations are destined to improve soon, and it is worth noting that Mary's site of study was a consulting organization on the cutting edge of management studies, just as Leathe's site was a contracting agency performing high-level data analysis and report writing in which labor potential had to be maximized for the organization to survive.

As other organizations restructure to improve their value in the sphere of production, professional writers (and allied compositionists) can strive to improve composition's enactments and writers' subjective work identities by underscoring the ways in which value in the economic sphere always interleaves with values in the ideological and political spheres. Such considerations carry at least the following implications: the flattening of hierarchy should logically entail a redistribution of profits among contributors to value; as more workers (including writers) enjoy greater roles in discovering new linkages between needs and solutions, they should also have a say in the workplace cultures they "write" in so doing; because professional authorship (discussed at length in chapter 7) will increasingly incorporate users into the authoring (and hence production) phase, organizations will need to reconceptualize their consumers philosophically, repositioning them from targets to sources. These implications may appear utopian, yet the logic of enhancing composition epistemology and practices as this archaeology suggests makes them wholly pragmatic, as this chapter and those following will make clear.

Writing and Power

To speak of writing and power is to invoke the political sphere, a sphere around which composition has cut a wide berth during most of the twentieth century. This berth helps explain the plight of compositionists generally as portrayed by Susan Miller: because composition has remained ancillary to the "real" intellectual work of English departments, its teacher-scholars have remained marginalized in academic power structures. Miller addresses the mechanisms and epistemologies undergirding this marginalization at length, reminding us that we have much at stake in this matter as concerns the status of all writing teachers and researchers at work in the academy. From another perspective, James Berlin reminds us that not to address the interconnections of power and writing is to do our students a great disservice:

> Colleges ought to offer a curriculum that places preparation for work within a comprehensive range of democratic educational concerns. Regardless of whether students are headed for the highest or the lowest levels of the job market, we ought to provide them at least with an understanding of the larger operations of the work force. ("English Studies" 223)

As discussed in chapter 2, the principal reason why composition has never undertaken such political projects hinges on university structures in general (as they replicate the structures of "scientific management") and English department structures in particular (as they maintain a hegemony of literary studies over writing studies: Sullivan and Porter's "curricular geography" appropriately locates those genres of writing associated with the workplace as always secondary in English department structures and practices, including allocation of resources.) Reading their geography gives one pause (see figure 2, chapter 2), if only to reconsider representations of literary studies (and composition) as somehow independent of the workplace and the formation of workers, for example. As argued extensively in current critical theory, by reinforcing the "author function" that establishes systems of discursive (and aesthetic) exclusivity, literary studies work to reinforce the cultural status quo and workers' placements (and purviews) in workplace cultures.

At the same time, the unidirectional arrows from professional writing to the workplace signal a vital element of writing that has remained largely unexploited in the academy: the element of power as it inflects discursive work. With the turn towards theories of subjectivities in the humanities and in English literature more specifically, the inextricable relation between knowledge and power has been a recurring focus. Thus a cultural studies perspective in literary interpretation might focus on rereading the canon for the ways in which power has represented itself and solidified ideological support under the aegis of "knowledge," for example. The power/knowledge unity has thus provoked valuable classroom experience for students in the realm of discursive consumption, while affording very little experience in the realm of discursive production—in spite of entreaties by such scholars as Lester Faigley to reconsider "the subject" of composition.

This lacuna in classroom discursive experience derives from several sources, several of which are outlined in Dias et al.'s *Worlds Apart: Acting and Writing in Academic and Workplace Contexts.* The authors discuss the texts produced by writers in workplace settings (see particularly p. 226–30) as always already imbued with power, both within the organization and on the part of the organization, in contrast to the demonstration texts students produce in academic writing forums. Because workplace writing *constitutes* realities and because these realities are always filled with power relations, this discursive form is most fertile for investigating the composition of the subject in discourse, which necessarily entails investigating how class interests are "played out through particular institutional forms and balances of power," as Frow puts it in the chapter epigraph. Conducting such investigations will require ongoing collaboration among academics and professional writers, which in turn will require inventive research designs and novel conceptualizations of partnerships. If academics maintain the epistemological allegiance that the field of composition demands—that is, composer-centered research that eyes the trivialization of any discourse with skepticism and any positioning of writers that relieves them of responsibility and rights towards agencies at work as unacceptable— then fears of cultural reproduction often raised in discussions of "service" writing should rest allayed. And if predictions by labor researchers such as Robert Reich are even vaguely on target, then it will be in the best interests of most high-value organizations to deem writing subjects and writing cultures part and parcel of the enterprise.

In chapter 8 I discuss rationales, dynamics, and epistemologies of research on discursive subjectivities in the contact zones between the workplace and the academy, after a look in chapter 7 at representing discursive work in the workplace and reconfiguring professional writers' expertise as implied by this archaeological work. Clearly, much work lies ahead in knowledge movement between the academy and the workplace. To prepare such work, we might extrapolate from this class of professionals known as professional writers to posit a new theoretical class of "discourse specialists." Such a class would enable us to designate writers' work with more precision than the terms "knowledge worker" or "information worker" voiced by cultural studies scholar Tom Moylan in the chapter epigraph. As valuable as these terms have been in enabling cultural studies to counter monetary capital with cultural capital in knowledge/power struggles, neither quite captures the specificity of professional writing, its discursive roots, and its actors' subjectivities. In *A Theory of Discourse*, James Kinneavy reviews some of these discursive roots along with terms he considered in naming his project, disqualifying "composition" in 1971 because of its limiting connotations (4). Nearly three decades later, in the light of composition's exciting and provocative reconfiguring of its "subjects" and with the possibility of more adequately investigating "formations" beyond academic walls, we might return to this pioneer's quandary and deem that our project now merits the mantle of "discourse" and our writers the title of "discourse specialist."

Melding Composition with Discourse Studies

In *Composition in the University,* Sharon Crowley reviews the "process movement" critically, noting its collusion with current-traditional epistemology:

> The easy accommodation of process-oriented strategies to current-traditionalism suggests that process and product have more in common than is generally acknowledged in professional literature about composition, where the habit of contrasting them conceals the fact of their epistemological consistency. A truly paradigmatic alternative to current-traditionalism would question the modernism in which it is immersed and the institutional structures by means of which it is administered. (212)

The institutional structures that administer composition are those of the scientifically managed university and of the narrowly defined English "as literature" outlined above. The postmodern alternative to the modernism of composition entails broadening its borders to include all discourse as it is produced and consumed and all composers as both subjects and agents of discourse. Doing so allows us to rethink composition fundamentally as an inquiry into discursive subjectivity and to posit as one of composition's aims that of enhancing composers' capacities to perceive and reflect upon their subjectivities as they take form among specific determining discourses, most notably those of the workplace. Nearly all college and university enrollees will assume active lives as symbolic analysts, and as such will assume specific positions as both agents and subjects in circuits of discursive production and consumption. A truly paradigmatic alternative to current-traditionalism could begin with this fact alone to problematize the ways in which all who study writing enter into discourse and sustain positions therein.

For those whose professional status will be that of "writer" and for future professionals in other classes, too, theories of subjectivity in discourse rendered accessible through case studies and reflexive work in the classroom could become valuable knowledge for assessing later agencies in organizational processes. The domains of such theory will evolve as we all struggle to come to grips with entry into discourse, but at the very least we can begin with partial domains as various disciplines and fields have developed them to date. Against the background of chapter 1 and this chapter's introduction as each sketches postmodern approaches to understanding subjectivity in domains from the psychological and the sociological to the political, ideological, and economic, I sketch some ideas for exploring subjectivities of writers as part of discourse studies. The discussion makes use of researchers' topics and themes, selected researchers' work, and recent trends in composition to suggest ways in which composition studies might meld with discourse studies more generally, the better to garner political and epistemological clout within the academy and without.

Psychological and Sociological Subjectivities

If we accept the postmodern tenet that the workplace writing subject takes form among the discourses that obtain in any given organizational culture, then part of our task as compositionists becomes that of tracing the ways in which a writer's "I" gets deployed by the discourses in a local culture. Within the confines of a classroom, such tracing is impossible, yet approaches to and mechanics for such tracing are perfect topics for classroom work. Gwen's research on self-documentation demonstrates that practitioners in many professions come to their work fully versed in documenting their work—to avoid litigation, to substantiate steps taken in a process, and so forth. Writers rarely receive such instruction. However, writers in classrooms are frequently required to keep journals on their readings or writings—as a basis for class discussion, as springboard material for "transactional" writing, or as a nongraded discursive effort in tandem with the graded. The practice of "journaling," now common in composition, might be refocused in some cases to help writers trace their subjectivities in completing other discursive tasks. One imagines a course in which writers must complete a project, collaboratively or singly, and during which they also keep meticulous journals on their decisions, actions, processes, etc. Workshops could be dedicated to analyzing the "I's" of the journals along the lines of the analysis in chapter 1, to help writers perceive the social forces entering discourse through the "I's" they posit and to help them perceive forces that could not enter through these "I's." Conducting rhetorical analysis of the writing tasks as assigned in conjunction with these journal analyses could lay the groundwork for writers who will later compare on-the-job assignments with subjectivities they are able to document.

At the same time that we ask composers to identify and characterize these subjectivities, we might ask them to focus portions of journal entries on their affective response to composing work on the project with which they are engaged. Based on documentations of affect, we might revisit cliché concepts such as "writer's block," for example, to map discursive forces at work to produce, sustain, or undo such blocking. Most valuable in this exercise would be not so much the "unblocking" as tracing the discursive impulses that appeared to engender the initial stasis as well as those that enabled writing. At opposite ends of our grand narrative spectrum lie the mental turmoils of the singular artist at grips with the muses and the workaday writer churning out prose; in between lie many narratives, many discourses, and their subjects, which can enable us to construct impetuses in instrumental discourse as personally powerful as the mythical impetuses of artistic creation. Catherine Belsey speaks of a "concept of a dialectical relationship between concrete individuals and the language in which their subjectivities are constructed" to support "the concept of subjectivity as in process" (66). Such journal work could form valuable baseline documentation for exploring such a dialectical relationship, while framing "process" within composing in ways that revise the modernist underpinnings noted by Sharon Crowley. Writers in various local workplace cultures who undertake journal work on subjectivities-in-process might likewise compare their entries with the many representations of psychological and sociological realities in chapter 5, the better to imagine new unities.

Political Subjectivities

In exploring convergences between feminist research and postmodern theory, Patti Lather speaks of "seeing subjectivity as both socially produced in language, at conscious and unconscious levels, and as a site of struggle and potential change" (118). At unconscious levels, subjectivity is produced by workplace discourses that position subjects in specific ways with respect to other subjects in the local culture and which implicitly specify subjects' ranges of action in organizational work. Identifying these discourses and positions—that is, shifting them from the unconscious to the conscious—is a difficult task best achieved in workshop environments. To prepare such work in the classroom, we might prompt readings of first-person accounts similar to those discussed above, this time with an emphasis on implicit shaping of authority—in its scope and nature. If the future workplace of symbolic analysts is to be one of high-value, then clearly authority must be allocated on the basis of knowledge rather than organizational position, even if this allocation is temporary and malleable in tandem with other factors. Moreover, because writers are a class of professionals that nurtures a particular self-consciousness with respect to one's relationships to the discourses in which an "I" appear, studying writers will need methods to help them glean contours of this local authority within larger discursive arenas.

One method entails revisiting the concept of "voice," a mainstay of modernist thought yet particularly fecund for postmodern interpretations because of its metaphorical nature, as demonstrated by Carl Leggo through the questions he asks that reframe "voice" in postmodern terms. If we free "voice" from the essentialized notions of subjectivity typical of modernist thought, that is, that writers find their "true voices" connected with some essential, innate characteristic, then we can begin to hear other murmurings. In "Voice Lessons in a Poststructural Key," Linda Brodkey and I took up this task, drawing on the material language theory of David Silverman and Brian Torode that provides interpretations of subjects' appearances in discourse as always inflected by the power relations with other theoretical subjects. Their analysis is grounded in Louis Althusser's notion of the subject as interpellated by ideological state apparatuses and seems to respond to critiques of Althusser's somewhat mechanistic structuralism precisely by tracing the shifting power relations from moment to moment in discursive appearances. One begins by understanding a "voice" as the relationship between a discourse and its identifiable subjects, then by way of articulation theory to discern "how ideological elements come, under certain conditions, to cohere together within a discourse, and a way of asking how they do or do not become articulated, at specific junctures, to certain political subjects" (Hall 53). For writers building their repertoires of techniques for tracing contours of their subjectivities in discourses in which they are implicated, understanding a voice as carrying vestiges of state apparatuses that position us all with respect to each other by virtue of power rather than knowledge can foster an acuity for hearing these voices in mundane workplace discourses.

A glance at the multiple discourses and underlying discourses identified by researchers in chapter 5 provides a preliminary array of discourses likely to be encountered by writers in workplace cultures. Multiple discourses—from business discourse to legal discourse to news discourses, by way of many incidental discourses along the way—will shape the voices of organizational documents; underlying discourses with intentions from the (ostensibly) benign to the flagrantly malignant will likewise direct voices. Practicing writers can benefit from contemplating the voices turned up by archaeologies and analyzing them with the critical skills nurtured through discourse studies. Even before entering workplace cultures, writers might analyze extant examples of workplace documents for the voices they air and the attendant subject positions of culture members. David Jolliffe's readings of workplace documents for identity formation, using Norman Fairclough's notion of "interdiscursivity," might aid readers in framing and elaborating such analysis, particularly as he links agency as *implied* in training documents as contrasted with real organizational purview (347). In classrooms, writers might tap the practice of journaling once again to frame similar readings and to compose individual techniques for constructing such frames, perhaps using double entries to react to and analyze affective responses in the process. Beyond the walls of the classroom and in the interest of shaping professional class solidarity in the interest of change, writers might share observations on subject positions in workplace discourses by means of discussion lists and other virtual forums, an idea forwarded by Cynthia L. Selfe and Richard J. Selfe Jr. and addressed at greater length in chapter 8.

Ideological Subjectivities

Though analyses of political subjectivities frequently subsume analyses of ideology (as Hall's comment above implies), it is worth our while as part of an inquiry into discourse production to create a separate category, if only to demystify the notion of ideology and to name it as a force immanent to all discourse. Catherine Belsey defines ideology as "the sum of the ways in which people both live and represent to themselves their relationship to the conditions of their existence" (42), thus establishing ideology as a force with which we all contend. As chapters 4 and 5 demonstrate, when professional writers undertake analyses of workplace cultures in which they are (or might be) members, the representations that they compose give them the *occasion* to ponder their conditions of existence within the organization and with respect to other professional classes which they otherwise simply would not have.

When we narrow ideological analysis to workplace cultures, conditions of existence range from the purely physical "cube city" (Adam, final ethnography) inhabited by most professional writers to economic and political conditions in the processes of production. In his three spheres of class formation discussed earlier, Frow underscores *relations* among classes, in the process identifying " semiotic constructions of the subject form" (106), which suggests discerning more fully the ways in which the professional class of writer take form via using the appearances of an "I" in writers' depictions of their relationships to the conditions of their workplace existences. Because class formation is always in process (albeit with certain characteristics that remain fairly constant), questioning processes (and hypothetical end products) can aid writers in discerning the subjectivities they are invited to and obliged to inhabit in the workplace. Workshops and virtual forums seem indispensable to such questioning and to inquiry into the range of interests which this professional class claims and thereby uses to establish relations with other professional classes. Particularly in the context of high-value production, writers and researchers will want to follow the leads of Frow and others who seek to uncover relations between ideological value and value in other spheres. One might, in fact, devote an entire course to such theoretical inquiry, rendered rich by case studies and richer still by pondering the moments when "discourse" understood in the modernist sense takes on fuller significance through postmodern framings. The effects of discourse outlined in the last two sections of chapter 5, from withdrawal of engagement to heightened senses of awareness regarding self-documentation to the production of waste, constitute ideological shaping of subjectivity that certainly bears scrutiny.

Patti Lather sees ideology as "the stories a culture tells itself about itself" (2), suggesting that an analysis of ideological subjectivity as discursively shaped incorporate observations made by autoethnographers on the stories workplace cultures tell about themselves. Intrinsic to ethnographic methodology since the interpretive turn has been the principle of *reflexivity*, the ongoing consideration of the researcher's social, political, economic, cultural, and other origins as they influence perception of and inscription of a culture. As James Clifford states it, "every version of an 'other,' *wherever found*, is also a construction of a 'self'" (23, emphasis mine). Clifford's point was to signal the movement of ethnography in 1986 into areas previously reserved for other discursive practices (e.g., sociology, literature, cultural critique); a central thesis to this archaeology is that one might easily enlarge this realm to include so-called instrumental discourses. With each positing of an "other" via the products of an organization comes a construction of the writerly "self," which, when compared with inquiries into subjectivity suggested above, can yield insight on the writers' workplace lives, the salubrity of their workplace cultures, and the agencies that take form through the practices and structures that discursively shape conceptions of the "other."

This point seems particularly relevant to the "ethos" of composing, addressed at length in chapter 7, and to revisions of "process pedagogy" that heed Sharon Crowley's critique of it. According to Zora Neale Hurston scholar Michelle Smith-Bermiss, Hurston's approach to autoethnography was one that underscored the process aspects of such writing:

> She had a very studied "anti-scientific" approach. She rejects the illusion of scholarly impartiality and looks at ethnographic writing, and particularly autoethnographic writing, I think, as a process rather than a revelation. She doesn't sit and say, "Well, I've noted x number of facts and observed this amount of time and so I know something, concrete and finite," but rather this is something that gets worked out again and again. (in class, 3/18/98)

Because she understands "process" in ways that dislodge it from end products, in ways that in fact defy holding up any one artifact as exemplar—the better to situate writing as a valuable ongoing reconstruction of selves and others *and* the epistemologies that link them—her approach to autoethnography could reinvigorate process pedagogy. By integrating the concerns of autoethnographic subjects in process into discourse studies designed for writers, we might imagine curricula that will serve writers in the workplace as they ponder their discursive subjectivities and plan courses of action to reshape them as they deem pertinent.

The notion of reflexivity is invaluable to autoethnographers, too, as they train "new eyes" to view familiar surroundings, constructing new "I's" in the process. Whether or not professional writers are formally engaged in cultural analyses of the workplace, guarding against lethargy in interpreting workplace cultures and the constructions of one's subjectivity within them seems vital not only to personal mental health (Challie, final ethnography) but also to a sense of connection to the ongoing processes of professional class formation sketched above. This aspect of subjectivity is explored at greater length in the discussion of intersubjective research in contact zones in chapter 8.

Economic Subjectivities

Discourse studies focused on economic subjectivities might seem quite foreign to the field of composition, yet the imbrication of economic class relations with those in the political and ideological spheres make such studies indispensable. These studies would begin with an organization's bottom line and then break it down into its components, tracing salaries for all professionals involved along with their contributions to the organization's product. To the extent possible, analyses of end value and value added by contributors would be conducted. Such analyses would both render visible the subtleties of division of labor and more importantly delineate the symbolic capital that various classes of professionals bring to the organization's goals and missions. Symbolic capital, for writers, translates into fungible contributions to an organization's end products and to its local culture, an aspect often elided by current-traditional understandings of discourse as mere communicative packaging.

Through such explorations of subjectivity as shaped and reshaped through specific organizational structures and practices articulated to varieties of discursive conditions, composition could begin to realize some of the goals staked out by compositionists eyeing the postmodern condition. In the following pages are presented some ideas for specific curricula aimed at these goals.

Designing Professional Writing Curricula

One of the many boons of the emergence of composition as a field has been the broadening of the conceptualization of curricula at the postsecondary level. At most U.S. colleges and certainly at research universities in the twentieth century, curricula have been for the most part construed narrowly as bodies of knowledge to be imparted to students, usually by various departments who claim dominion over particular ways of knowing. This concept of curriculum, termed by Eisner and Vallance the "academic rationalist," has its roots in university structures dating to the twelfth century (Holmes). Yet other concepts of curricula exist, tied to different philosophical traditions and focusing less on predetermined bodies of knowledge and more on other aspects of teaching and learning in institutionalized settings. One such concept identifies the focus of curriculum to be students' "self-actualization" (Eisner and Vallance), and one of composition's achievements has been to validate this concept as part of college and university curricula. With the advent of process pedagogy and composer-centered instruction, students' self-actualization has assumed new epistemological status—which is no small issue in light of the forgoing discussions of subjectivities and earlier discussions of discursive selves. The ideas for writing course conceptualization that follow, grounded in researchers' analyses of workplace cultures, assume such an approach to curriculum development.

Like the ideas for exploring writers' subjectivities above, these writing courses envision a paradigmatic alternative to current-traditionalism suggested by Sharon Crowley. She expands upon such curricular alternatives:

> Many universities and colleges already offer an array of upper-division courses in creative, technical, and professional writing. I would like to see this array of courses supplemented by a vertical elective curriculum in composing, a curriculum that examines composing both in general and as it takes place in specific rhetorical situations such as workplaces and community decision making. . . . The topmost reaches of an undergraduate curriculum in composing would study histories of writing, debate the politics of literacy, and investigate the specialized composing tactics and rhetorics that have evolved in disciplines, professions, civic groups, women's organizations, social movements and political parties—to name only a few sites where such investigation could fruitfully take place. (*Composition* 262)

The ideas for courses that follow could be used at both undergraduate and graduate levels, dovetailing with the kinds of histories, debates, and investigations sketched by Crowley.

Organizational Studies for Writers

We need courses that explore the constellation of organizational structures and processes of information flow within them, conceived not for managers who oversee these structures and flows (as so many courses in organizational studies are) but for writers who will tap into them, use them in their writing to enhance values in the organization, and monitor them as they imply new links between needs and solutions and as they reflect the workplace cultures that writers write. Because writing instruction in the United States has for so long been grounded in singular authorship, writers' views of writing as linked to systems thinking—one of the crucial components of a symbolic analyst's education, according to Reich (230)—are underdeveloped. Writing courses in on-line environments hold great potential to help students reconceptualize authorship as plural and their places in it as complex; if we can add dimensions to these courses that incorporate elements of organizational systems, "systems thinking" may become integral to understandings of authorship much in the ways that it is already integral to understandings of phenomena in other disciplines preparing students for the workplace. (Ironically, English departments, which customarily assume progressive stances on campus and cultural issues, send their charges into the workplace with similar stances, perhaps, yet with little in the way of the institutional knowledge and strategies needed to promote these stances, as compared with graduates from other disciplines.) We need courses that equip writers intellectually with knowledge of organizational pasts and presents.

In the research sites represented in this archaeology alone, we can see organizational structures and practices varying dramatically depending upon the size and nature of the organization, from the informal structures and ad hoc practices of small businesses to the rigid, hierarchical structures and protocol-laden practices of most trade associations, by way of vast government structures that target the public as audience through layers of mediation or public relations firms that target the public as consumer in the interests of a client—with a wealth of implications for writing along the way. Researchers' topics and themes in analyzing the workplace cultures of these sites suggest that we include in courses on organizational studies the genesis and forms of mission statements, policies, and organizational procedures, as writers write them and live them. Case studies could provide valuable concrete examples *in situ* and could allow comparisons with subcultural dynamics as sketched in archaeologies such as this (see chapter 4), perhaps even highlighting the dynamics resulting from specific players and organizational alliances. What kinds of documents do specific organizations author? What are the origins, the evolutions, and the effects of these documents? What kinds of relations and ideologies do they authorize? What connections can be made, theoretically and historically, to other discursive work, including the discourses of surveillance and panoptics of the nineteenth century as they shaped the ideological panoptics of increasingly archaic organizational structures at the end of the twentieth century? What ideas do such connections spur among writers for the kinds of value they will seek in high-value organizations?

Cultural Histories and Traditions

In addition to studies of contemporary organizations, we need historical studies of the deeds and effects of organizations. This would include copies of documents and depictions of contributors' roles in elaborating them, if possible, as these documents constitute deeds and frequently track the effects, both planned and unforeseen, as they ripple through local and larger cultures. Writers could also benefit from analyzing documents that record these deeds. Alongside any discursive representations that organizations might want to furnish, research by independent historians focused on discursive constructions in historical contexts could aid discourse workers enormously. Such a course would explore this general question: Where and how has writing (and different kinds of writerly subjectivities) been shaped in organizational America? To be eschewed would be the cliché accounts focusing on a "great man's" vision and its enactment through the organization in favor of the day-by-day discursive operations and writers' roles and subjectivities in them, not unlike the historical accounts of daily French life by Braudel.

Writers could not only study these accounts but reenact scenarios, perhaps role-playing to collectively reproduce discursive moments, then compare this reproduction with studies of discursive subjectivities in other courses and with historical contexts surrounding these accounts. As we approach an age in which whole generations of writers have no familiarity with such tools as carbon paper or Liquid Paper, reenactments that link specific technologies with specific organizational forms, missions, and the discursive subjectivities they produced could provide writers with great insight on their current technologies and the forms and subjectivities linked to them. Johndan Johnson-Eilola's observations on the ways in which hypertext composing in workplace settings affects cultural dynamics are pertinent:

> In traditional cases workers experiencing difficulties or having questions about their task are likely to consult a colleague or supervisor for help. But because the integrated hypertext and task allows them to find quickly the information they need to complete their task, workers are less likely

to consult a source outside their currently assigned work area or task (that assignment can be explicit or implicit)—physical, social, and mental patterns and processes lose distinction. (*Nostalgic* 82)

As workplace composing becomes increasingly hypertextual, we will need courses in cultural histories and traditions that track changes in organizational social patterns alongside changes in writing technologies, to enhance writers' understandings of their discursive work as ideologically shaped by the technologies channeling it. Alongside such courses could come inquiries into specific industries, and the discursive practices and traditions associated with them. Such studies might enable writers in different kinds of industries to nurture senses of subjectivity tied to valuable discursive traditions and intellectually strong enough to resist the scuttling of tradition by Taylorization. The case of Red's local newspaper office installing time clocks for reporters comes to mind.

Christina Haas analyzes histories and traditions of writing through the lens of technology studies, suggesting ways in which such studies could dovetail with writing courses aimed at imparting wisdom on cultural histories and traditions:

> Today's writing technologies have a heritage that can be traced back to the earliest tools of writing. At each "stage" of a contemporary writing technology's development, theories of use and practice shape how it was, and is, developed. . . . The effects of any given technology—here, computer tools—will multiply in complexity with every level of development and every new use to which the technology is put. Unraveling the threads of technology development and use, through historical as well as empirical studies, will be the kind of interdisciplinary project that Technology Studies can pursue. (229)

One might retrace the histories and powers of writing in ways similar to that of Henri-Jean Martin, who traces ways in which cultural processes and understandings of written discourse have intertwined through the ages. We might ponder, with Martin and many others, the ways in which interpersonal subjectivities shifted dramatically with the advent of the printing press as it reshaped the dissemination of writing and hence constructions and understandings of authorship (see Woodmansee) and as it shaped a new autonomy for readers. And as we ponder ways in which subjectivities will be reshaped by the printing press's twentieth-century equivalent, the computer, we might also reconsider the implications of reader autonomy and reading formations. Tony Bennett and Janet Woollacott's discussion of reading formations, valuable in probing the ways in which curricular choices shape subjectivities in discursive consumption, could in this way be linked to studies of writing formations and their shaping of discursive production. Such studies seem necessary, given the fact that historical events such as the invention of the printing press have constructed reading as a solitary act, pushing us to conceptualize writing similarly, when current thought in both the workplace and the academy tell us that such a conceptualization is woefully inadequate. As subjects who not only produce discourse but also inhabit subjectivities that discourses have produced, writers dwell in circuits of production and consumption subtly shaped by organizational histories and traditions, raising questions of intertextuality much in the way that such questions have been linked to literary authorship yet broadening the database to include texts drawn from virtually any discursive practice or tradition relevant to a particular workplace culture (see discussions by Brady and by Selzer on intertextuality and professional writing).

Collaborative Composition

For years, Andrea Lunsford and Lisa Ede have been exhorting us to conceptualize composition as a collaborative endeavor and to offer more courses affording students the experience of composing collaboratively and reflecting productively about the processes involved. "If men and women in the work force frequently write collaboratively," they say in *Singular Texts/Plural Authors,* "should not writing teachers help prepare them for an important part of their job?" (13) Lately, Their position has been echoed by numerous scholars in composition (see, for example, the collection of essays edited by Reagan et al.), and by scholars outside the field such as Robert Reich, in his discussion of collaboration as being among the four skills most vital to symbolic analysts:

> Learning to collaborate, communicate abstract concepts, and achieve a consensus are not usually emphasized within formal education, however. To the contrary, within most classrooms in the United States . . . the overall objective is to achieve quiet and solitary performance of specialized tasks. (233)

Almost as stark confirmation of the ways in which the enduring effects of public schooling's Taylorization in the twentieth century have increased the rift among social classes, he continues:

> Yet in America's best classrooms, again, the emphasis has shifted. Instead of individual achievements and competition, the focus is on group learning. Students learn to articulate, clarify, and then restate for one another how they identify and find answers. They learn how to seek and accept criticism from peers, solicit help, and give credit to others. They also learn to negotiate—to explain their own needs, to discern what others need and view things from others' perspectives, and to discover mutually beneficial resolutions. This is an ideal preparation for lifetimes of symbolic-analytic teamwork. (233)

Reich is not referring to writing classrooms (since so few writing courses are constructed on a fundamentally collaborative model), yet his comments hint at the potential of such courses when teamed with concepts such as writing as a mode of learning—anticipating ways in which writers in organizational settings can bring their expertise to bear on organizational value. Lunsford and Ede frame observations not only with respect to writing's relations to epistemology (and hence value) but also with respect to the issue of discursive selves so central to this archaeology:

> For teachers of writing, however, the most immediate need is for a pedagogy of collaboration, one that would view writing as always shared and social; writers as constantly building and negotiating meaning with and among others; and evaluation as based at least in part on a "range of selves" and on communal efforts. ("Collaborative Authorship" 438)

The dynamics of collective procedures and writing discussed in chapter 4 illustrate the degree to which writing is always shared and social, as do the kinds of writing displayed in the opening sections of chapter 5. Clearly, this archaeology confirms Lunsford and Ede's claim while displaying "ranges of selves" that might be pondered in elaborating not only evaluation but also the kinds of knowledge rendered possible through such courses, a point explored in chapter 7's discussion of writers' expertise. Integral to collaborative writing in today's classrooms are, of course, computers—the technological development that has revolutionized writing and reading formations as no other development since the printing press yet while remaining narrowly conceptualized in much writing curricula.

Computerized Composition and "Informating"

In her discussion of the shift in the organization of industrial life from the earlier "automated age" inherited from the industrial revolution to the "informated age," Zuboff observes the danger of archaic organizational forms in this new age:

> Unless informating is taken up as a conscious strategy, rather than simply allowed to unfold without any anticipation of its consequences, it is unlikely to yield up its full value. The centerpiece of such a strategy must be a redefinition of the system of authority that is expressed in and maintained by the traditional industrial division of labor. (309)

Her reference to "value" resonates with earlier discussions of high-value economies and the need to better prepare symbolic analysts, and the workplaces they enter, for such work. The systems of authority to which she refers locate authority in hierarchical position, rather than in the knowledge produced through the exercise of one's profession. Clearly, the implication is once again for flattening hierarchies to best exploit workers' potentials.

Other implications abound. As a stand-alone machine and without adequate curricular goals and contexts, the computer merely speeds writing and knowledge production processes, depriving writers of rethinking their writing as fundamentally as the computer is reshaping writing. Stuart Selber's "Beyond Skill Building: Challenges Facing Technical Communication Teachers in the Computer Age," grounded in a survey of actual computerized composition courses on a number of campuses, exposes the limits of computerized composition without adequate contextualization—not just for technical communication teachers but for *all* writing teachers. Selber lauds the efforts of educators who integrate "literacy and humanistic concerns" into the conceptualization of computerized composition; such concerns are vital to professional writers as they study writing, reconstruct its conceptualization in the informating age, and ponder its role not only in organizational authority but also in organizational authorship, explored in chapter 7.

Johndan Johnson-Eilola links studies such as those by Selber on classroom instruction with current organization of workplace computing in "Relocating the Value of Work: Technical Communication in a Post-Industrial Age." Using Reich's discussion of symbolic-analytical work as touchstone, he updates earlier approaches to substantiate the "value added" by technical communicators, in the process sketching lines of inquiry that might enhance our understanding of the writing of workplace cultures in the computer age. He analyzes, for example, recent trends in industry such as "reengineering" as in fact a newfound focus on communication, a domain in which writers, writing scholars, and writing instructors have been generating knowledge and hence value for years. His analysis suggests probing further the kinds of knowledge that writers always bring to a workplace context tacitly and pondering the implications for rendering such knowledge explicit; as we do this we should simultaneously explore and expose the ways in which this knowledge is inextricably bound to other knowledge, other aims, and other subjects.

Johnson-Eilola extends his analysis of computer-mediated composition and its instruction in *Nostalgic Angels: Rearticulating Hypertext Writing* to note various ways in which the advent of hypertext necessitates inspecting the technological subjectivities engendered by it, observing that "in order to construct hypertext as a socially empowering technology, we have to expand our vision to the social, mapping the world and living the map" (173). The mapping he suggests could easily draw on discourses such as workplace archaeologies provide:

> In hypertext discourses, what escapes is often the social milieu in which the technology is developed, used, and remade. Critical theories and pedagogies of hypertext must begin mapping these uses, users, and discourses against each other—the endless task of cognitively mapping local to global that is only ever struggle, never resolution. (240)

As we draw such maps, we can in the process reexamine some of our catch-metaphors for writing. To the metaphorical characterizations of writerly selves as "reverse prisms" and "channels" in solitary production can be added those of "nodes" or "links" when writers' work takes place in networks, in systems of information and knowledge. Consider Starla's role of scanning major newspapers daily for work-worthy information, or Albert's role as "in charge of the public image of the organization" on the World Wide Web. The position of node in information flow is no small charge, given that information often functions as capital in an organization's value. As we design curricula that prompt students to reflect upon these metaphors and their implications, we would do well to include in our designs elements that would prompt students to conceptualize such nodes and links as multidimensional, to virtual forums that inform writers as a class of professional, for example. Says Cynthia Selfe:

> For nondominant groups, e-mail is a particularly potent site for discursive exchange because it ameliorates some of the geographic barriers that hinder collective action, providing direct access to individuals and other groups who share dissatisfactions, concerns, and solutions. In this way, e-mail also serves as a possible site for individual agency, resistance, and collective action based on the rhetorical articulation of shared ideological positions. (278)

As we represent discursive work among ourselves and to our students as inevitably bound to classes in formation, developing courses that enable writers to build positions on and within such formations is indispensable.

Pondering Discursive Shards and Imagining New Writing Vessels

The melding of computer technology and writing has shaped professional writers' work in local cultures as fundamentally as did the reorganization of those cultures along Taylorist lines early in the twentieth century. As the discussions in part two and this chapter intimate, moreover, computerized writing has enormous implications for the shapes of discursive subjectivities to come. Psychological and sociological subjectivities will be shaped by the ways in which entries into computerized, webbed discourse will change with advances in technology. Political subjectivities will change as writers are able to forge new alliances beyond the boundaries of workplace cultures, with writers in other cultures and with allies in the academy. Ideological subjectivities will change as computerized writing enhances the ways in which subjects can construct representations for themselves of their conditions of work lives. Ultimately, the discursive scenes of workplace writing could serve as invaluable empirical records of the constructions of "self" and "other" that organizations and their discourses engender and promote. Surely, such constructions will figure prominently in the century ahead as we find ourselves compelled to explore genuinely the constructions of self and other that lie at the core of inequitable—even hostile—relations within the nation and beyond it. The multidisciplinarity of discourse studies as a field makes it rich with potential for such explorations, and composition's focus on discursive production, rather than discursive consumption, positions it as a promising part of such studies.

As we ponder discursive shards from archaeologies such as this one and as we attempt to imagine new writing vessels, we can perhaps rectify the long-standing belief in English departments that composition is somehow "contentless." In the impoverished forums of English classrooms, writing does often appear a mere vehicle for expressing thoughts. but in workplace writing, the "content" of composition is the work it effects, the realities it mediates, and the subjectivities it shapes. The more often we can represent discursive work in this light within the academy, the more we can garner support from colleagues in other disciplines and from agents in positions of academic stewardship and public oversight. Composition made remarkable strides in representing (and revising) understandings of discourse production in the last three decades of the twentieth century, and as technological advances continue, the potential for composition studies to yield more knowledge and more value for the academy and the workplace seems great.

These same technological advances, however, can collude with current-traditional epistemologies of composition as forwarded by most English departments to reproduce an understanding of writing as contentless, of the shaping of subjectivities through discursive work as a by-product rather than a fascinating, vital focus. Writing in "Distant Voices: Teaching and Writing in a Culture of Technology," Chris M. Anson says,

> With the potential for the further automation of writing instruction through the use of telecommuting and other technology-supported shifts in instructional delivery, composition may be further subordinated to the interests of powerful subject-oriented disciplines where the conception of expertise creates rather different patterns of hiring and material support. (275)

He is referring to the trend in scientifically managed academic environments to reduce full-time faculty ranks through part-time employees capable of serving the "powerful subject-oriented disciplines." Of course, these disciplines lie elsewhere than English at present, but discourse studies could very well rise in prominence with the growing recognition that "the subject" is a subject vital not only in the ideological but also the economic and political spheres.

As we continue to demonstrate how vital this subject is, and can be, we will vest our students and our collaborating professional writers with an expertise on a par with those from other disciplines. To do so, we will have to re-present writing in workplace contexts, too, the topic of the next chapter.

7 REPRESENTING DISCURSIVE WORK IN THE WORKPLACE

The basic triad of elements (writer, audience, text) that we have
distilled from classical theory is not sufficient to explain or to
model the practice of rhetoric in today's economic world.
—Mary Beth Debs, "Corporate Authority"

If you have a master's in English, you should be an *expert*.
—Bernie, in class, 2/2/93

Bernie's comment, voiced in the second class meeting of the first offering of the course Cultures of Professional Writing, reflected his central aim in returning to graduate school: to develop expertise on a par with the legal writers whom he regularly edited in his workplace. His progress reports, research, and comments in class occasionally referenced the second-class status that he lived in professionally and which he found unfulfilling. Over the years, such concerns about status have been echoed by the large majority of course participants, and many of them have addressed this phenomenon directly in their research, as discussed in chapter 4. Whether living workplace lives as "functionaries," "ghosts," or "support staff," professional writers experience their status as second-class to "subject matter experts" and other colleagues from various professional classes. And whether or not one empathizes with their affective response to this condition, as writing scholars and as writers who know firsthand the power of writing, we should be prompted to probe the (mis-)representations underpinning such status.

Composition epistemology as conveyed through teaching practices that reduce the locus of writing expertise primarily to formal qualities surely has much to do with the misunderstandings of writing beyond the walls of the academy. If we imagine the curriculum vitae of professionals from all classes in any given workplace, their formal writing instruction, in perhaps 95 percent of the cases, holds one element in common: Composition 101. And as earlier discussions argue, the representation of writing conveyed through most generic composition courses over the years has remained essentially formalist, current-traditional, and modernist. Recent college graduates may have benefited from writing intensive courses in various disciplines or writing across the curriculum (WAC) courses, but the standard for measuring the epistemology of writing remains composition. Recent innovations in composition instruction that make use of draft and revision, peer response, "freewriting," and the like may have enhanced professionals' understanding of writing *processes* yet done little to prompt understandings of writing as a unique form of meaning production and of discursive engagement as shaping realities rather than merely reflecting them.

Moreover, other professionals who have benefitted from writing instruction under the process paradigm and in content areas will have used writing to build knowledge in content areas with immediate applications in organizational contexts. The MBA looms as the most unequivocal example; a survey of course topics and applications associated with them in other disciplines would certainly yield similar examples. The professional writers in this archaeology, who hold degrees almost exclusively in English, bring no similar "content area" knowledge to workplace cultures. (Other archaeologies might reveal degrees in areas such as communications, for example, in which case the melding of communications knowledge with writing knowledge produces a unique kind of "content," but here again, popular conceptions of "communication" as messages following unilinear paths from senders to receivers represents communications specialists' expertise, also, as essentially formal.) Professionals with degrees in business, government, engineering, organizational psychology, and the like enter the work force with a knowledge of some subject area linked closely with an organization's products or the management of its production. Because these employees have expertise that allows them to originate the products of their organization or to situate these products historically and in the marketplace (as in the case of legal services, say), their status hovers above that of writers, who handle "only" the discourse surrounding these products.

As writing teachers, we might be moved to re-present discursive work to the workplace by the effects on writer psychology bound up in representations of writers' work as purely formal: withdrawal of engagement, low morale, frustration, resignation, and insecurity (see chapter 5). Or as workplace managers, we might be moved to seek a new re-presentation in the interest of reshaping dynamics between the individual and the organization (see chapter 4) and hence potentially enhancing the value that will be generated in the workplace. Or as writing scholars and professional writers, we might be moved to represent discursive work to the workplace by sheer dismay at the poverty of current models as compared with the richness of writerly experience. Whatever the motivations, we can begin by revisiting theories of authorship, in the hopes that a cultural construct so broadly constructed from multiple roots can serve as intellectual meeting place for people reapproaching writing in twenty-first-century organizational contexts.

Representing Authorship

In chapter 2 I presented a brief account of the ways in which the "author function," as Foucault would term it, has worked culturally to establish domains of discursive exclusivity, locating writing from students and workplaces in the lower realms. Academic debates about "authorship" as a concept reifying the transcendent ego have been filtered to a broader public through media focus on such catch-phrases as Barthes's now famous "death of the author" (*Image, Music, Text*). Like Nietzsche's murder of god, Barthes's homicide has provoked strong responses, variously motivated, no doubt, yet galvanized certainly by the apparent evacuation of individual will from discursive acts. To popular representations of scholarly inquiry gone awry, one might counter with Richard Freed's observation: "the so-called death of the author, however, doesn't mean his demise, only that the scribe is always already circumscribed" (212). Mass representations of the "author" resist an equation with "scribe," of course, yet even this semantic sticking point might be argued through historical investigations that locate scribes as part of a larger authoring process (Woodmansee); in the hermeneutical tradition, moreover, the *most* hegemonic texts were products not of original individual writing but of transcription of the divine word.

Yet the conditions of circumscription in authorship, as popularly conceptualized, have remained largely physical rather than ideological. Just as Composition 101 serves as a cultural reference point for most professionals reflecting on the nature of writing and composing, so have literature courses focusing on the works of fiction or poetry, published under the names of individuals, shaped most people's notions of authorship. In addition to scholastic experiences, popular framings of authorship via best-seller lists, book signings, and the like contribute to an understanding of the author as the solitary, originating, published writer discussed in chapter 2. By such measures, professional writers are never implicated in authorship, the realities of their discursive work reflecting precisely the antithesis, as represented in Sharon Crowley's ironic comment cited earlier: "there's writing, which is the simple ordering and recording of thoughts or information and which can be done as easily by a secretary or a committee or a machine or a technical writer" ("writing" 97). The title of "secretary" signals not only a gendered position but also a functionary one, two traits that distinguish professional writing as often practiced. That professional writers often compose collaboratively (even if not by "committee") and allocate part of the writing process to machines (by virtue of having mastered software that their bureaucratic masters haven't mastered) additionally places them outside the realm of authorship as popularly construed.

Crowley refers as well to "technical writers" in parodying our broad cultural constructions, evoking images of techno-functionaries charged with the apparently transparent task of documenting other people's realities. And as unlikely to most people as this particular realm of professional writing might seem in enlarging notions of authorship, some of the most provocative work on linking authorship theory with authorship practice has come from this realm. By way of example, if the image of a near automaton suggested by Crowley seems too hyperbolic, Jennifer Slack, David Miller, and Jeffrey Doak render the hyperbolic real: "We want robots!" stated an industry recruiter for technical communicators on their campus (31). The authors demonstrate convincingly how technical writers are never functioning as near machines in an uncircumscribed space, whether or not their coworkers, or even the writers themselves, acknowledge it. Reviewing communications models in order to demonstrate the shortcomings of the "transmission" model, the authors draw upon articulation theory to point out that communication always "articulates" all subjects implicated in the process to power and knowledge, albeit in varying ways depending upon institutional location, local practices, and so on. Slack, Doak, and Miller designate all technical writers authors by linking this theory with a Foucauldian theory of authorship focusing not on flesh-and-blood subjects but on their discursive counterparts in circuits of discourse production:

> Whether they desire it or not, technical communicators are seen as variously adding, deleting, changing, and selecting meaning. Again, whether they desire it or not, they are always implicated in relations of power. Their work is at least *complicit* in the production, reproduction, or subversion of relations of power. This is necessarily the case, even when the acceptance of the transmission or translation model may occlude the nature of the work they do. Technical communicators *are* authors, even when they comply with the rules of discourse that deny them that recognition. (31)

My own experience as a technical writer illustrates some gains for organizational writers, their readers, and organizations when we problematize the authorship of instrumental discourse. When I worked as a technical writer in the railroad industry, I was charged with revising operating rules (in collaboration with a committee of fifteen content experts) to render them readable for employees of high school education or less. That job not only sent me to readability research to discover the reductive, simplistic, purely formal principles underpinning readability formulae, it also enabled me to see how elements such as document design could radically change reception of text. (McKenzie's study of the redesign of plays in the eighteenth century as "forms effecting meaning" [Chartier] comes once again to mind.) As I was beginning my foray into narratological theory at the time, the experience also enabled me to read the operating rules as a text presenting real readers with an implied reader, with whom they would or would not identify and hence engage with the text. In conjunction with this implied reader, of course, was an implied author for the text, whose image I shaped as I conducted my research and as we completed our collaborative revision, establishing in the process new textual formulations of users' places and purviews in the relations of power at work in this organization.

It is perhaps precisely because technical writing has for so long been understood as the unproblematic representation of some preexisting reality, in which the writer's task is to perfectly mirror that reality in discourse, that the field has responded to social constructionist tenets that dispel the mirror metaphor with provocative re-presentations of authorship such as those offered by Slack, Miller, and Doak. One of the germinal theoretical pieces in the field is Carolyn Miller's "What's Practical about Technical Writing?" in which she observes the Greek understanding of rhetoric as an art (or *techne*), which reverberates with researchers' representations of themselves as writers in chapter 2. In discussing practical rhetoric, Miller provides historical analysis, observing two associations attributed to the "practical" deriving from classical Greek usage: a "high" sense which "derives from the Aristotelian concept of praxis and underlies modern philosophical pragmatism, [and which] concerns human conduct in those activities that maintain the life of the community" (15) and a "low" sense having to do more with accomplishing mundane activities of "the world of work" (15), by people unconcerned with theory. Noting the system of slavery in place in the culture that gave birth to such distinctions (it was the slaves who performed most of the mundane activities while free male citizens partook in activities concerning the life of the community), Miller wonders rhetorically if "we might question whether this association should prevail" (15).

Of course, the association does prevail, and one of the enduring debates in technical writing circles has centered on the motivations of technical writing curricula: the academy's designs or the workplace's needs. Proponents of the latter have sought high praxis by bringing "theory" into their classrooms in forms as apparently neutral as document design theory, for example. Proponents of the former have leaned towards the social constructionist theories such as those invoked by Slack, Miller, and Doak and which seem eminently more promising for reshaping broader cultural perceptions of authorship. Until we can re-present the seemingly "low" practical dimensions of authorship as *always* implicated in "high" practices imbricated in broad, deep, vital cultural issues, a slavery of another form will endure—the slavery of workers to ideologies that misrepresent their work, manifested not coincidentally through the ongoing formation of a professional class consisting mostly of women (see chapter 2).

This archaeology not only argues for professional writing curricula that are motivated by both the academy and the workplace, it proposes some novel forms in chapters 6 and 8. Integral to these forms, as might be expected, are professional writers as emissaries, border workers who move between both cultures to inform each. Here the social force of "teacher" that frequently enters discourse through the writing self, documented in chapter 2 yet rarely mentioned as part of writers' roles in organizations in chapter 4, can prove extremely valuable: part of our professional writing curricula should focus on the roles of professional writers in teaching discourse theory to the workplace and in teaching workplace cultures to the academy. Such a positioning of "student" subjectivity seems vital to me, as I have argued in "Teaching Technical Authorship." At the same time, professional bodies such as the Society for Technical Communication (the largest professional organization for professional writers in the country) will have to define, promote, and lobby for the understanding of the discursive work of the workplace as *constitutive* of realities rather than *reflective* of them, as I have argued in "Toward Technical Authorship." Particularly in an age in which electronic updating of the forms of authorship seems to progress geometrically (and thus demands so much effort merely to keep abreast of these forms), such positioning will prove difficult. Yet if we are to re-present discursive work in the workplace in ways commensurate with our scholarly understandings of the workings of discourse and our writerly sensibilities while embroiled in discursive work, such a project seems essential. To support it I extend these observations on authorship and return to the narratological frame presented in chapter 1 to sketch a model that does justice to the scope of professional writing and which might enable us all to re-present authorship to audiences beyond the walls of the academy.

Representing the Domain of Professional Authorship

The narratological model depicted in chapter 1 and used throughout this archaeological research reflects popular understandings of authorship as described above, which is to say solo textual production, primarily in the realm of fiction or poetry, disseminated in book form to a largely anonymous audience. Although the model aids inquiry into nonfiction authorship through its delineation of textual and extratextual authors, it proves inadequate for apprehending the complexities of workplace authorship. If we contemplate workplace authorship against chapter 4's discussion of document processing, subcultural dynamics, and cultural stabilization and change, for example, the section "Dynamics of Collective Procedures and Writing" underscores the frequency with which multiple "authors" contribute to documents which may be published anonymously or under the name of an organizational player who in fact wrote none of the content. More and more often, the audience for a text in the workplace has actually provided input into the authoring process: usability and readability testing in technical writing stand as the most striking example of this phenomenon, and a glance at the lists of organizational products and kinds of writing in chapter 5 reveals other ways in which audiences play a role in authoring. In his "Intertextuality and the Writing Process," Jack Selzer asks "Cannot the audience be seen as author, too?" (177), and the archaeological work of researchers in this book documents several ways in which audiences are authors. One of the most striking examples, and without doubt a presaging one, is that of Gary's study of Web site authorship, which includes regular updates of electronic "textual" representations as a direct function of users' responses to the current form. The webmaster's guiding principles in "authoring" are thus responses from the audience.

The *ways* in which the audience becomes part of the authoring process and the *positions* that audiences are afforded in the process are many and polemical. If the audience is positioned merely as consumer, the writer's role is reduced to "low practice": adjusting appeals for maximum consumption. Yet such is rarely the case, given that professional writers are always balancing audience response with organizational concerns and priorities, as reflected by the list of skills and by the dynamics of collective procedures and writing discussed in chapter 4. This multivalent positioning of professional writers has led Sullivan and Porter to characterize them as "audience advocates," applying the metaphors of "arbitrator" or "negotiator" to elaborate this positioning (414). Their metaphors dovetail with those proposed by Slack, Miller, and Doak, who speak of technical authors as "advocates for their constituencies: their employers, clients, and audiences" (33n).

These metaphors for professional writers' workplace identities have wide-ranging implications, which go beyond the pragmatics of authoring organizational texts to the changing epistemologies of composition. Speaking of the "disappearing boundaries" between audience and authorship, Louise Wetherbee Phelps puts it this way:

> The difficulties [in accounting comprehensively for social dimensions of writing] foreshadow the imminent replacement of dialogic interaction (an exclusive, cooperative relation between writer and reader mediated by text) with a more fully contextualized, polyphonic, contentious model of transactionality that encompasses multiple participants and voices along with situation, setting, institutions, and language itself—and finds it hard to maintain firm boundaries between self and other. (156)

In referring to a model of "transactionality" Phelps evokes the work of WAC researchers James Britton and others on "expressive" vs. "transactional" writing, grounded in the Prague Linguistics Circle's model of communication that posits one sender and one receiver for any act of communication. The model is unidirectional, unabashedly modernist in its representation of "communication," and remarkably similar to Chatman's narratological model presented in chapter 1. Against the archaeological findings in this book and the theoretical discussions above, I have revised Chatman's model and named it for the specific brand of discursive work that grounds this archaeology: the domain of professional authorship. (See figure 3.)

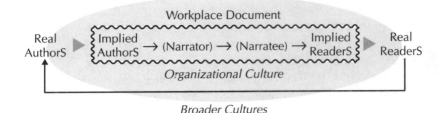

Fig. 3. The Domain of Professional Authorship

To approximate the complexity of professional authorship, this model depicts many real authors for any one "text," which is rendered here with wavy boundaries to signal that more and more often, texts are electronic, less fixed, and frequently "under construction," to borrow from popular Web site jargon. Many real readers figure in this model, too, some of whom contribute to authorship through their feedback, some of whom do not. The implied author and implied reader of this model are multivalent, since the texts of professional authorship are frequently *consulted selectively* rather than read in their entirety, unlike the implied author and reader of the earlier narratological model which presumes linear and complete readings. As in the earlier model, the implied author is understood as the "implicit image of an author in the text, taken to be standing behind the scenes and to be responsible for its design and for the values and cultural norms it adheres to," to recall Prince's definition in chapter 1 (*Dictionary* 42). The professional writer, in this model, is both maker and monitor of the implied author.

In addition to providing a "more fully contextualized, polyphonic, contentious model of transactionality" as per Phelps's requirements, this model restores to workplace writers their rightful place in authorship, wrested from them through composition epistemology spawned at the turn of the twentieth century by the needs of high-volume macroeconomic production and postsecondary curricular design that sundered writing selves from their writing. For as makers and monitors of the implied author of a document, professional writers should be vested with rights and responsibilities regarding the values and cultural norms the document adheres to. Such a position in the domain of professional authorship has wide-ranging implications for writers' expertise—as they exercise it on the job, as we shape it with them through collaborative research, and as they represent it to colleagues in the workplace.

Representing Writers' Expertise

In the past ten years, the field of rhetoric has produced compelling arguments for renewed focus on the ethics of composing. At the 1997 Conference on College Composition and Communication, for example, some twenty sessions were devoted explicitly to issues of ethics in composing. Recent textbooks in technical writing such as Lay et al.'s *Technical Communication* emphasize the importance of a technical document's *ethos,* a topic rarely broached in earlier textbooks in this field. Articles in scholarly journals abound, exploring the ethics of composing either directly or tangentially as part of other discussions.

Among these articles is James E. Porter's "Developing a Postmodern Ethics of Rhetoric and Composition." Like Mary Beth Debs, whose chapter epigraph notes the inadequacy of the rhetorical triangle inherited from classical times, Porter recognizes the inadequacy of an ethics presuming universal precepts that theoretically precede discursive events. Porter reviews Aristotelian epistemology to note that "for Aristotle, arts of production (like poetry and rhetoric) were distinct from the practical arts (like ethics and politics)" (209). He also notes that this view has remained the "dominant" view within rhetorical studies, which helps account for the recent focus in composition theory and practice. Composition, granted legitimation through alliance with rhetoric, has found itself claiming terrain that classical rhetoric does not bestow. That much composition instruction as practiced in this country in this century likewise ignores the *effects* of composing has retarded the emergence of *ethos* as a valid and vital focus for compositionists.

Yet the scholarship on the *ethos* of composing makes overwhelmingly compelling arguments for locating this topic at the center of composition's agenda—in both classroom instruction and in research. Steven Katz, for example, has conducted research on technical memos composed during the Third Reich that describe the design of vans to transport people to their deaths in terms of the "number of pieces loaded" (255). Katz's argument is that the very genre of technical documentation offers an *ethos* that legitimates such wording, since in some versions of technical discourse the writers not only have no say in content, they actively work to objectify subjects and to occlude agency—in compliance with discourse conventions. Katz concludes his analysis by fleshing out questions for compositionists:

> The question for us is: do we, as teachers and writers and scholars, contribute to this *ethos* by our writing theory, pedagogy, and practices when

we consider techniques of document design, audience adaptation, argu-
mentation, and style without also considering ethics? (271)

Yet considering ethics as part of composing, in the double bind
created by classical rhetorical theory and current-traditional composition epistemology is no easy task, as James Porter makes clear in his
essay cited above. His "postmodern ethics" includes an "ethical composing process" that discards classical notions of universal values preceding composition and which positions the composing event among
pulls from the individual, a discipline/field, the community, and tradi-
tion/culture. Porter notes that such a composing process "necessarily
involves the ways that knowledge, power, and ethics intersect" (222).

Such a conceptualization of composing processes makes eminent
sense against the grounding of this archaeology, since professional writers' purview, within the domain of professional authorship, includes
shaping and monitoring a document's *implied author,* taken here to be
roughly equivalent to a document's *ethos.* Though one might argue that
these two concepts differ somewhat in their roots, to the degree that
they designate the values conveyed by a document they are equivalent.
An added advantage of speaking in terms of implied authorship is that
it supports the conceptual reframing of authorship, in the academy and
in the workplace, to extend it to instrumental discourse, to include multiple contributors, and to take into account the *effects* of discourse as
they reverberate within and beyond local cultures. To speak in terms
of implied authorship in a domain of professional authorship is to take
into account the pulls on writers in ethical composing processes noted
by Porter. Such a theoretical framing also prompts ideas for reconceptualizing professional writers' expertise, which I will sketch with respect to the model above.

Expertise as Shaper and Monitor of Implied Authors

Katz's example of an implied author that seems unthinkable yet is in
fact made possible by conventions at work in a particular kind of discourse may seem to be an extreme example, yet when the discursive
shards turned up by researchers in this archaeology are considered for
the possible unities they might form, examples nearly as extreme as
Katz's take form. Scanning the kinds of writing documented by researchers in chapter 5's first section, one can imagine memos and correspondence composed by professional writers who have gleaned valuable information about the topic at hand through writing about it yet

whose purview in voicing this information is restricted. That is, their writing processes might have produced knowledge deemed extraneous to the immediate task by supervisors yet potentially significant in the long run, or in a slightly different application, or with a slightly different audience, and so forth. Composing an implied author that ignores these possibilities is tantamount to fostering a culture that sanctions ignorance, yet as discursive work is currently represented in most workplaces, most decisions about implied authors—about the cultural norms and values conveyed through writing—are beyond writers' rights.

Katz's research is ultimately not about individual agency so much as the ways in which agency is prefigured and constricted by discursive structures; a writer's need to develop acuity in perceiving such prefiguring and constricting should go without saying. Equally important is the need to develop acuity in perceiving convergences between discursive structures and organizational structures and to glean ways in which discursive practices and organizational practices take shape among these structures. By developing such acuities, writers can monitor the congruences among the values and norms that the local culture seeks to foster and the values and norms that result from authoring processes—the better to inform other culture members and the better to exploit writerly talents to their fullest in the interests of the organization and its members.

Developing such expertise clearly requires some experience and instruction in organizational analysis, as suggested in chapter 6. It also hinges upon the ongoing representation of writing in the workplace as an engagement in the production of meaning rather than merely its transmission and the work of writers as already imbricated in cultural production and reproduction. Such representations are not just claims in the interest of a professional class in formation, they are indicators of ways in which reconfiguring writers' expertise as discursive work can benefit the local culture. As writers develop acuity in discourse analysis along the lines sketched here, their daily encounters with discourses of the workplace will take on a greater theoretical dimension, leading some, for example, to interpret discursive bits as seemingly banal as e-mail as valuable indicators of an organization's climate, as Challie did in her research for the Cultures of Professional Writing course.

Shaping implied authors will entail theoretical inquiry into any discourse forms that emerge in given cultures, as discourse specialists compose among these forms. One can imagine the complexity of such work against the backdrop of chapter 5's discussion: multiple discourses will require inquiry through fieldwork and perhaps archival work, to glean origins and groundings of such discourses and to identify suitable implied authors; underlying discourses will require evasive tactics at worst (by writers who find themselves in discursive scenes that target them as members of a race, gender, etc.) and enhanced complexity of composing processes at best as writers come to appropriate grips with these discourses.

Monitoring implied authors will ultimately mean expanding loops of information flow, so that discourse specialists can provide contributors with feedback and status reports, as an organization's documents become artifacts for analysis and reflection upon discursive instantiation of culture by all interested culture members. Such reconfiguring of information flow runs antithetical to rigid hierarchical workplace cultures, of course, but such structures are already archaic in high-value economies, even if they prevail for the moment. As networks of composing become increasingly complex through virtual collaboration, the information flows between centers of organizations and their peripheries will change as a matter of fact; anticipating such changes and configuring them as part of conscious discursive work can only serve both writers and the organization.

For such expertise to be acknowledged and become actualized, significant re-presentations of the nature of writing and discourse work will have to take place. Here the frequent dovetailing between writers' experiences as writers and as teachers proves serendipitous, allowing us to imagine writers instructing coworkers in current discourse theory much as writers in the past have instructed coworkers on formal issues in prose. Those professional writers and aspiring writers who hold no formal experience as teachers nor anticipate any should be able to draw upon subject positions as teachers and learners that they frequently occupy discursively if not organizationally, the better to convey to colleagues the complexity of work long believed to be relatively superficial because of inadequate representations.

The frequent forays into the realm of technical writing that so many professional writers make can aid them, too, as they ponder implied authors amid the discourses of their workplaces and the enactment of those discourses as technology configures and reconfigures it. Indeed, Carolyn Miller speaks of a need to elaborate a "rhetoric *from* technology": "the ways in which values and thought patterns developed by technological work extend to and pervade other cultural arenas" ("Learning from History" 307). Professional writers will need such a

rhetoric, and self-conscious employment of technology while composing the implied authors that convey local cultural values could turn
up shards to be used in elaborating it.

Expertise as Coordinator of Real Authors Articulated to Implied Authors

In the domain of professional authorship, most writing is collaborative, uniting several contributors, often from diverse backgrounds and
ways of knowing, to produce the "text" and its implied author. The
dynamics of collective procedures and writing as depicted in chapter
4 limn the complexity of such a task: document processes are inevitably many and varied, inflecting prose forms through disciplinary review, subject to organizational players' ad hoc tactics, and at times
flowing counter to vital information flows. Subcultural dynamics take
form depending upon divisional allegiances, varying approaches to
knowledge and its production, and struggles to shape and resist institutional constructions of subjectivity; cultures change and restabilize,
requiring socialization of workers, new learning, and inevitably introducing new players. Among such cultural dynamics, professional writers must coordinate efforts.

   Local cultural dynamics, for writers and for professionals from
other classes, have been rendered even more complex in recent years
through the innovations in technology and the work effected through
it. The potential for technological developments in the areas of hard-
ware and software at times appears boundless, and the effects on real
authors as they use this technology often go unnoticed, as noted by
Johnson-Eilola in his discussion of hypertext:

> The machine seems to anticipate the user's needs, responding like a
> shadow to every wish and movement. The machine is never completely
> absent, but it becomes increasingly difficult—pointless, it seems—to re-
> flect on the operations of the machine, like thinking about breathing.
> Functional hypertexts are defined, socially and politically, in this poli-
> tics of amnesia. (*Nostalgic Angels* 50)

That only one researcher in this volume focused primarily on the influence of technology on the practice of professional writing (Albert)
confirms perhaps the degree to which computer-mediated authorship
has become as second nature as breathing. Yet such internalization can
indeed engender a politics of amnesia, which underscores the need for
writers and scholars to be developing a rhetoric from technology to

raise technology's subtle shaping of subjectivity to the conscious level and to aid practicing writers in coordinating cultural authorship as technology progresses.

Clearly, such coordination will require the kinds of teaching about discourse theory and effects as outlined above as well as ongoing inquiry into discursive production. This coordination will also entail occupying organizational subject positions such as "diplomat" (Jeff), as writers interact with various real authors. As noted in the previous chapter's discussion of writing curricula, writers are usually ill-prepared for such roles, having learned writing most often in singular authorship modes. Clearly, this lacuna must be rectified within the academy; at the same time, we can begin representing plural authorship of singular texts more adequately in the workplace.

One way to do so is to extend Susan Kleimann's work on workplace cultures and review, using her notion of "contributory expertise" (68) as a leverage point. Kleimann proposes this term based on observation of hierarchical and collaborative review processes at the General Accounting Office. Her subjects were not professional writers but rather professionals from other classes who composed reports through elaborate review, yet her notion of each contributor bringing to the composition special knowledge about technical aspects, legalities, front-office aims, and audience has great import for enhancing our knowledge of *writers'* contributory expertise. Once we conceptualize writing as work that not only reflects but constructs realities, that draws upon diverse discursive practices and traditions in the inscription of local cultures and the construction of implied authors whose norms and values could have wide repercussions, and that assumes discourse as an apparatus for the production of meaning, the representation of writers' contributory expertise in coordinating real authorship looms a vast undertaking that will require extensive and ongoing research.

The work of several researchers in this text suggests self-documentation as one way to track writers' contributory expertise, with Gwen's perhaps the most compelling. In an attempt to explore such self-documentation, I designed an MA course entitled "Composing Collaboratively for Publication," in which course participants self-selected groups within which to compose an article for publication in a forum of their choice while keeping detailed journals of their contributions both individually and collectively in moving the project along. Reading these journals and comparing them with my own class observations and selected audiotapes of collaborative composing sessions yielded a number of categories of expertise that writers employ tacitly quite often yet which go unnoticed in workplace cultures precisely because they are tacit and often rapidly deployed. For example, in addition to tapping expertise in textual composition most frequently associated with writers, writers collaborating with other contributors often tapped expertise in actively shaping and reshaping review procedures and dynamics as they proceeded, deferring consensus (see Burnett) on key issues when appropriate and adjusting composing appropriately. They would tap attitudes, beliefs, and emotions to glean "insight" (see Morgan and Murray), and they would use oral discourse in a variety of ways to structure and support composition (Henry "Documenting Contributory Expertise"). Writers on the job no doubt deploy many different kinds of expertise of this nature, in ways that vary from culture to culture and in ways that cut across cultures. If we can represent this expertise more fully in its complexity, we can display to workplace colleagues the work that is entailed by coordinating real authors' contributions to a singular text and its implied author.

If writers are represented in the workplace as employing their expertise not only in document processing but also in cultural processing, they will be positioned to tap the research and theory on composing that has burgeoned in the last two decades to enhance these cultural processes. Writing processes generally associated with individual cognitive processes of composing such as planning or brainstorming, when transposed to collective authorship, can well yield novel networks and review among various contributors, enhancing their contributions. Finally, whether motivated by the contributions of real authors who are also simultaneously intended users of organizationally authored products or by their responsibilities to cultures beyond their organization gleaned through monitoring implied authorship in organizational documents, professional writers working in the domain of professional authorship will want to develop and represent their expertise as mediators between a given local workplace culture and larger cultures in which any work has its effects. Some ideas concerning such expertise are presented below.

Expertise as an Intermediary Between Organizational Cultures and Larger Cultures

In archaic organizational structures inherited from a previous economic age, most information flow of any import beyond organizational borders is handled by professionals from classes such as management. In the informated age of electronic networks, such flow is nearly impossible—and highly counterproductive—since it fails to tap the skills of workers such as writers who can interpret and act upon information in novel ways. Concerning information coming into the organization, consider Starla's job of combing major newspapers each morning for news pertinent to her division and her organization. As a writer who also collaborates in shaping information that will travel from her organization through various media to larger cultures and who draws upon ways of knowing and learning specific to writers during such discursive work, she interprets this information in unique ways. Her expertise includes reading as a writer, and thus imagining discursively constructed realities that might take footing in what she reads. This expertise has direct connections with "reading formations" discussed as part of writing curricula in chapter 6, and with ideology, since ideological discourses "work more through selective attention than through outright suppression" (Rosaldo 87). As discourse workers interpret and act upon information as it moves between workplace and larger cultures, the representations that they make to themselves of their relationships to their conditions of existence are always at work, and it behooves us all, as writers and researchers, to probe interplays between these representations and such intermediation.

Concerning the effects of organizational authorship on larger cultures and professional writers' roles in these effects, Mary Beth Debs offers one scenario:

> In writing, for example, about new products or policy decisions, the writer is acting as a spokesperson for the organization in transcribing what is, in effect, a preexisting reality (the product or policy developed by the organization): It is the company's message and to a large extent the organization's vision or knowledge that the writer is sending. (166)

In characterizing a writer's work as "transcribing . . . a preexisting reality," Debs sketches a scenario of cultural inscription, of mediation between the organizational and the discursive effected by writers. Her selection of "products" as example might prompt us to muse upon the organizational products and kinds of writing discussed in chapter 5. Though products such as editorial pages and recruitment brochures might seem relatively innocuous, inquiries into the ways in which such products represent internal realities and position external audiences with respect to these realities by course researchers Jen and Hart, respectively, reveal the construction of a variety of relations between organizational cultures and the larger cultures in which they are located. In the case of a job announcement newsletter, audiences are positioned as protégés of the organization; in the recruitment brochures, as young scholars enamored with tradition yet desiring change. As intermediary agents between organizations and audiences, writers shape these relations and monitor them to ensure their success—which in turn guarantees the solvency of the organization. And if we take relationality as a generative topic in studies of cultural construction and reproduction, we can ask ourselves how the relations that get shaped through this mediation among cultures might become in turn foci for inquiry in the ideological plane: how do the subject positions offered to audiences through an organization's discursive representations reverberate through larger cultures? What conditions of existence do they imply and where do these conditions fit in systems of value within organizations and beyond them?

In the discursive shards of chapter 5 alone, dozens and dozens of representations, attendant positions, and relations among them are suggested; other archaeologies would produce hundreds more. In the domain of professional authorship, the relations thus established become topics for critique in the ongoing progress of workplace cultures and critical topics for culture members striving to maintain the solvency of the organization. In this sense, the roles of "advocate" and "mediator" suggested by scholars in professional writing seem vital, since these roles focus explicitly on the circuits of discursive output and feedback and the knowledge that can be constructed in these circuits. These roles should prompt writers to nurture expertise in demographic interpretation as it can feed such knowledge, to draw on circuits particular to, say, government writing that position the public as primary audience reached through complex mediation, and to envision composing for multiple and serial audiences as constructions of self and other—to recall earlier comments by ethnographic theorist James Clifford and composition theorist Louise Phelps.

Such constructions of knowledge in the domain of professional authorship will dovetail with knowledge of oneself as a member of a professional class in formation as discussed in chapter 6 and with self-knowledge as a writer whose subjectivity is an in-process construction amid the discursive structures and practices of given workplace cultures. To enhance this knowledge, writers, as "nodes" and "links" between organizational cultures and larger cultures, will want to develop expertise in participating in on-line forums composed of other writers in other cultures, the better to frame reflections on discursive selves and others (see Jillian in the appendixes; Selfe and Selfe). In representing this facet of writers' expertise in the workplace, writers and scholars collaborating with them will probably want to point out that discursive constructions of self and other are not only ethical considerations but considerations in the generation of a culture's value.

Representing Writing's Interests

In an individual writing conference with George, he told me of perennial writing classes offered in the military headquarters organization where he worked. In these classes, expert instructors from outside the organization would review principles of style and usage and run their charges through exercises designed to reduce nominalizations, passive voice, and the like. The classes were fine as refreshers, George claimed, but nearly all of the writers with whom he collaborated had long since mastered such fundamentals and rarely wrote in the passive voice or converted action to stasis in their prose. The reports to which they contributed, on the other hand, were riddled with such constructions, and therein lay the rub: problems in style were the result of cultural processes that included regular obfuscation of agency and disciplining of inferiors by superiors through discursive intervention that effaced their "voices." (For a fuller discussion, see Henry and "George.") Yet because "writing" in this culture was represented widely as an individual endeavor (albeit conducted serially in a "chop chain" of review) and the "work" of discourse as essentially the transmission of information, the culture's occasional engagement with discourse instruction came in the simplistic form of individual tutelage in prose style. George's MA thesis explored this phenomenon in depth, making provocative suggestions for local writing practice and instruction that would make use of reader-response theory and thus exploit one of the elements of the domain of professional authorship more fully. His work demonstrates the enormity of the rift between the academy and the workplace in understandings of discourse and its workings, and suggests some of the work which remains to be done in representing the interests of writing in the workplace.

The most immediate channel for doing so would seem to be professional writers who circulate between the two zones. To represent their expertise in postmodern modes of composing more fully to their coworkers, they will need instruction in various aspects of discourse as outlined in chapter 6 and they will need concrete examples drawn from their daily work as illustration—hence, once again, the enormous value of cultivating varying approaches to reflexive practice and to documenting one's engagement in collective procedures. Based on such documentation, professional writers may draw upon teacherly subjectivities to demonstrate ways in which social constructionism takes form in specific cultures. As they inhabit these teacherly subjectivities (many made available through discourses with which they maintain connections), other subjectivities are likely to be offered within organizational structures, in particular those of managers.

Lena's research most directly addressed this aspect of professional writing. When she interviewed the director of the association where she was observing document processing and production, the director lamented the fact that several of the able writers on staff would leave after a few years, having exhausted possibilities for promotion and for learning. If they wanted to remain with the organization, she predicted, their only option would be to move into management. This option is obviously at work in many cultures, judging by advertisements I receive regularly from outfits offering seminars in organizational communications and publishing. Titles such as "publications manager," "public relations manager," "communications manager," and the like, wrought in part by the complexities of composition in an informated age, presage organizational positions in which the writer is positioned as a "manager" of discursive production. In such an era, it seems critical that we represent discursive production as already imbued with complex cultural processes, local and larger, and that we contemplate the ways in which new "management" positions can heed such representations.

One possible avenue is through integrating our theory, research, and instruction on discursive work with Frow's notion of professional classes as always classes in formation discussed in chapter 6. Undergirding formations, he suggests, are ideological class relations, in which semiotic constructions of the self take form and in which a sense of self-identity and identification of the social other emerges. As discussed earlier, writers' practices of journaling and reflective commentary on their writing can enhance work in this sphere enormously. Frow's juxtaposition of ideological class relations with political class relations and economic class relations should prompt us to seize the latter as a highly pertinent sphere for representing writing's interests in workplace cultures. Precisely because workplace cultures are configured most strongly by economic forces, we will need to point out the ways in which these forces, ultimately concerned most centrally with the production of *value,* are inextricably bound to forces and values in the other two spheres. Now that we have dispensed with notions of writing as purely transmissive and with discursive work as merely functional, it remains our task to demonstrate repeatedly the ways in which values in the ideological sphere relate to values in the economic sphere. As we undertake this work as part of composition's subject, we will need to devise strategies in the political sphere, a central topic of chapter 8.

8 INTERVENING IN CULTURAL PRODUCTION AND REPRODUCTION

Roy: How'd you like to go to Washington and work for the
   Justice Department? All I gotta do is pick up the phone, talk
   to Ed, and you're in.
Joe: In . . . what, exactly?
Roy: Associate Assistant Something Big. Internal Affairs, heart of
   the woods, something nice with clout.
Joe: Ed . . . ?
Roy: Meese. The Attorney General.
Joe: Oh.
Roy: I just have to pick up the phone . . .
                              —Tony Kushner, *Angels in America*

Ito: The chance.
Grace Jones: To refigure the self.
Ito: To appropriate.
Grace Jones: The accoutrements of power.
Ito: To articulate.
Grace Jones: A new identity.
                           —Dorinne Kondo, "Bad Girls: Theater,
                Women of Color, and the Politics of Representation"

In Dorinne Kondo's performative version of ethnography, Janice Ito, "a young assistant professor who is thrilled with her new job at the Mount Olympus of scholarship, Ivy University" (52), team talks with Grace Jones as the two stroll down a fashion designer's runway, clad in Issey Miyake dresses and carrying Uzis. Ito is bent on academic success yet struggling with various ideological and pragmatic demands that go with the job; Jones is her pop idol, suddenly materializing in her world to serve as both inspiration for her articulation of a politics of representation and foil to her conceptualization of political identity in narrowly academic terms. The chance to refigure the self—to articulate a new identity—comes to those who inhabit given identities creatively, we glean from Jones's later comments when Ito objects to Jones's having donned a leopard-skin suit and brandished a spear in *Conan the Barbarian*.

As one of the contributions to Behar and Gordon's *Women Writing Culture*, Kondo's essay takes up the complex issue of the politics of representation within the field of ethnography, and the character of Grace Jones in Kondo's performative ethnography prompts musings upon autoethnographic projects. As noted in chapter 3, when Mary Louise Pratt popularized the term in English circles, she defined autoethnography as "a text in which people undertake to describe themselves in ways that engage with representations others have made of them" (35). To articulate a postmodern, feminist, autoethnographic identity, Kondo's scene implies, subjects should be prepared to engage with the identities that specific cultures regularly offer, even if these identities as initially offered appear objectionable.

Such is the engagement with identity that the domain of professional authorship would currently seem to require of professional writers. That is, given the ready-made subjectivities of "functionary," "support staff," "ghost" (chapter 4), or even "robot" (Slack, Miller, Doak) that are offered to professional writers most often by workplace cultures where writing is represented as essentially reflective of rather than constitutive of realities, where discourse is a mode of transmission rather than an apparatus for the production of meaning—these representations linked to reductionist notions of authorship fostered by both the academy and by popular media—the most salubrious tactic would seem to be to engage with such subject positions in order to revise them. Depending upon the culture and positions that are offered, engagement may mean little more than putting up with limiting notions of identity until one can move to a better culture. (This tactic has been voiced by several of the researchers represented here, particularly those working in cultures which are customarily the most top-down and constricting: trade associations.) Such cultures will undoubtedly resist revision from the bottom up, certainly from one lone agent whose professional class carries so little clout, which should prod academics who prepare such agents for their positions to investigate other means of intervention in local cultures and in cultural processes.

Intervening in cultural processes beyond the walls of the academy may strike compositionists as foreign, but in professional writing scholarship such a mandate has been taking form over the last few years, leading Rachel Spilka to speak in 1993 of "influencing workplace practices" through curriculum design and research. That professional writing scholarship should be the field to forward this mandate derives not only from its object of study but from the methodologies that have most informed this study. From the earliest ventures into workplace cultures by academics in rhetoric and composition, the primary fieldwork methodology has been ethnography (see Odell and Goswami), and at least two approaches to ethnographic inquiry—applied ethnography and feminist ethnography—lobby explicitly for intervention in the culture under study. In "Applied Anthropology and Post-Modernist Ethnography," Agneta M. Johannsen notes that "applied anthropology is mainly characterized by intervention" (71), observing in the process that "interpretive anthropology especially focuses on the principle that to characterize people in any way is to intervene in their lives" (77), which has been a principle at the heart of feminist anthropology, amply demonstrated in *Women Writing Culture*. As professional writing scholars seeking rigor both in our methodologies and in our positioning with respect to epistemologies tied to those methodologies, it makes perfect sense to recognize intervention in cultural processes as part of our work.

It also makes sense to take up the issue of cultural intervention within the broader landscape of postsecondary curriculum design. To speak of cultural processes in terms of cultural production and repro-

duction is to invoke the work of Pierre Bourdieu and Jean-Claude Passeron, who in *Reproduction in Education, Society, and Culture* return
to Bourdieu's notion of a *habitus*, "the product of internalization of
the principles of a cultural arbitrary capable of perpetuating itself after pedagogical action has ceased and thereby of perpetuating in practices the principles of the internalized arbitrary" (31). Bourdieu and
Passeron use habitus to characterize the ways in which the French
educational system reproduces class distinctions even when federal interventions have been taken to prompt more egalitarian access to high-
status disciplines. Though their interpretations of class formation strike
one as oversimplified in the light of class scholarship since the book's
publication, their observations on educational institutions' unwitting
collusion with forces in the sphere of production that reproduce the
status quo are well taken. Such observations implicate curriculum design and return us once again to the realm of curriculum theory. To
the element of students' *self-actualization* as part of curriculum noted
in chapter 6, ethnographic inquiry as framed in this archaeological work
lobbies implicitly for adding *social reconstruction* (Eisner and Vallance), since work at the level of discursive constructions of the subject always entails work at the level of social systems as intertwined
with discursive processes. Sidelined earlier in the century as invalid
curricular material during the Taylorization of the academy and particularly of writing instruction, social reconstructionism is likely
to reemerge as cultural forces so closely allied with Taylorization wane
in the informated age.

As this shift occurs, composition will be positioned to take advantage of it in novel ways by virtue of having taken on discursive constructions of subjectivity as one of its foci. In so doing, composition
commits itself to inquiries into the replication of status quo subjectivities within educational institutions and, by extension, to the interventions necessary to aid students in achieving their maximum self-
actualization. With respect to professional writing, at the very least,
compositionists have a mandate—grounded in this composer-centered
field—to investigate the ways in which status quo subjectivities required
by the workplace in an earlier economic era are replicated through *current* discursive practices, to strive to revise these practices, and to share
these investigations and rationales for revision with students. Primary
to this rationale is the principle that the writing subject has been shaped
dramatically and systematically by current-traditional composition
epistemology and institutional locations of writing instruction that

sunder "real" selves from their discursive representations in specific ways—intervening, as it were, in the subject's range of possible entries into discourse.

Countering the effects of this protracted and systematic intervention will require diverse and equally protracted efforts, given the scope and depth of these earlier forces bearing on discursive subjectivities. Yet the time for such counterintervention would seem ripe, owing to at least three developments in the past decade or so: (1) theories for apprehending the complexities of discursive constructions of subjectivities—of the ways in which the social constructionist elements of language and discourse practices shape our identities—have finally made their ways to composition studies; (2) the shifts in our national economy, particularly as global capitalism has positioned U.S. economy, render earlier subjectivities required by the workplace archaic and even counterproductive; (3) developments in technology have revolutionized discursive circuits, opening channels for reshaping subjectivities and for reimagining rhetorics, as Carolyn Miller's observations noted in the previous chapter underscore. I discuss some implications of each of these factors against the backdrop of this archaeology below.

Discursive Sites of Intervention

The most immediately relevant discursive site for investigation and intervention is the writing subject. In chapter 6 ideas are presented for repositioning this subject as part of the larger project of re-presenting discursive work in the academy. In the pages that follow, these ideas are extended for their applications in an interventionist approach to writing subjectivities in the realms of the individual, of a professional class, and of virtual forums.

Individual Sites

When conceptualized as a site at which social forces struggle to enter discourse, the "I" of the professional writer stands as a key point in intervening in cultural reproduction. The erasure of the "I" through current-traditional composition epistemology has been roundly seconded by workplace discursive practices, judging by the reports of researchers in this book, rendering this site somewhat inaccessible. Yet through rethinking authorship as a part of instrumental discourse and conceptualizing a domain of professional authorship, the purview of the professional writer's "I" becomes clear: "real" authorship entails "managing" the many contributors to an organizational document (including in some cases end users providing feedback) and imagining the document's ultimate effects in local and larger cultures, as noted in chapter 7. Otherwise stated, the "I" of the real author, even when not evidenced in texts, becomes politically and poetically positioned among many social forces in extremely complex ways. Intervening in cultural production and reproduction entails equipping professional writers for such positioning intellectually in classrooms and collaborating with them later in the ongoing processes and products in which each "I" becomes implicated.

If we ponder Louise Phelps's observation on the "disappearing boundary" between authors and audiences and if we accept the validity of extending to instrumental discourse James Clifford's observation that every positing of an "other" in discourse is a simultaneous construction of a "self," then clearly one of our projects in the academy must entail assessing various discursive practices and traditions for their potential in intervention. That is, in addition to imagining courses in organizational studies and classroom work on students' "I's" as material, we might comb discursive horizons for practices and traditions that offer occasions for deconstructing notions of the "I" as an originating, transcendent ego. Most traditions in English work against such positioning, paradoxically, which is one reason why collaborative composition courses hold such promise. But in addition to such courses, we might nurture course design that makes connections with fields that traditionally position writers as spokespeople rather than transcendent egos.

Ethnography and folklore are two such fields, based on my experience in this archaeological undertaking. While it is true that each of these fields currently replicates in scholarly publications the "major author" mode that academic notoriety requires, they nonetheless demand of these authors a cultural validation of tales uncommon in most English studies: the ethnographer and the folklorist employ methodologies explicitly to this end, thus constructing an "author" who is directly responsible to local cultures. And while Ph.D. writers in these traditions display such responsibility in writing *about* cultures, professional writers could display such responsibility while writing *within* cultures.

We can prepare grounds for interventionist action via the individual writer by writing such responsibility for cultural validation into our composition epistemology and practices. James Zebroski and Nancy

Mack have observed the power of ethnographic writing in heightening critical consciousness among students; what I am signaling is the power of such writing for heightening collective consciousness among all of us who convey fundamental philosophies about writing subjects through the very conceptualization of courses. My experience in teaching such a course (at the undergraduate level) has taught me that a recurrent focus becomes that of the writer's ways and means of validating observations on a culture. Even writers who do extremely well in courses positioning them as independent originators of writing have difficulty learning how and when and why to seek cultural validation for discourse depicting a culture. In the domain of professional authorship, such a discursive identity is indispensable.

Equally indispensable is an individual identity that assesses the culture with respect to larger cultures. The politics of representation, as ethnographers know, requires an ongoing questioning of who speaks for whom, to whom, and under what conditions. Just as rethinking ethnography in the postcolonial era has led some ethnographers to eye the uses of ethnographic representation with vigilance, so might our course work with individual writers in this tradition foster a similar vigilance over cultural representations and reproductions via instrumental discourse in workplace cultures. Because the workplace culture is always situated in our larger culture, such vigilance is not only justified but necessary. The work on *ethos* cited in chapter 7 speaks to this issue, as does the burgeoning research on writers' subjectivities as shaped by computers. As Cynthia and Richard Selfe observe, "We are already constituted both as technological and cultural subjects, created in part by the machines we ourselves have created and written continually in our discursive practices on these machines" (352). Part of our interventionist project as technological and cultural subjects surely must entail monitoring the contours of individual subjectivity as technology shapes it, combating the politics of amnesia as we develop our rhetorics from technology. Sharing the knowledge produced through such monitoring among professional writers, scholars, and other members of the workplace constitutes an intervention in individual subjectivity as compelling as any other in composition history.

Catherine Belsey speaks of the "displacement of subjectivities across a range of discourses" (65), and as I scan the lists in chapter 5, I can imagine the ways in which subjectivities are displaced across some of the specific discourses of the workplace represented in this archaeology. I imagine writers encountering discourses from other professional classes and from other intellectual traditions, working to effect meanings that the professional writer must interpret. When I review representations of themselves as writers in appendix B, though, they seem unprepared to theorize relations between displacements and responsibilities. If we glance through the appendixes further, we can see that professional writers are quite capable of working within the ethnographic writing tradition to produce discursive subjectivities allowing entry to such theorizing. Part of our work in intervening in cultural reproduction should entail our working with these writers to probe how such writerly subjectivities take form as part of a professional class.

Class Sites

My work as instructor of Cultures of Professional Writing each term entailed constructing tables similar to those in appendix B and appendix C so that course participants could see how their work compared with that of peers and so that they might begin to glean contours of writers as a professional class. If we are to intervene effectively in cultural production and reproduction, investigating the contours of this professional class as they solidify and shift is indispensable. Such investigations can proceed from many points of departure. Depicting the production of all writers in a course as a set supports in-class discussion of the *terms* of the set. Whereas I have chosen topics and themes as valuable to a discussion of organizational and discursive features deemed pertinent by professional writers engaged in organizational analysis, one might equally devote tables or charts to the specifics of whole writing projects undertaken by a group of professional writers. Doing so would enable even finer discerning of the current scopes of writers' purview in the domain of professional authorship.

Comparing organizational charts across workplace cultures also supports enhanced understandings of professional writers as a specific class. Inevitably, these organization charts show writers situated on the margins of their cultures, or at the lower echelons. Comparing their positions in workplace cultures with those of professionals from other classes, along with study of the educational backgrounds and workplace experiences required (or professed) by other professionals, could enable a critical consciousness at the level of discursive formations, which in turn might enable the envisioning of intervention in the name of a class's value to the organization. As an individual, it is often difficult to discern where and how such values are constructed, yet as a class, such constructions are more easily discernible by virtue of the relations and recurrent positions rendered visible.

As a site of intervention in cultural production and reproduction, the professional class of writers currently offers little leverage in workplace cultures because of its low status, yet this status could change with shifts in organization of workplace cultures towards high value. For those cultures seeking high value configurations to support new production of knowledge, employing writing as a mode of learning and discourse as an apparatus for the production of meaning, the professional class of writer could re-form with greater status and say in cultural production. In his discussion of class formation, John Frow speaks of class interests as "hypotheses, more or less rationally calculated (or miscalculated)" (105). As a site of intervention, we might hypothesize the interests of professional writers as they fit in workplace cultures. Chapter 6 implies hypotheses in the ideological sphere, grounded in the symbolic capital with which we provide professional writers and always already linked to discursive constructions of self and other as our composition epistemologies enable them. This capital can be parlayed in the sphere of production when discursive representations are recognized as a site where not only cultural capital but also economic capital take form. The political world turns on such a principle, but perhaps because composition epistemology has for so long eschewed politics under pretense of neutrality, professionals trained in writing have been at a loss to identify and act upon political agendas in the interests of their class.

Such work would seem to lie before us, and as we undertake it, we would do well to hypothesize interests that heed all the relations of the domain of professional authorship. The onus of explaining the interrelatedness of "users" and "authors" might fall to writers in their roles as discourse teachers, and to this end it behooves us all to take up such topics regularly in discursive forums conceptualized not just for colleagues in the academy but for discourse workers in various contexts and at various levels. At least one hard-copy forum in which academics speak to professional writers (and vice versa) on issues of cultural production and reproduction would be a valuable first step in hypothesizing this class's future interests. Virtual forums will be indispensable, both as means of drawing together writers dispersed geographically and as means of exchanging information on the monitoring of cultural production immediately and at will.

Virtual Sites

If considerations of writers as a class of professionals enhance our understanding of writer subjectivities through the organizational factors introduced, then considerations of virtual sites of representation enhance our understanding of writer subjectivities by expanding the "organizational" beyond traditional structures. In fact, such expansion may be influencing organizational dynamics in ways unbeknownst even to organizational players at the tops of organization charts, if Shoshana Zuboff is correct in her predictions about the ways in which "informating" is changing the nature of the workplace. That is, even in the absence of organizational restructuring for high-value production (as evidenced by most of the studies in this archaeology), ad hoc restructuring may be at work through new flows of information. The fact that organizations already employ software to monitor employee Internet use in a twenty-first-century enactment of nineteenth-century panopticism clearly signals new information circuitry. Discursive reach among workplace culture members, it would seem, has been revolutionized by the Internet in ways still to be explored.

So have writers' touchstones for style, judging by Gary's study of World Wide Web site maintenance by a job bank and software provider. With no previous professional writing experience, Gary went to his site with notions of style garnered from instruction in writing in the English essay tradition, only to find tantalizing guidelines offered by "writers" from business and marketing grounded in one principle: what kind of writing invited and sustained visits to the site. On one level, such an observation points to the market discourse that drives many workplace cultures (see chapter 5), yet on another level, the observation augurs progressive conceptualization of cultural discursive production that brings audience and users into the authoring process. By bringing audiences into real authorship of a culture's discursive products, one might argue, intervention in cultural reproduction is made possible in ways hitherto impossible.

Such scenarios for intervention have existed for some time in the realm of technical writing via feedback procedures aimed at usability or readability. It seems inevitable that these scenarios will expand to other domains, if only by virtue of the cultural porosity enhanced by the Web. And indeed, major public institutions are increasing "transparency" by placing documents on the Web and integrating them into cultural processes. Though the content of these documents is no doubt carefully screened, the accessibility might in many cases reposition users, particularly if we think of the government sites represented in this archaeology (see appendix B). Other possible scenarios include forums in which outsiders to an organization might post commentary on that organization's engagement with respect to the larger culture; such publications already exist in hard-copy form, of course, but the Web offers means for collecting and threading them in novel ways.

Concurrent with such virtual interventions that bring audiences into authoring in valuable ways will be virtual interventions linked to the class of professionals known as writers. Now this class can share information among its constituents concerning their conditions of existence; writers can represent these conditions to other writers much in the ways that participants in Cultures of Professional writing have represented such conditions to one another in flesh and blood. Using these virtual forums constitutes ideological intervention and invites contributions from discourse workers in the workplace and the academy. Cynthia Selfe proposes using forums such as e-mail in ways specific to intervention in cultural reproduction, to "support discursive forums that serve to flatten more traditionally constructed hierarchies in business, organizations, and governments by connecting individuals directly to decision makers and to the information used in making decisions" (258), which dovetails with observations above and elsewhere in this archaeology concerning circuits of information flow in the domain of professional writing. Selfe sees such virtual forums as part of a larger trend in the postmodern era in which grand narratives (which always work ideologically through selective attention) are enfeebled through the multiplication of discourses (and hence alternative narratives), which in turn offer more opportunities for agency and resistance (285). Focusing some narratives on the interests of professional writers as a class, how these interests do and do not connect with interests of other classes (and indeed with ultimate audiences in the domain of professional writing), and where and how these relations figure in values produced and sustained through local cultural work can perhaps bolster interventions by writers in realms previously excluded to them. At least some of these narratives should be grounded in the *petits recits* such as found in archaeologies, enabling individual writers, perhaps, to link the *petits recits* from other locales to their own, cognitively mapping their positions ever more globally.

Organizational Sites of Intervention

The chapter epigraph from *Angels in America* is in part about the construction of exclusive realms through networking, in this case political networking between New York and Washington in the mid-eighties. The character of Roy Cohn (based on the real-life New York attorney and power broker), facing disbarment, needs a well-placed pawn in the Justice Department to represent his interests—hence his offer to clerk Joe Pitt. The vituperative Cohn is dishonest, maliciously evil, and extremely powerful, being well connected within the Republican Party not only to Attorney General Meese but even via Nancy Reagan to the President. As the play unfolds and we witness Cohn's Machiavellian tactics, we come to realize, as does the naive Joe Pitt, that Cohn indeed has only to pick up the phone to place a player in the upper echelons of a major government organization.

This representation of political networking manifested by actors as emanating primarily from the professional class of attorney requires no willing suspension of disbelief on the part of a Washington audience, for our days are dappled with similar discursive scenes, be it through the local press or through occasional unfortunate real-life encounters. (Edwin Meese, attorney general under President Reagan during the Iran-Contra debacle and current activist against freedom of speech on the Internet through his support of the Communications Decency Act, was named to my university's Board of Visitors by Republican governor George Allen; in 1999 Meese became Rector.) In many organizations in and around the Washington area, particularly those associated with government or its lobbying, selection, and positioning of huge numbers of organizational players has much more to do with political interests than with relevant expertise. Organization charts that benignly depict these players and positions, never hinting at the interests or networks behind them, offer little more than faint intimations of the complexities of organizational authorship.

Such were the organizations studied by 32 of the 84 researchers in this archaeology (appendix C). Another 36 studied organizations in the private sector, where players' interests are admittedly tied more closely to market demands, and organizational authorship is thus shaped by different kinds of politics: here professionals from business classes and others wield the strongest influence in cultural production and reproduction. The remaining researchers studied educational institutions and nonprofits, encountering the political shaping of authorship in varying degrees depending upon the topics and themes explored. Even in this last category, where the play of politics often appears most innocent, the forces bearing upon organizational authorship as researchers could discern them in just one semester nearly always suggested further lines of inquiry into the interests behind these forces. (See the abstracts of researchers in this category, along with the topics and themes they explored in appendixes B and D.)

The issue of interests as represented through organizational authorship cannot be overemphasized, neither as theoretical insights on class formations as intricately tied to relationality of interests across economic, ideological, and political spheres urges *empirical* inquiry into the conditions underpinning such relations (see Brodkey, "On the Subjects") nor as scholarship in the informated age on professional writing poses questions not easily answered in an era of shifting organizational and discursive formations. Computerized composition scholars Cynthia and Richard Selfe pose such questions, and although they use the title "technical communicators" to designate organizational writers largely because such writers are most easily associated with electronic composing, we can substitute the title "professional writer," as I have done elsewhere in this archaeology, not only to tap the valuable scholarship coming from technical writing but also because the titles are often used synonymously and interchangeably in organizational settings. Selfe and Selfe ask:

> To whom are technical communicators responsible? Their corporate employers? The public who uses the corporation's products? The professional societies to which they belong? Who is responsible for the information that technical communicators produce? Who controls the information technical communicators produce? Why is this so? Whose interests are being served in controlling information and in defining the various roles and responsibilities of technical communicators in the way that we now do? (330)

As inscribers of cultures, managing organizational writing in the domain of professional authorship, professional writers are responsible to large numbers of people in ways that are occluded by current roles and responsibilities as configured in most organizational settings. Hence we are not only justified in claiming rights to interventions by professional writers and their discursive collaborators in cultural production and reproduction, we are obligated—even impelled—to do so in the interest of knowledge both theoretical and utilitarian in an era of changing discursive and organizational formations. Deborah Brandt observes ways in which literacy is always multiply "sponsored," noting that different kinds of sponsorship construct subjects differently. If we revisit the sites discussed in chapter 3 and the work and positions documented in them for the ways that literacy sponsorship is already shaping subjects, we can imagine interventions (and can hypothesize class interests) to form new unities from this earlier archaeological work, as follows.

In commercial organizations (see appendix C), part of writers' work should entail a philosophical situating of the local culture vis-à-vis larger cultural trends, as writers manage implied authorship. The philosophy invoked would be one not only of ethics and civic humanism (see Thomas Miller) but also of pragmatism, as the local culture seeks optimum articulations with norms and values evidenced in larger and exterior cultures. Even in businesses such as public relations firms, whose sole *raison d'être* is the discursive representations of outside clients, organizational authorship entails negotiating these representations in consumer cultures. Because such cultures are always imbued with mediations of representations emanating from other sources, the professional writer must select and deploy clients' representations judiciously. Otherwise stated, the writer engages in ideological work, and intervention in such work entails at the very least theorizing the terms of selection and deployment.

As an example, Ann, who works as a writer for a public relations firm, extended her work in Cultures of Professional Writing into an MA thesis, in which she explored the processes whereby an all-female business shaped the voices of all-male clients for various media. Her inquiry naturally took her to feminist theory and works such as Belenky et al.'s *Women's Ways of Knowing* in order to depict the kinds of knowledge about discursive forms that she and her colleagues had built over the years and to contrast this knowledge with that of their clients. Part of their work entailed *teaching* their clients about discursive features in the realm of public relations, and herein lies great potential: as we collaborate with such writers through academic liaisons, the theories we harken to imply specific kinds of responsibilities, relationality, and alliance with other groups, defined in part by professional class and also by gender, race, and other traits.

The interests of such groups might enter the domain of professional authorship via the circuits open to users, consumers, and other audiences implicated in organizational authorship. As such, interventions by professional writers may well entail taking the position of "advocate" cited earlier. If we recall Jeff's discovery through his interviews with engineers that technical editors in his culture were unwittingly undermining the engineers' authority by unstringing noun strings, we can imagine future scenarios in which those noun strings might indeed *need* to be unstrung for interpretation by a nonengineering audience. In the role of advocate for audiences (and end users), his editing work could even entail pursuing questions and objections raised in their interests (or that he would anticipate in their interests) within the organization.

Alongside the role of advocate might be considered the role of lookout—as writers positioned as nodes or links with extraorganizational cultures scan discursive horizons for information and knowledge that shapes the local culture. Starla's job of clipping daily news items she deems relevant to her organization represents a form of intervention with great potential, depending upon the ways in which organizations position these writers in information flows and the ways in which educational institutions prepare them intellectually.

Professional writers might also intervene in those cultural processes that are more self-contained within an organization. Some researchers in business cultures studied in this archaeology have already done so, either literally through discursive intervention or philosophically through themes addressed in their organizational analysis: Nyck composed formal policy regarding employees' duties and rights and had it instituted at his office, and Red harkened in his ethnography to newspaper industry traditions being scuttled at his newspaper through the introduction of time clocks for reporters. Rex noted ways in which discursive practices reinforced certain organizational structures at his site of study, thus implying possible interventions by writers should those structures support counterproductive values, and Lisa similarly identified a reproduction of cultural values through discursive practice. In her final ethnography, she states: "Since discursive practice is defined as rationalizations used for the production of meanings, it would then follow that the editing process is yet another set of rationalizations for rationalizations previously constructed (the written text)" (12).

We can imagine similar conceptualizations of intervention in government agencies and institutions as depicted in appendix C. Seeing these conceptualizations through to realization might prove more difficult, given the frequent layers of bureaucracy and politically motivated decisions. George's insightful suggestions for introducing some instruction in reader-response theory at his military headquarters organization as an alternative to the pointless instruction in prose style went unheeded, yet it remains a valuable intellectual intervention as we elaborate our understandings of organizational authorship and ways of integrating audiences into authoring circuits. Other researchers in government settings conceptualized similar frameworks for interventions in discursive practices: Helen through her analysis of magazine editors' construction of implied authorship as replicating certain cultural norms and values, and Gloria through a similar analysis of implied authorship in correspondence composed across divisions at the Library of Congress. Pragmatic interventions in such sites will undoubtedly require sustained efforts on the part of professional writers, perhaps in concert with professionals from other classes, which is all the more reason to cultivate connections with these classes under the aegis of shared values.

In the trade associations represented in appendix C, intervention seems relatively unfeasible, except when writers are positioned such as Kyle was to solicit and edit articles for the association's publications with a fair amount of license. But as noted earlier, his professional purview as a writer was the exception rather than the rule in this category of workplace. More often, content of even the most mundane nature is carefully monitored, owing to the hegemony of political discourse in local practices, and if writers and their allies are to conceptualize intervention, their efforts would be better placed in intellectual interventions by writers in their own discursive, theoretical, and political understandings—since in most cases they will leave such workplaces for better employ after short stints.

Finally, the category of educational institutions as organizational sites for intervention strikes most closely to home for those of us with a direct stake in the goals of these institutions. Writers' work and positions in these institutions as depicted in appendix C lobby for intervention in curriculum design and classroom practices, of course, yet they also lobby for intervention in extracurricular circuits (see the abstracts of Alice, Emma, Jillian, Julie, Lee, and Marla). To do so, one might draw upon the work of Anne Ruggles Gere on the "extracurriculum," which identifies the need for academics investigating and teaching discursive practices in classrooms to learn from the practices of grassroots community writing groups, formed in the name of a cause. She says: "As we consider our own roles of social agency we can insist more firmly on the democracy of writing and the need to enact pedagogies that permit connections and communication with the communities outside classroom walls" (91). Her stance is echoed by James Slevin in terms of the very disciplinarity of composition studies:

> At the heart of the educational practice I propose is a reconceptualizing of disciplinarity so that its intellectual work is located in encounters with students and in the projects that arise from these encounters. What we need is a sense of disciplinary work that supports and even makes possible these developments, a sense of "discipline" that allows literacy workers (teachers *and* students) in various institutional sites (academic *and* nonacademic) to feel the importance of what they do and to recognize their connections with one another. (160)

Intervention, along such lines, would entail deconstructing the philosophical boundaries that accompany the institutional boundaries of our colleges and universities in ways that admit and legitimize instrumental discourse elaborated in workplace cultures. Such interventions have already been proposed—perennially, in fact—yet usually in ways that suggest the kinds of collusion in cultural reproduction discussed in the chapter introduction. The interventions I refer to valorize instrumental discourses as topics of critical analysis to be undertaken in the elaboration of writing formations. As such, they will position their students not as uncritical subjects but as future inscribers of workplace cultures, tasked with the enormous responsibility of scrutinizing the discourses and discursive practices implicated in such inscription for the norms and values they produce and reproduce.

To ignore this extracurriculum is tantamount to political suicide for discourse workers, given the recent trends at the national level among students towards undertaking postsecondary education concurrent with work. At my state university, for example, the majority of students support themselves partially through jobs and take five or six years to complete an undergraduate degree. Recent federal subsidies for similar structuring of tertiary education in community colleges augurs similar scenarios which, when considered alongside the numbers of people pursuing advanced degrees in discourse studies while holding full-time jobs, compels us to theorize this situation. Such engagement dramatically limits a person's time and opportunities for edification in cultural issues or for civic engagement, which renders Mary Beth Debs's suggestion in chapter 4 that the organization has become the major arena for public life for the individual in modern Western civilization simultaneously tantalizing and ominous. With the increased speed in cultural processes effected through computers, political implications of the products of authorship can be easily overlooked, meaning that whether or not we admit it, writers in workplace cultures are engaged in political work by default. Surely, it behooves us to investigate the discursive contours of this work in the academy.

In tandem with technological developments, other cultural processes have increased in speed, including those processes that make use of professional writers in a post-Fordist era of flexibility. The flexibility of labor produced by recent national economies clearly benefits organization players at the upper echelons at the expense of those in lower positions (Harvey). If we are to align ourselves epistemologically and politically with discourse workers whom popular (and academic) ideologies would position in these lower positions as functionaries, then it becomes our work to take up intervention in cultural production and reproduction as part of our job as compositionists, cultural scholars, and certainly as academics in professional writing. If we do not, scenarios such as the one composed by Kali, based on her real-life witnessing of hiring and firing and enacted by course participants during a writing workshop, could well become a recurrent tale among professional writers. Her scenario depicts a Kafkaesque culture in which writers are fired and (perhaps) rehired so frequently through management snafus that they are inured to termination:

> *Kali:* Here's the setting: battleship-grey walls with rose flecks that are an attempt to add cheer but end up looking like blood stains. The floor plan is obviously cubes, but they're attached in such a way as to resemble a maze as well. Everyone is walking around holding clipboards. Alan enters in a whirl, like a Tasmanian devil.
>
> *"Alan":* Has anyone seen Mary? I need to find Mary. I need to *fire* Mary. I don't want to, but someone upstairs messed up and I have to. Tell Mary I'm looking for her.
>
> [he exits; Mary enters]
>
> *"Mary":* Has anyone seen Alan? He needs to fire me so I can get back to work. I need to get all this done before I go.
>
> [Alan reenters]
>
> *Alan:* Mary. There you are. You're fired.
>
> *Mary:* I know.
>
> *Alan:* I don't want to be the one to tell you but I have to.
>
> *Mary:* I know.
>
> *Alan:* It's nothing you've done.
>
> *Mary:* I know.

Alan: You're a great employee.
Mary: I know.
Alan: Three weeks.
Mary: I know.

—discussion in class, 4/9/97

Reforming Discursive Formations and Recapturing Intellectual Dominion

In this workshop, Kali's fictional scene was conducted as a class activity in tandem with discussions of Dorinne Kondo's ethnography cited in the chapter epigraph. The workshop was suggested by guest scholar Zofia Burr, who melds poetry writing with critical writing in constructing her scholarship, which is otherwise grounded strongly in African-American studies, women's studies, and cultural studies. In introducing herself to the class, she stressed that she saw the dichotomy "creative writing/critical writing" as a false dichotomy against which she struggled, and the workshop produced provocative "plays" of the kind cited above that bore out her argument. Writers worked both creatively within the approach of performative ethnography proposed by Kondo and critically against the backdrop of a semester's fieldwork and analysis in a given workplace culture. Our goal in the workshop, much like the goal in Kondo's essay, was to shift momentarily to another mode of composing in the interest of gleaning something about underlying relations in culture. As Professor Burr put it:

> The live experience [of a staged scenario] really models for you the kind of problem you have as a writer to begin with: How are people who are situated in different places going to get into this? How am I going to represent people situated differently from myself? All of that. It's all about being in relation. And the thing about figuring a drama, as opposed to figuring a poem, is that you really do think about bodies in relation to each other saying things that are potentially defining. (in class, 4/9/97)

In Kali's scene above, the exchange between Alan and Mary is potentially defining of the whole class of professional writers if we don't intervene to reconstruct composition epistemologies and liaisons among discourse workers that recognize and theorize the creative and critical elements of composing instrumental discourse. Through their discursive work, professional writers daily reproduce (and potentially reconfigure) the terms of being in relation in their specific culture, yet because we have been remiss in recognizing such socially constructive acts for the inscription of culture that they are, writers such as Mary find themselves wholly expendable. With the rise of the professional managerial class (see Harvey) has come a construction of organizational authorship in which those most versed in writing find themselves most distanced from authoring by their lack of authority. As discourse workers, we should seek to reclaim this dominion for fellow writers, and we should concurrently reshape writing formations critical to exercising authority and responsibility in the domain of professional writing.

We can begin by connecting curricular writing formations of professional writers with reading formations such as discussed in chapter 6 to the ends of producing writers who are creative in their constructions of reality via instrumental discourses and are equipped with theories and cultural awareness of the most critical sort. If I have seemed overly dismissive of courses in which students write *to* an instructor *about* literature and other texts, I should emphasize here that I see such work as crucial, given the imbrication of reading formations and writing formations. When such courses are conceptualized as *complementary* to the constructions of writing formations rather than constitutive of them, they can aid writers enormously. Indeed, invaluable work takes place in courses with carefully selected texts and contextualization that enables situating these texts amid cultural (and multicultural) processes past and present. Courses such as those described by Richard Miller or Phyllis van Slyck, in which the classroom setting is construed as a "contact zone" in which the cultures coming into the classroom with students become a part of curricular material, enable negotiations of representations and repositionings in light of multiple theories and multiple perspectives among those students. Such reading formations can link with writing practices in valuable ways, as writers in organizational settings tap discursive theories and experiences to make decisions in the ongoing inscriptions of workplace cultures.

When scholars and educators such as Miller and van Slyck use the term "contact zones," they invoke the autoethnographic project, since the term became popularized by Mary Louise Pratt in the same essay that transported autoethnography from anthropological to literary circles. And indeed, spatial tropes have often been employed to depict discursive work under the postmodern umbrella, since one feature of postmodern discourse is that of border crossings. These tropes have enabled insight in particular with respect to cultural differences grounded in ethnicity and regionality, for example, for obvious reasons: particularly if students from various "zones" are present in one classroom, experiences and interpretations emanating from these zones can be aired. But a similar task with respect to professional class is more difficult to accomplish, both because most students in most classrooms are not yet fully vested members of those classes and because academic structures are such that once class formation does begin with specialization, students encounter only students of their own specialization and class in formation.

It would seem that we need tropes to complement autoethnography's "zones" for conceptualizing and engendering exchanges between the academy and the workplace in the name of cultural interventions and under the aegis of authorship in instrumental discourse. Because the "zone" has proven a productive trope and perhaps to articulate more easily the knowledge generated through this trope, we might think in terms of "space," particularly in an age of virtuality and its forums. Working within the philosophical tradition, Jacques Derrida has spoken of a "becoming space" that Patti Lather draws upon in conceptualizing inquiry that bridges postmodern and feminist theory: "A science capable of grasping the continual interplay of agency, structure, and context requires a 'becoming space' . . . where we can think and act with one another into the future in ways that both mark and loosen limits" (101). Forming such a space, against the work of this archaeology and in pursuit of bringing to organizational authorship the theoretical and pragmatic attention it deserves, would require players from both academic and workplace contexts constructing theories of practice that explore the interplay of both structure and agency in the processes and products of authorship. Kurt Spellmeyer has asked, "Are we prepared to recognize nonspecialists as genuine collaborators in the making of knowledge?" ("Inventing the University Student" 44), and this archaeology answers his question with a resounding "We must." Collaborating genuinely—thinking and acting with one another—will of a necessity entail inspecting the terms of "being in relation" of which Zofia Burr speaks, which should push us relentlessly—as members of the class of discourse workers—towards mapping the continual interplays among the ideological, productive, and political spheres shaping our being and in which cultural values take form.

Tony Bennett has spoken of "strategic interventions within the operating procedures and policy agendas of specific cultural institutions" (32), and while he is thinking more of interventions among players from a variety of professional classes usually positioned in more powerful positions than writers in organizations, his appeal applies to professional writers in their day-to-day inscriptions of culture. As we take steps to enhance the theorizing of and ongoing empirical research in organizational authorship and as we conceptualize new reading and writing formations to prepare discourse workers for their positions, we would do well to acknowledge the lack of political impetus to act that we have provided to date. Such a lack looms large, given the degree to which we have shaped political interpretations in reading formations in recent years. Kondo's play is illustrative: the character of Janice Ito is invited by Grace Jones to *try on* the accoutrements of power, which we realize can be little more than a temporary fitting for Ito in current political arenas. Compared with the character of Roy Cohn in Kushner's play, at least, the real political clout of Ito is negligible.

As for Cohn, he is facing not only disbarment but also his impending death, though he refuses to admit it. He has contracted AIDS through homosexual sex, we glean, yet he forbids his doctor during the diagnosis (under threat of destroying the doctor's practice) even to pronounce the word "homosexual," since such a representation of Cohn in his circles of power would mean his undoing. Thus *Angels in America* informs us not only about political networking to construct and maintain realms of exclusion but also about the politics of representation. Reading the play in 2000, in the age of protease inhibitors that offer extended life until perhaps even a cure for AIDS is found for people infected with HIV, we remember the early years of the plague in which the play is set and the pointed refusal of the Reagan administration to respond quickly to this disease. Gay interpretations of this refusal point to the equation of AIDS with homosexuals in the mideighties and long-standing homophobia in the Republican Party which condoned gay genocide through selective inattention. Had interventions in research, treatment, and education occurred earlier, such interpretations argue, many who have died might still be among us, and the epidemic that now sweeps the world might have been mollified.

The character of Cohn illustrates a particular kind of politics of representation, in which personal gain or the gain of a select group is inordinately augmented by blocking comprehensive and multidimensional interpretations of social facts. Such interpretations have long been at the core of feminist theory, African-American studies, gay studies, cultural studies, and others, yet the power suggested through such reading formations hasn't been connected with writing formations. One of the reasons for this failure is that for all of the work in the ideological sphere, the political sphere has been pretty much ignored—while the sphere of production is positioned as some kind of afterlife to which academics have neither interest nor purview. In so doing, compositionists have repeated an "innocence about power" (Berlin, *Rhetorics* 80) which has consistently plagued composition epistemologies. Yet when we rethink ideological constructions of authorship through the ages and institutional enactments of composition that relay current-traditional epistemology, the spheres of production and politics loom as terribly neglected elements in the approach to discursive constructions of subjectivity. Surely one solution to this problem is through the establishment of a political action arm of the Conference on College Composition and Communication, as Sharon Crowley argues (240).

One of the effects of the institutional departmentalization of composition into English earlier in the century, to recall the argument in chapter 1, was that the relationship of mentor between professors and students was severely undermined, since professors now found themselves with so many students from outside of their field and the professorate was being pushed towards research in the academic rationalist tradition—that is, publications on their own topics of interest, often rarified and esoteric—thus limiting energy and time that could be invested in mentoring. As we refashion composition epistemology and imagine new institutional forms adequate for apprehending the complexities of organizational authorship, certainly we will want to redress this positioning of professor and students. Probably the identity of "mentor" will prove inadequate, since student writers (who will often be simultaneously workplace writers) will be bringing experiences and expertise into the classroom which will in fact constitute much of the curriculum—and so we must seek new relationships adequate to our task.

We will want to seek new relationships (and alliances) with students and professors from other professional classes, too, given that many of these people are deeply implicated in discourse work, in specific ways owing in part to their disciplining, in part to the contexts, and in part to the contours of the classes in formation to which they belong. Occasions for many other kinds of archaeological digs will present themselves, and it behooves us to nurture them as they might enable writers to *act* in their workplace cultures with greater and greater sophistication and political savvy. If, with Branden and with all other discourse workers with whom we explore organizational au-

thorship we seek to foster a critical relationship with our own discourse, we will need to explore relentlessly the ways in which individual
discourses meet with structures and practices *in situ*. Not to do so is
to succumb to reductionist ideology in our own fields and by extension
in our own lives. When we imagine the becoming spaces that we will
create to mark and loosen discursive limits, we might take one archaeological shard as talisman, Leigh's comment that she "always wants
writing to be part of her life" (appendix B), a life, like all of our lives,
that will be increasingly composed by the workplace cultures that writers write.

APPENDIXES

WORKS CITED

INDEX

Appendix A
RESEARCHERS' PROFESSIONAL WRITING BACKGROUNDS

Organizational Print Publications (including editors, copy editors, editorial assistants)
>1993: Bernie, Challie, Itsy, Jan, Kolar, Nancy
>1994: Hart, Jen, Leigh
>1995: Brenda, Daisy, Grace, Helen, Karla, Kelly, May, Phoebe, Tess
>1996: Diane, Holly, Kyle, Nyck, Starla, Sue
>1997: Adam, Chet, Corinne, Lena, Maggie, Mary
>1998: Heather, Jackie
>1999: Anita, Ella, Ginger, Jane, Meg

Public Relations/Policy
>1994: Ann
>1995: May
>1996: Andrew, Ray
>1997: Carolyn, Lena
>1998: Kirsten

Technical Writing/Technical Editing (includes Web site design and writing)
>1993: Ellie, Jeff, Joe, Rex
>1995: Sarah, Tom
>1996: Albert, Norma
>1997: Ana, Carolyn, Chet, Kali
>1999: Adria, Anita, Amy, Joanne, Leathe

Analysis Writing and Correspondence
>1993: George, Lisa, Mandy
>1994: Cass, Hart, Liz, Rachel
>1995: Gloria, Tom
>1996: Andrew, Lois, Starla
>1998: Megan, Ravi
>1999: Leathe

Research Writing
>1993: George
>1995: Gloria, Gwen

Journalism
>1993: Nidean
>1995: Daisy, Karla, Kelly, Marla
>1996: Mack, Red

Journalism (continued)
>   1997: Carolyn, Maggie
>   1998: Jackie

Teaching
>   1993: Anne, Lisa
>   1994: Lee
>   1995: Kelly, Marla
>   1996: Alice, Jihad, Kate
>   1997: Chet, Elaine, Janice, Julie, Lara

Graphic Design
>   1993: Challie
>   1997: Mary

Freelance, Self-Employed Writing
>   1993: Branden
>   1997: Janice

Academic Writing (solely)
>   1995: Jillian
>   1997: Gary

Appendix B
RESEARCHERS' TOPICS IN SELF-ASSESSMENT AS WRITERS, SITES OF RESEARCH, AND RESEARCH TOPICS AND THEMES

Researcher/Background	Topics in Self-Assessment	Site of Research	Research Topics and Themes
Adam Editing	Worked as a contributing editor for arts and entertainment magazine; good at interviewing and incorporating quotes; good at dialogue; prone to agonizing; uses deadlines; needs practice	Publishing company	"Customer service"; morale; turnover; isolation, alienation of department within company
Adria Technical writing	Creative writing undergraduate degree; technical writing career means learning technical knowledge; enjoys document design, end-user documentation; designs Web pages and corporate literature; agonizes over phrasing, fears sounding stilted; "my academic writing . . . sounds strange"	Military contractor	Socialization, modes of communication, high turnover, visibility of technical writers' work
Albert Technical writing, World Wide Web writing	Development in high school advanced placement English; influence	Government think tank	Virtual workplace and split subjectivity, representations of self, writer as go-between, accountability

Researcher/Background	Topics in Self-Assessment	Site of Research	Research Topics and Themes
Albert (continued)	of college professor; better writing when not nervous about risks; mainly e-mail now; in charge of public image of organization; functional writer—observe, experience, write; humorous narrator		
Alice Teaching, academic writing	Early development; journals, storytelling, poetry; writes and reads for students and publicly; interest allows immersion; challenge of research	Fourth-grade classroom	Research projects and multicultural issues; library's lacunae, parents' books; nonnative speakers and literacy roles
Amy Technical writing	"Never thought of myself as a writer"; writes Powerpoint presentations, Web pages, and brochures; enjoys letter writing; "enterprising"; wants to improve as a writer	Electronics representative	E-mail communications, shaping cultural norms and values
Ana Technical writer	Technical writing for military contracts; woman, minority, and non-techie in military-industrial complex (status through English degree); writes fiction in personal life for release, satisfaction, development	Military contractor	Gender, race, and organizational status and position; document review, budgets; technical writer's knowledge

Researcher/Background	Topics in Self-Assessment	Site of Research	Research Topics and Themes
Andrew Policy and public relations writing	Career change; experience in reading and writing of program proposals, procedural initiatives, and speeches, in addition to editing and proofreading; would like to write for an association, public relations; grammar and writing served earlier career (writing as valuable professional skill)	Campus police department	Formalization of policy, training, remodeling of culture, control of information
Anita Technical writing	A "writer-in-progress"; handle topics coherently, in an organized format; "soup-maker," presenting other people's information; good ear, weak in rules of grammar; fun with words and ideas	Maritime office	Meetings and writing projects, efficiency, communications
Ann Public relations writer	Not a "writer" ("public relations specialist"); writing equals poetry or literature, "publication"; satisfaction seeing writing in print; two types of writing; professional: newsletters, press releases, brochure copy (creativity, scrutiny, frustration); personal: proposals for nonprofits (satisfying, purpose, responsibility, pride)	Public relations company	Instruction in writing; organizational function of lessons; all women; "feminine"; status; voice, vocabulary

Researcher/Background	Topics in Self-Assessment	Site of Research	Research Topics and Themes
Anne Video- grapher, full-time student	Teaching as a profession perhaps an error (job market); narrator questions the self- analysis instrument	Boys' prep school English class	Personal/academic writing, gender roles
Bernie Editor	High school writing as expressive outlet; self-satisfying; more effective form of commu- nication than speech; writing vs. other professions	Professional association headquarters	Topics for organiza- tional publications, linear and lateral thinking, lobbying
Branden Independent tourism writer	High school writing influen- tial; equates writing with Shakespeare; published widely; selling her writing	Government travel agency	Documents as possessions in bureaucracy
Brenda Press and professional writing	Developed early (age eleven); writing is fiction, a certain length; finds it easy, enjoyable; process involves trans- lating, solving puzzles; some- times humdrum; motivated by deadlines; looks forward to re- sponse; schooling; following a project	Association	Magazine editing and review processes, Post- its, editors' review styles
Carolyn Technical writer, journalism	Values essential— must believe in document; enjoys writing to educate (experience as feature writer); experience in interviewing; currently working collaboratively on a user's manual	Information technology consulting company	Communication gaps between departments, influence of gaps on writers' performance

Researcher/Background	Topics in Self-Assessment	Site of Research	Research Topics and Themes
Cass Contract writer, government	Excelled in research papers in high school; writing commercials for radio; seven years preparing documents for government contracts (coordinating requests for proposals; memos, board reports, research ideas); pursuing MA in teaching of writing and literature to teach composition or technical writing eventually	Government agency	Director's management of projects, fax, communications, government hierarchy, employee affect
Challie Graphic designer	More comfortable with creative than technical writing; capable yet difficulty implementing ideas	Professional association headquarters	E-mail message types, Continuous Quality Improvement in organization, efficiency through e-mail, performance
Chet Editing	Needs improvement in writing skills; interest/passion for this art form; mediocre in nonfiction, poetry, technical writing; have "verbal acuity"; likes writing fiction most, but earning a living?	Government-related publishing company	Deadlines and quality; teamwork, cooperation, sacrifice
Corinne Editing	Difficulty conveying emotion as an editor; investigative, artistic, organizer; functional skills: cultivating, problem solving, producing, collaborating, administering, scheduling	Public relations office of historic house	Restructuring and editing, perpetuating image, old production practices

Researcher/Background	Topics in Self-Assessment	Site of Research	Research Topics and Themes
Daisy Journalism, public relations, editor	Journalism, news releases, public service announce- ments, brochures, features; others' evaluations of her; enjoyment; writing poetry provides ful- fillment; dead- lines; early development; goal to teach	Newsroom of biweekly	"Live" culture vs. textbook, observed quietness in the field site, experience, interactions
Diane Organization publications editing	"Conventional organizer, artistic creator, social helper" (Holland); undergraduate training in jour- nalism; perhaps more an editor than writer; satisfaction in effecting results	Education association headquarters (communi- cations department)	Strategic planning in "disheveled" culture, publication processes, management vs. writers and editors, turnover
Elaine Academic, newsletters	When writing, a good writer ("ele- gant simplicity"); needs audience and deadline, though (why her novel remains unfinished); juggling mother- hood and writing; great emphasis on page one in com- posing; newslet- ters; emotional high from crafting words	Corporate history writing company	One script's evolution, academic/corporate views of writing, should/can this com- pany do advertising?
Ella Legal support writing	Assemble note- books, design databases, orga- nize, summarize; no creativity, presently; still developing; importance of proofreading; adapted style (shorter sen- tences); creating family Web pages	Law office	Managing documenta- tion for outside client: volumes of old docu- ments, drudgery, lack of autonomy

Researcher/Background	Topics in Self-Assessment	Site of Research	Research Topics and Themes
Emma Teaching	High school training in "notecards and outlines"; later, "writer-based"; still later, "audience issues"; not a "gifted" analytical writer, so uses lots of drafts and hard work	Elementary school	Teachers' and administrators' writing; hierarchy, distance, tensions
Gary Academic	Early development (grade school); enjoys researching, drafting, and revising; enjoys poetry and creative writing; doesn't call self writer ("true writers write all the time"); methodical, precise	Internet job bank	Writing and editing by "non-writers," new issues in writing brought by Internet
George Writer/editor (fourteen years)	Childhood writing; high school contest; occupational pleasure is clear and useful writing	Military headquarters organization	Ghostwriting, document review procedures, writer psychology, readability
Ginger Legal support writing	Personal writing is journals, poetry, letters, e-mails, classes, editing others; professional writing is legal-secretarial, revisions, collaborative, never originated by self; strong in grammar, sentence structure; "pride"; future goal to be editor or technical writer	Law office	Legal culture, drudgery, humor, sarcasm

Researcher/Background	Topics in Self-Assessment	Site of Research	Research Topics and Themes
Gloria Professional writing, library	Innovation, experimentation, self-motivation on the job; autonomy, variation; interdisciplinary; research, self-discovery; discipline	Library of Congress	Reference correspondence, self development, autonomy, service, timeliness, styles
Grace Copy editor, public relations writer	Developed early (age eight); many genres; student writing vs. literary; BA in English; analyzing others' vs. original work; volunteering; correspondence; promotional copy; editing	Society's journal publications office	Manuscript review policy and procedures, culture's three subcultures, history
Gwen Medical writer	Writing requires much research; writing since childhood; schooling important; literature an important influence; family influences; many skills; variety and learning on the job; thoroughness; patience and understanding required; seeks a contribution to society	Psychiatric research hospital	Documentation of and by workers, intrigue, surveillance, professional development
Hart Corporate editor, writer	Hearing an "internal editor" and "voice of doom" while writing; comparison with *Hamlet, The Firm, The Road Less Traveled*; humor is a refuge; deadlines as motivation; natural affinity for language; writing self withered while corporate tool; writing is hard work	University public relations office	Representing change and tradition, office status in university hierarchy, conflicts, writers' roles

Researcher/Background	Topics in Self-Assessment	Site of Research	Research Topics and Themes
Heather Magazine writing	Switched from MA in literature to professional writing and editing; practical, realistic, goal oriented, with artistic, creative streak; has difficulty with long papers, lead sentences for news stories; "just starting out as a writer, with room for improvement"	Association publications department	Writing and editing magazine; isolation of staff, physically and culturally
Helen Editing, organization magazine	Schooling; job led her to pursue professional writing and editing degree; variety; purpose; artistic endeavors	Law enforcement training facility	Magazine publications office, editors' differing approaches, implied authorship cf magazine
Holly Newsletter writing and editing	Editing while writing, overview and notes; perfectionist and organizer, needs clear idea and right conditions; deadline helps; writing and discovery; originality and creativity not strong suits; perhaps a better editor than writer	Newsletter publisher	Decisions and authority in process, turnover, management lacunae
Itsy Editorial assistant, federal government	Childhood writing; "structured and unimaginative writing" in federal government; wants work in publications	Small business management office	Office dynamics, newsletters, family metaphor, miscommunication
Jackie News, magazine, public relations writing	Artistic, social, enterprising, conventional (Holland model); work has fostered talent in creative	Association publications department	Publishing bimonthly newsletter, staff/"volunteer" dynamics, "news" role in a public relations setting, writing style defined by roles

Researcher/Background	Topics in Self-Assessment	Site of Research	Research Topics and Themes
Jackie (continued)	nonfiction, interviewing, headline writing, problem solving; future goal: technical writing, publishing, teaching, advertisement copywriting		
Jan Editor	Not a writer, yet; writing as genetic; literary vs. professional writing (herself)	Professional association headquarters	Issues management teams resulted in no change in writing process, memo use in organization, management vs. employees
Jane Research/ editing	College experience in visual arts; "Can I call myself a writer if I don't excel at multiple types?"; clinical research associate; ghostwriting; editing children's book	City government agency	Red tape, document cycling; strategically missed deadlines
Janice Creative freelance	Early development; writing as therapy; penchant for humor writing; enjoys workshops and group processes; enjoys close observation and analysis	Newsletter/ book fulfillment company	Business letter in small family company, family conflicts, no second generation business writers
Jeff Technical editor, environmental engineering company	Meeting deadlines is crucial; good at organizing large documents; prefers writing humorous essays about people ("male Erma Bombeck")	Environmental engineering consultancy	Culture clash, technical staff vs. editors; status; expertise and interactions; noun strings
Jen Editor, publications specialist	Two "types" of writing, personal and professional; personal: journals (enjoyment, therapy, relaxed,	Government employment newsletter publisher	Purpose of editorial pages, office style and writing style, all women, feminine attributes, authority, validation

Researcher/Background	Topics in Self-Assessment	Site of Research	Research Topics and Themes
Jen (continued)	most clear); professional: job writing and editing (analytical, exacting, "technical-mindedness," "structured"); writing means expressing self		
Jihad Teaching, business memos	Identifies purpose and sticks to it; edits a minimum; does not revise ideas; favors uncomplicated language over fancy; as non-native speaker sometimes uses Arabic writing approaches; recent shift to word processing	Fast food headquarters and franchise	Writing forms and instructions, implied readers and voice
Jillian Academic writing	Satisfaction; solutions to problems in others' writing; exploration; reformulation; academic writing is unfulfilling	Internet list	Shift in e-"culture" over time, users' self-representation, register
Joanne Technical/ publications writing	BS in technical writing/editing; marketing writer in computer industry; integrating art and text; simple style; analytical, scheduling skills; company newsletter; "social, artistic, enterprising"; social interest; collaborative skills; provides financial security	Technical contractor	Documenting of tech contracting work, changes in technology and documentation
Joe Documentation specialist	Technical writing is a challenge; diplomacy and negotiating;	Software development company	Corporate style manual, representation, users, audience

Researcher/Background	Topics in Self-Assessment	Site of Research	Research Topics and Themes
Joe (continued)	rewarding; creator, problem solver (writer working on programmer's product)		
Julie Teaching, community college	Lots of reading and thinking about conventions (academic and business); composed a computer manual; experience in industry and many written genres of workplace	Community college classroom	Work writing influence on school; perceived applications, similarities, value
Kali Information and analysis writing	Easily adapts styles; uses investigative and conventional skills for work writing (mostly factual tables and charts); uses speech-pattern sentences for personal and informal writing; artistic, social, enterprising	Military contracting company	Job insecurity and writing quality, self-imposed standards, planning departures
Karla Journalism, pubs	Artistic skills; schooling; newsmagazine writing; free-lancing; fulfillment; narratives of changing jobs, validation; goal is to write fiction	Association publications division	Newsletter production, editorial board's intervention, corporate politics
Kate Teaching, academic writing	"Solid" writer—others' estimation; precision, readability, thoroughness, yet lacking spark; not a "creative" writer (humiliation); more comfortable in third person than	University writing center	Tutor styles, writing center services, English department culture/ writing center culture

Researcher/Background	Topics in Self-Assessment	Site of Research	Research Topics and Themes
Kate (continued)	first, would like to meld first person and third in this course		
Kelly Copy editor/ writer, publications	Teaching compo- sition; freelancing; journalism; pub- lications; variety and volume of work; creative writing interest; "painful"	University publications department	Changes in publications process to "teams"; time, pressure; different participants' viewpoints
Kirsten Magazines, public relations writing	Influence of college instruc- tion by magazine writer; interviews and research lead the writing; nonprofit writing to raise public awareness; future goal: marketing or public relations writing	Association magazine publications division	Publishing monthly magazine, work ethic, standards, collabora- tive and solo work
Kolar Editorial assistant, public relations	No assessment provided	U.S. senator's office	Hill culture, press office writing, fabri- cation, socialization
Kyle Writing and editing, organization magazine	Practice and perfection (edit- ing association magazine); edit- ing others; devel- oping style (easy to read, clear, concise); true love is humor (D. Barry); e-mails a favorite place to write—not literary or poetic, but fun and understandable	Association communica- tions de- partment	Magazine publication, turnover, publication processes and creativity
Lara Teaching, kindergarten	Working with kindergartners; artistic theme strong in Holland model; difficulty in expression at times; write funny	Elementary school	Composing school plan collaboratively; difficulties, poor management of collaborative writing

Researcher/Background	Topics in Self-Assessment	Site of Research	Research Topics and Themes
Lara (continued)	letters, emotional poetry, determined letters to Congress		
Leathe Technical/ report writing	Working independently, analyzes, conceptualizes, and organizes information; creates tables; writes data up without theorizing; dislikes proposals, prizes "time flexibility"; likes data analysis	Research and technical development company	Culture of a "flat organization"; chain of command; project cycling, iterations
Lee Teacher, writing center director	Writing to learn, writing and reading; writing to explain, provide information at work; journal for exploring, examining feelings; notes, letters, and lists in "everyday life"; lacks discipline; revises a lot; playing with words	Writing center	Tutoring vs. computer lab, evaluating software, organizational location and conflict
Leigh Editor, government	Professional writing means editing other people's writing, style to government standards; memos are "structured writing" (a formatting technique) (persuasive memo to boss got money for graduate school); academic writing includes hypertext fiction, a struggle and is revealing about self as writer (vulnerability, flow, catharsis); writing always part of life	U.S. cabinet speechwriters	writing processes, writer's references, "idea factory", metaphors, civil servant vs. political

Researcher/Background	Topics in Self-Assessment	Site of Research	Research Topics and Themes
Lena Teaching, high school	Enjoys language, "putting it together"; "scaled-back ambitions" (great novels, MFA vs. MA in professional writing and editing); likes to observe, describe, draw conclusions	Nonprofit educational publications company	Management style, editors' decisions on manuscripts, career advancement for writers means moving into management
Lisa Analyst, English as a second language teacher	Understanding through writing; writing as means; writing and investigative skills; non-native speakers in American work culture	Bank	Style: marketing and prestige; commercial loan vs. operations; family symbolism; gender, conflict, morale
Liz Staff assistant	BA in French; MA underway to expand professional scope, improve writing skills; difficulty with long documents; strengths: creativity and variety of style, persuasive writing; uses e-mail extensively	World Bank editors	Writing style, editors' work, organizational division's status, support staff/professional staff
Lois Marketing, organization memos	Career change; striving to improve skills; writer is a "reverse prism"; "stories demanding to be told" (a narrative of writer as vehicle); trying to find own voice	Telecommunications company's virtual office	Face-to-face and virtual cultures, top-down vs. bottom-up
Mack Journalism	Not a writer: not paid or regular; enjoy researching more than writing; deadlines help; newspaper experience produced "journalese" and enhanced	Personal 'zines	Writers' aims and backgrounds, anti-school, who are the audiences

Researcher/Background	Topics in Self-Assessment	Site of Research	Research Topics and Themes
Mack (continued)	understanding of writing process; telling stories to teach and delight; miss thrill of news writing		
Maggie Journalism	Good at conveying facts; never writes about self; succinct; likes to use quotes; editor (very different from writing); personal writing friendly, familiar, unrestricted; lost some creativity	Publications company	Standards, author-editor-colleague exchanges, technology of virtual publishing processes, auto-didacticism
Mandy Secretary	Not yet a writer (must "produce"), so "aspiring" writer; African-American woman; attending school and working at two jobs currently	Industry association headquarters	Waste in document publishing and distribution; sexism, racism
Marla Journalism, academic writing	Academic and journalism primarily; BA French/English; graduate courses for credentials; teaching, counseling, creating, relating; community ties	Secondary school	Communications in school; administration, teachers, students, parents and information flow
Mary Editor, graphics, freelance	Editor of college undergraduate paper; published freelance essayist; suspense novel in circulation; journal keeping with illustrations; would like to write and illustrate children's books	Management consultancy	Elitism, mentoring, perks, turnover, (non-?) hierarchy, stress, deadlines

Researcher/Background	Topics in Self-Assessment	Site of Research	Research Topics and Themes
May Public relations/ marketing writing	Schooling developed skills and interest; journalism; interviewing; corporate writing; education to enhance and rectify	Hospital	Public relations writing, agendas of different divisions
Meg Marketing writing/ editing	Business writing conveys concise messages; managing content for fourteen Web sites; writer/editor for two internal publications; corporate public policy and government marketing writing; e-mails, faxes, letters; intimidated by creative writing	Global information company	Monthly program/ activity report, managing/controlling work expectations
Megan Academic/ fund-raising	Influence of parents and teachers while young; eleventh grade: art of sentence structure; college major in creative writing; undertaking MA in professional writing and editing to sharpen skills	University foundation office	By-laws, direct mail, memoranda of understanding, acknowledgements, vagueness in discourse, personal yet universal appeals
Nancy (editorial assistant) and Ellie (technical writer)	Nancy: developed early (age six); writing as personal; sense of inferiority; must be interested in topic Ellie: direct, clear, logical; writing is a puzzle; hopes for a varied writing career	Educational facility planning company	Collaborative document process, proposals, family roles

Researcher/Background	Topics in Self-Assessment	Site of Research	Research Topics and Themes
Nidean Journalist; full-time student	"Never boring," even if matter is dry; "chameleon penner"; writing ability helps in all professions	Fitness training facility	Language use to manipulate, brochures, notions of self, gym discourse
Norma Technical writing and editing	Late bloomer, early anxiety, stress, punishment; worked hard at this difficult skill; interrupted college; enjoys tech writing most; updating and revising textbooks;would like to use ethnography to develop freer style	Doctor's office	Coded entries on patients, time, industry standards
Nyck News and information editing	Currently stagnant, needs a deadline or a demander; gets ideas for stories, poems, screenplays, but doesn't write them down; dreamed of writing since fourth grade; may use writing as therapy; adopts voice of humorous narrator in the self-assessment	Capitol Hill info provider	Formalizing culture through writing, responsibilities and pay, credentials and professional identity
Phoebe Professional writing, business, poetry	Ethnography will be "confessional" (Van Maanen's categories); MFA vs. MA in professional writing and editing; poetry; "doing everything" in office writing; writing as therapeutic; schooling; newfound passion for editing	Writers' organization	Interoffice correspondence, artists as managers, alliances in culture, upheaval

Researcher/Background	Topics in Self-Assessment	Site of Research	Research Topics and Themes
Rachel Foreign language assistant	Early employment; artistic skills and writing; "knack" for technical writing, business writing; tenacity, autodidactic; long-term goal: write full time	Embassy defense section	Reports, letters; author credit; military structure and writing; gender divisions
Ravi Academic/ freelance	Taking pride in one's work; the thrill of being published; getting a paycheck; has written two plays, many poems, travel notes and essays; rereads his work	Software development company	"Unconventional" office management, training, collaboration, work dynamics
Ray Policy and public relations writing	Creative and fiction on own time—desires more time for "independent, introspective, and nonconformist" writing; at work: press summaries, press releases, memos, letters; perhaps too self-critical; similar technical writing in future?	Small town police department	Revising policy, oral vs written culture, organizational dynamics, writer as "shield" for chief
Red Journalism	"Descriptive writer," visual thinker (mother a painter); newspaper experience: writing approaching spoken style and now reads as a writer; writing is an art, for fulfillment; rhythm and rhyme are therapeutic	Daily newspaper	Journalist culture and professional development, management vs. reporters, "trust," surveillance

Researcher/Background	Topics in Self-Assessment	Site of Research	Research Topics and Themes
Rex Editor, technical writer	Writing is artistic; enjoy team atmosphere yet independent; seeking new job	Illustrations department, national monthly	"Boundaries," phys- ical, social, linguistic; captioning; veterans vs. novices; management vs. employees
Sarah Technical writing, academic	Enjoyment; inter- est; writing to learn; intellectual stimulation; social contact (through inter- views); organiz- ing; ordering; variety of tasks; deciding whether to switch to freelancing	Freelancers	Project acquisition and management in current economy, isolation, interactions with editors and others
Starla Public relations, news analysis	Prefer nonfiction to fiction, humor (Dave Barry); enjoys writing profiles; work (other people edit) vs. home (freer); "audio" writer (sentences and musicality)	Financial services company communica- tions department	Organizational hierarchies; press releases; problems in information flow, review processes
Sue Organiza- tion editing and writing	Earlier days, enjoyed writing for writing; now, job requires much writing in formats and "govern- mentese"; others' opinions are a plus; lack dis- cipline; moody; writer's block; deadlines are a plus, private writing suffers; writing as therapy	Military field office	Review and dissemina- tion system, office alliances, breakdowns in dissemination
Tess Writer/ editor, organization publications	Publications; enjoyment; many tasks; learning skills on the job; creative writing, poetry; convic- tion; "painful"; wants to find her professional culture	Travel business	Corporate culture and writers' cultures, association vs. cor- porate writing, inter- viewing for new job

Researcher/Background	Topics in Self-Assessment	Site of Research	Research Topics and Themes
Tom Professional/ technical writing	Developed early (age four); wants and fears feed-back; comfort, loss, invasion; people who influence; giving power; finds academic writing esoteric; narrator uses metaphor and irony	Community college senate	Memos' form and function: organization structure and power

Appendix C
WRITERS' WORK AND POSITIONS BY NATURE OF THE ORGANIZATION

PRIVATE BUSINESSES AND CORPORATIONS

Size*	Researcher	Writing Work Documented	Writers' Positions in Organization
L	Adam	Compiling health care reference materials	Writers and editors in either publishing division or operations division
M	Adria	Composing and updating software life cycle documentation, corporate literature, Web site copy	Technical writer [researcher], a Web site developer, in thirty-person headquarters of defense contracting organization, coordinating virtual teams around the country
L	Amy	Composing e-mails to customers and coworkers	Sales representatives in five-person office coordinating requests and information from fifteen other offices
S	Ann	Public relations writing	Owner (founder), project coordinator, editor, graphics specialist
M	Carolyn	Composing software documentation	Technical writers in documentation and training team
S	Chet	Producing publications on government procurement	Owner (founder), editor, attorney, assistant editor/production manager, printer
S	Daisy	Interviewing, writing copy, editing	Associate publisher, editors (managing, feature, sports, copy), reporters

*S = less than 15 employees; M = 15 to 100 employees; L = more than 100 employees

Size	Researcher	Writing Work Documented	Writers' Positions in Organization
M	Elaine	Writing corporate histories	Historians: CEO, archivists, project managers, writers
L	Ella	Composing interoffice memos, client letters, document charts, file indexes, tables of contents	Legal assistant [researcher] of attorneys in eight-person team, 500-person firm
M	Gary	Composing and updating Web site	Marketing executive, webmaster, technical writer
L	Ginger	Composing form agreements, memos, and letters	Secretaries [researcher], legal assistants of attorneys in firm of over a hundred
M	Holly	Editing newsletters	Editor in editorial department of twenty, newsletter publications company
S	Janice	Getting clients, promoting their publications	Owner (CEO), secretary, public relations writer, marketing writer, printer
L	Jeff	Editing engineers' copy, proposals	Technical editor in team of seven, engineering organization of over a hundred
M	Jen	Writing, editing, proofing copy	Writers, editors, and editorial assistants in biweekly newsletter
M	Jihad	Writing memos and business forms	Managers and employees from other professions
M	Joanne	Composing manuals and on-line Web page, migration plans, drafting on shared drive	Documentation manager of staff [researcher] in six-person team of fifty-person organization
L	Joe	Writing software documentation; editing copy from other departments	Technical writers in team of four, part of software development organization of 150

Size	Researcher	Writing Work Documented	Writers' Positions in Organization
M	Leathe	Composing proposals and statistical analysis, Web sites	Technical writer/editor [researcher - one of four] in eighty-person government contractor
M	Lisa	Writing memos and correspondence	Vice presidents, loan administrators, operations assistant, assistant managers, customer service assistant
L	Lois	Writing memos and e-mails up and down organization to coordinate marketing	Salesperson in virtual office of eight, part of communications technology organization of over 300,000
S	Mack	Self-publishing 'zine issues	Independent (links with other writers via 'zine culture)
M	Maggie	Assembling books for publication by e-mail	Sponsoring editor, managing editor, project editor
L	Mary	Team writing management studies	Specialists, managers, associates, analysts (all MBAs)
L	May	Writing promotional brochures	Assistant vice president, marketing and public relations, hospital of over a hundred [researcher]
L	Meg	Writing internal and external reports, newsletters, Web sites	Vice president, director, senior manager [researcher], information associate in 250-person office of 16,000-person information company
S	Nancy and Ellie	Coordinating proposals, boilerplating	Technical writer/program analyst; liaison to exterior (clients) in five-person architectural consultancy organization
S	Nidean	Desktop publishing consulting	Outside consultant

Size	Researcher	Writing Work Documented	Writers' Positions in Organization
S	Norma	Documenting patients in office	Professionals in other professions
M	Nyck	Scanning and proofing transcripts of government documents, putting them on-line	Reporters, editors, chief editor, and managers in sixty-five-person on-line news and information provider
M	Ravi	Marketing software and telecommunications service	Marketing writers, technical writers, sales writers
M	Red	Reporting for and publishing newspaper	Managing editor, editorial editor, copy and bureau chiefs, copy editors
M	Rex	Indexing and abstracting illustrations	Indexers in illustrations division of national monthly publications office
S	Sarah	Self-marketing own writing and revising and composing organizations' publications	Niches: outside writers (selling their content) and consultants (working with organization's content)
L	Starla	Clipping news articles, writing press releases, newsletter	Communications specialists, PR director in seven-person communications division, organization of over a thousand
L	Tess	Writing newsletter, public relations, brochures	Writer in communications department in travel company of 2,300

GOVERNMENT AGENCIES AND INSTITUTIONS

Size	Researcher	Writing Work Documented	Writers' Positions in Organization
L	Albert	Managing Web pages, composing copy, managing e-mail and voice mail in virtual office	Technical writer/webmaster in 850-employee government think tank
M	Ana	Writing technical specifications, proposals, status updates	Technical writer, communications automation officer in operations department of information technology division

Size	Researcher	Writing Work Documented	Writers' Positions in Organization
L	Anita	Drafting, circulating, and editing short- and long-term projects; presenting progress in meetings	Technical writer consultant [researcher] to maritime headquarters; military personnel at various ranks in ten-person division
L	Branden	Collectively writing reports and press releases for public, composing internal weekly reports, editing and copyediting	Outside consultant [researcher] to policy and planning office in travel agency in department of commerce; staff writers in policy and planning
L	Cass	Composing requests for proposals based on input from many divisions	Contracting officer [researcher] in 250-person government agency on arms control and disarmament
L	George	Gathering data, analyzing it, writing in chop chain for officers' signatures	Program analysts and writers in military headquarters organization of 400
L	Gloria	Researching sources and synthesizing them for library patrons via letters and e-mail	Reference librarians in newspaper and current periodicals reading room of Library of Congress
L	Gwen	Writing grant applications, administrative renewals, memos, purchase orders, articles and books, statements, audio-visual presentations	Branch chief, writer/editor [researcher], and secretaries in branch chief's office overseeing twenty-nine-member staff
L	Helen	Editing submissions from the field for a law enforcement organization's magazine	Editors and associate editors in seven-person publications division of national law enforcement organization
M	Jane	Composing and editing monthly reports, newsletters, magazine articles, Web site copy, letters to citizens	Supervisor and editor [researcher] in two-person public affairs division of fifty-person city government agency
L	Kali	Writing reports, financial analysis technical specifications, computer tips	Direct-charge and over-head employees in various divisions of military contracting company

Size	Researcher	Writing Work Documented	Writers' Positions in Organization
M	Kolar	Ghostwriting statements, fabricating letters from constituents	Press secretaries and assistants in U.S. senator's press office
M	Leigh	Speechwriting for U.S. cabinet member	Civil servant speechwriters in cabinet office, team of five
L	Liz	Producing collective reports for external audiences, editing and revising copy from other divisions, writing internal memos	Report authors and editors (on-staff and contractual) from various divisions of World Bank staff of 9,500
M	Rachel	Composing wire reports and written reports for superiors' signatures, composing internal memos and assignments	Civilian and military employees in twenty-four-member defense attaché section of a foreign embassy
M	Ray	Writing public relations copy to exterior, policy revision within organization	Policy writer in support division of small-town police force
M	Sue	Processing and editing reports, checking forms and formats	Reports officer in government/military field office of twenty-five

PROFESSIONAL ASSOCIATIONS AND SOCIETIES

Size	Researcher	Writing Work Documented	Writers' Positions in Organization
M	Bernie	Producing four journals to keep constituency abreast of issues (writing and editing)	Authors (outside and on-staff) and editors (support staff in publications department) in association headquarters
M	Brenda	Evaluating submissions, accepting, editing, and publishing articles for bimonthly magazine	Director of publications, assistant director of publications, and writer/editor in three-person publications branch of communications department of association headquarters
L	Challie	Publishing monthly newsletter and e-mail exchanges in organization	Writers and editors, graphics expert [researcher], in 160-person association headquarters

Size	Researcher	Writing Work Documented	Writers' Positions in Organization
S	Corinne	Composing public relations materials for historic house	Director, marketing director, managers (special events, education, interpretation, media relations), administrative assistants, contract editor [researcher]
M	Diane	Writing, editing books, desktop publishing, proofing; composing public relations brochures and reports to constituents	Writers, editors, and editorial assistants in five-person communications department of twenty-person association headquarters
M	Grace	Coordinating manuscripts from authors and referee reviews in professional society's monthly journal, editing and copyediting	Manuscript coordinator, editor in "adjunct journal staff," team of eight associate editors and editor-in-chief
L	Heather	Publishing monthly magazine	Editor-in-chief, assistant editors, managing editor, senior editors, copy editors, editorial assistants
S	Itsy	Producing newsletters for constituents	Two writers, each in charge of separate newsletter, in five-person office of association
L	Jackie	Publishing newsletter for national association	Editor-in-chief, managing editor, associate editors, editorial assistant, photo assistant
M	Jan	Collectively producing perspective paper to represent constituency to Congress	Senior staff and support in eighty-five-person association headquarters
M	Karla	Publishing newsletter for national association	Editorial board, managers, project directors, writers, editors, copy editors, editorial assistants in media relations department of association headquarters

Size	Researcher	Writing Work Documented	Writers' Positions in Organization
S	Kirsten	Publishing magazine for national association	Senior vice president in communication, publications director, editors-in-chief, managing editors, in magazine staff of six, part of publications staff of seventeen
M	Kyle	Writing stories, coordinating and editing submissions from nonpaid authors, for association bimonthly magazine	Editor in seven-person communications department of thirty-five-person association headquarters
S	Lena	Publishing monthly magazine for science educators	Editor, managing editor, associate editor, design manager, editorial assistant, field editor
L	Mandy	Boilerplating, speechwriting, composing reports to constituents	Managers and staff support in ninety-person association headquarters

EDUCATIONAL AND NON-PROFIT INSTITUTIONS

Size	Researcher	Writing Work Documented	Writers' Positions in Organization
M	Alice	Teaching report and research writing to fourth graders	Full-time teacher in fourth-grade classroom in public school system
L	Andrew	Composing training policies and lessons, standard operating procedures	Professionals in other professions, part of university campus police office
M	Anne	Teaching writing in high school sophomore English	Student-teacher in tenth grade English class in boys' prep school
M	Emma	Writing administrative notes, memos, newsletters; writing notes to parents	Principal, secretaries, teachers, support staff in elementary school
L	Hart	Writing copy for alumni magazine, special reports, president's statements and other publications in university relations office	Editor of magazine, director of publications, publications assistant and desktop assistant in the communications department of university relations department

Size	Researcher	Writing Work Documented	Writers' Positions in Organization
L	Jillian	Posting comments in MBU, a public listserv on the Internet	Mostly academics at various institutions in United States and worldwide, in various positions
M	Julie	Composing literary analysis, research papers, response journals in community college composition class	Students anticipating majors in business, art, sociology
L	Kate	Teaching writing one-on-one, conducting group workshops in university writing center	MFA students with teaching assistantships in English department with tracks in literature, linguistics, professional writing and editing, and teaching writing and literature
L	Kelly	Writing copy and editing others' in variety of publications in university publications office	Director of publications, production manager, writers, editors, copy editors, and editorial assistants in fifteen-person office
M	Lara	Collectively composing an elementary school three-year plan mandated by county	Principal, lead teachers (in subject areas), reading teacher, kindergarten teacher [researcher]
M	Lee	Writing memos on daily activities, reports to central administration of college	Director of a writing center attached to English department in community college
L	Marla	Teaching journalism, writing to parents, overseeing school newspaper production	Full-time teacher in public high school of 1,100
M	Megan	Writing by-laws, memoranda of understanding, biannual newsletter, direct mail solicitations; acknowledgments	Annual fund director, director of development for donor relations
M	Phoebe	Composing memos and reports on office business for internal distribution	Office manager and assistant in administrative division and programs coordinator in program division of non-profit organization serving writers, teachers, and community

Size	Researcher	Writing Work Documented	Writers' Positions in Organization
L	Tom	Writing memos and reports	Chair of college senate, community college

Appendix D
RESEARCHERS' ABSTRACTS OF WORKPLACE ETHNOGRAPHIES

ADAM—A LESSON IN THE DANGERS OF WORKPLACE ALIENATION

A valuable illustration for employees attempting to understand the dynamics of their workplace cultures is a corporate environment that has undergone a difficult period of growth resulting in a dangerous level of alienation from others by one or several departments within the organization. This autoethnographic study provides the history and goals of a publishing company, documents several sources of the company's difficulties, and concentrates on the detachment of one department, customer service, during this troublesome time. It is the author's contention that conditions at the company compounded the feeling of alienation felt by his department. Additionally, conditions inherent in all customer service situations as well as attitudes maintained by employees of this particular department are discussed to illustrate that fault should be equally accepted by those employees and the company environment as a whole. Concluding observations provide an insight to the future of the company and how its improving conditions could be attained at similar organizations.

ADRIA—SOCIALIZATION, ACCEPTANCE, EMPLOYEE TURNOVER, AND WRITING IN A SMALL DEFENSE CONTRACTING ORGANIZATION

This paper centers on the author's autoethnographic research at a small defense contracting organization in which employee turnover has become so bad that it is practically a joke. The paper focuses on the relationships between employee turnover, socialization, and writing tasks. Employees at this company learn quickly that socialization plays a big part in employee happiness and ability to get work done. Gossip and actual information sharing become entwined, so that a short office visit for talking about the new employee down the hall can become a valuable source of information. Besides oral communication, written communication in the form of e-mail is the most valuable source of information, but it often falls short if those involved in the e-mail conversation have never met in person. Turnover itself has made a case for the need for more documentation, since so many people leave that important information becomes lost. Finally, speculations are made concerning the relationship between management and employees, and opinions are expressed concerning the problem of turnover.

ALBERT—SPLIT SUBJECTIVITY IN THE VIRTUAL WORKPLACE

This study investigates the role of the professional writer in a government think tank. The two goals of this study were to assess the "virtual " environment in this workplace through exploring the split subjectivity of the writers there and to address the dynamic nature of documents (specifically resumes) on the World Wide Web. My findings focus on the virtual buffers now a part of the hiring and firing process of employees, and on the psychologies of composing in the virtual writing environment. This study incorporates the writings of three postmodern theorists, Charles Altieri, Terry Eagleton, and Morris Dickstein, to support the ideas of split subjectivity, virtual discourse, and the mediated values writers and readers bring to authorship.

ALICE—USING THE WRITING PROCESS TO ENCOURAGE DIVERSITY: AN ETHNOGRAPHIC INSIGHT TO CLASSROOM CULTURE

This paper presents the findings from a classroom study that provided insights on the impact of the writing process on accommodating diversity and ability. The setting of the study is a fourth- and fifth-grade classroom in an urban elementary school. Students, parents, teachers, and administrators were interviewed and observed in the school setting and the results were described in field notes and written responses. Analysis of data revealed three significant points: (1) Students come from varied writing experiences that can have different values than their school experiences; (2) Students need to see themselves in the curriculum; (3) The writers' workshop format functions as a powerful tool for students to express what is important to them.

AMY—THE CULTURE OF BEA, PORTRAYED AND DEFINED BY E-MAIL

This study is an illustration of the culture of a branch office of an electronics sales representative. Using interoffice e-mails and organizational charts completed by each member of the five person office, the autoethnographer contrasts the team-oriented atmosphere perceived by office members versus the hierarchical structure of the office defined by corporate headquarters. The e-mails collected were categorized into five categories as follows: employee conversation (nonwork related), manager to subordinate instructions, comments to the office on outsiders' e-mails, and copies of e-mails sent to outsiders to keep everyone up to date. These e-mails were used to define the culture as team-oriented and were viewed using a sociolinguistic analysis. At the same time, the e-mails were contrasted against the culture defined in the organizational charts, which did not portray a flat organization. The author's analysis determined that there was a team spirit, but the office was still divided with managers and subordinates.

ANA—RACE, STATUS, AND WRITING CYCLING AT A MILITARY CONTRACTING FIRM

My experience as a technical writer at "D3 Corporation" allowed me to study the history of contracting and document review in tandem with hiring and firing. As money from one contract dwindled, employees in the lower echelons were let go (including one critical technical support person), while an expensive middle-manager was brought on, ostensibly for his power to land new contracts. By the time that four of the six minority workers in the company had been let go, my boss and I, the remaining two minority workers, felt some security—he because he had a strong track record in bringing in business and I because I was in fact the only one actually learning the technical intricacies of our projects through my writing. Towards the end of this study, upper management had begun cycling our documents to the new middle manager so that he could sign off on them and take money from our budget. At the conclusion of my study, my boss and I were interviewing for new jobs.

ANDREW—DEVELOPING A TRAINING CURRICULUM AND REMODELING THE INFORMATION FLOW: ONE ORGANIZATION'S APPROACH TO CHANGE

The Atlantic College Campus Security Police has changed the way it trains its officers and the way it disseminates policy and procedures to the line officers. This ethnography examines those changes, focusing on the training program that is presently in place, contrasting it to the previous arrangement. The paper also looks at the way in which directives are prepared within the organization as a vehicle to compare the director's leadership style to his goals and objectives for the organization. This work unit is, in some respects, a makeshift organization, carving and creating its culture as it goes. It has not looked at itself for the purpose of determining the value of the changes undertaken by its new director but instead relies on its intuition and experience to map its future.

ANITA—CONSTRUCTING COMMUNICATION

During the months of February through May 1999, I have been observing the maritime military division where I have been employed for three years. The data used for this ethnography include two sets of interviews with each division member, minutes from weekly division meetings, personal observations as both a participant and ethnographer, and incorporation of readings about ethnography research. I have studied how the nine members in my division communicate with each other about work issues. The theme that has arisen most dramatically is the lack of efficiency and ability to concisely explain projects to one another. The major focus of this ethnography—based on members' concerns during the first interviews—centers on weekly meetings held by the division; two other types of division meetings are included for comparison and contrast. Initial findings show that the weekly division meetings do provide a good opportunity for members to share their project information, but the structure of the meetings as they currently operate lacks the positive structure needed to enhance productivity.

ANN—EVERYTHING YOU NEED TO KNOW YOUR BOSS WILL TEACH YOU

This ethnography outlines the learning processes relative to writing as intertwined with learning processes relative to business success in a small metropolitan public relations firm. The ethnographer, also a subject of this study, examines a variety of writing samples and the manner in which lessons are presented as ostensibly limited to writing style. In addition to determining some of the acculturation purposes behind the lessons, the ethnographer attempts to address the spirit in which the lessons are received. Through both conversation with the authors and interpretation of the written lessons, conclusions are drawn as to the success or failure of the specific instructions and instructor.

ANNE—PREP SCHOOL BOYS WRITE: CULTURE IN CONTEXT

As one of only a handful of women on the campus of the Wilson School for Boys, a prep school serving Washington's elite, I used my student-teaching experience as subject for my ethnography. In particular, I focused on the kinds of writing and teaching practices for boys in Form III (ninth grade). Their regular teacher, Mr. Peters, was also a coach in several sports and drew upon his contact with the boys in this other venue to prompt their engagement in English through such classroom techniques as "paragraph wars," in which boys competed for the best paragraphs. My attempt to introduce journal writing was unsuccessful, which within the context of this larger ethnographic study I attribute to three factors: the journals seemed less "masculine" than the argumentative thesis writing of most other assignments; when the time necessary to complete them was weighed against the time necessary for school tasks deemed more central, the latter took priority; my status as student teacher, compounded by my gender in this all-male environment, did not lend weight to these journals. Treating the journals as both student assignment and data for my own writing enabled me to assess this "failure" with greater perspective.

BERNIE—TRIAL ATTORNEY WRITERS: ALL FACTS, NO FICTION

The researcher, an editor at an attorney's association engaged in lobbying Congress, studied the formats for reports written for four of the association's journals. These reports regularly followed the same recipes, with individual writers' slants on the issues made clear at times through selected quotes from interviewees. In addition, manuscripts prepared by trial attorneys regularly displayed a step-by-step, linear arguing process (just as these attorneys in interviews described a step-by-step composing process), whereas manuscripts submitted by transactional lawyers (engaged in contract and corporate law) showed evidence of more lateral thinking.

BRANDEN—DISCURSIVE ELITISM IN A GOVERNMENT TRAVEL AGENCY

As a participant observer in a government travel agency striving to become an influential voice both domestically and abroad in the tourism industry, I studied two documents—a booklet and a weekly report—as well as the writing of them to understand their significance in this local culture. My analysis draws heavily on organizational psychology, as a result of both Edgar Schein's readings for the class and the degree to which Schein's thought had influenced my principle informant, Diane, third in command in policy at the agency. In particular, organizational maneuvers among high-level players are interpreted in light of the past, present, and future orientations of the organization. The booklet I studied, now a year old, stood emblematic of past orientations of the agency for many, against which to measure subtly their differences. The weekly report to the secretary of commerce had a futurist orientation, elaborated by Diane but which incidentally allowed certain players to hold other members to projected roles in the organization, all the while elaborating their own.

BRENDA—THE MANUSCRIPT REVIEW PROCESS AT SCHOOL LEADER MAGAZINE: AN ETHNOGRAPHY OF POST-IT NOTES

This ethnography examines the manuscript review process of a bimonthly magazine published by a national, nonprofit association of school principals. The first section of the paper describes the unusual review process—which involves three editors and which takes place entirely on three-inch-square yellow Post-it notes— and gives the reader background information on the association, the magazine, the editors themselves, and the workplace setting. Later sections explore the content and scope of the reviews, workplace undercurrents present in the notes, and the gaps the Post-its fill in the absence of staff meetings, professional feedback, and other forms of communication. The paper also addresses the criteria editors use to rate manuscripts, and whether or not these criteria are sufficiently communicated to prospective authors. The ethnography ends with several recommendations for improvement based on the findings of the study.

CAROLYN—THE LAST TO KNOW: A TECHNICAL WRITER'S ETHNOGRAPHY OF A SOFTWARE DEVELOPMENT PROJECT

This ethnography focuses on the flow of information on a large software development project at a technology consulting firm. I took notes during staff meetings and conducted in-depth interviews with members of the three subcultures working on the project—the Testing, Development, and Documentation and Training teams—and examined numerous artifacts from each group. I demonstrate how these subcultures discover and disseminate information about the software among themselves and with others on the project. I uncover gaps in this communication and demonstrate that members of the Documentation and Training teams are excluded from the information sharing process and are the last to learn about important developments and updates. As a technical writer on the project, I became strongly positioned as a member of the subculture most affected by this ineffective communication. This study raises questions about why the gaps in information sharing occur, how they affect employees' morale and work, and what action could be taken to open the channels of communication.

CASS—MANAGING INFORMATION, MANAGING PROJECTS, MANAGING AFFECT

This ethnographic study focuses on the management style of a supervisor for an information management office in a small government agency. It outlines his career, describes his management style, and uses interviews with colleagues to examine how he motivates and finesses both his employees and those outside of his office using various tools and techniques (both verbal and written) to manage projects. By examining this facet of the workplace culture, the author attempts to correlate well-known and respected management styles with this man's apparently successful style. In particular, his humorous demonizing of bureaucratic processes via comments and drawings with his staff creates a "we're all in this together" aura that masks subtle manipulations.

CHALLIE—ELECTRONIC MAIL COMMUNICATIONS AS TRAITS OF A CORPORATE CULTURE

This two-month-long study of electronic mail in an association workplace began because the researcher (myself), a new employee and a Macintosh user, had limited access to e-mail. A survey was developed and given to approximately one-third of the staff; recipients proportionately reflected the hierarchical divisions on staff. In addition to the surveys, the author saved the 253 e-mail messages she received over the two-month period. Because survey results showed dramatic differences in private message use among departments, the author focused on all-staff messages: ones sent to everyone in the organization. Most of the all-staff messages were general internal information that was not urgent. The next most frequent category was externally related FYI. Further analysis discusses the types of messages sent by each staff level. Series of messages on the same topic—called "strings" in this paper but commonly known as "threads"—were also studied. Analysis of the message threads and usage patterns led the author to recommend changes in the work processes at the study site, such as increasing the number of incoming fax machines, making a much-referenced paper listing of addresses an electronic copy only, and updating software training procedures.

CHET—JUST DO IT . . . NOW! AN ETHNOGRAPHY OF A SMALL PUBLISHER

This ethnography is the study of the writing culture at Quill, Inc., a small-staffed publications house in Tysons Corner, Virginia. I began this study with the intent of determining how a writing and editing staff of five persons could successfully produce a relatively large amount of material under strict deadlines. Because this is also an autoethnography, I wanted to confine my observations and findings to precise and accurate work habits and behavior, independent of personal knowledge about this particular process. What I discovered almost immediately after beginning to record field notes, was that that approach would not be practical or constructive. My findings show responsive attitudes, teamwork, and talent to be the cogs of Quill's production machine under deadlines, the factor that most prompts good, clear editing and writing. The culture is as unique as the personalities of its inhabitants; Quill's functional writing process is dependent on five individuals performing as a collective whole.

CORINNE—A MOUNT VERNON ETHNOGRAPHY

The Programs Department of Mount Vernon is responsible for all public perception of Mount Vernon. My ethnography focused on how their writing reflects that mission, and how the "presence" of George Washington influences the work that they produce, notably in its various reflections of civility. The lack of cohesiveness as a department, which I observed while working as an outside contractor, could be attributed to the individual nature of members' approach to projects. My ethnography makes some observations and suggestions to improve the process, specifically the creation of a production/publication department with a formalized procedure for approving, supervising, reviewing, and editing projects.

DAISY—BEHIND THE BYLINES: LESSONS LEARNED FROM THE JOURNALISTS AT A SMALL WEEKLY NEWSPAPER

This study, conducted over an eleven-week period, describes the newsroom work environment and the journalists employed at a small, twice-weekly newspaper. There are eight primary informants in different writing and supervisory positions at the paper. The journalists provide their thoughts and opinions on writing preferences and styles, give advice to prospective journalists, explain their training to enter the profession, discuss future aspirations, and describe what it takes to be successful as a print reporter. The experiences of these reporters are also compared to those of the author, who was a journalist for several years, and to those of other professionals. It is hoped that this study can serve as a teaching tool for journalism instructors at the secondary and postsecondary level. For journalism students, it can serve as an in-depth guide to some of the realities of newspaper journalism.

DIANE—STRATEGIC PLANNING AND THE PUBLICATION PROCESS: ATTEMPTING TO DISCURSIVELY ORDER A DISHEVELED CULTURE

"NCHE," a medium-sized higher education association, located in the same building as more than twenty other higher education associations, has been involved in intense strategic planning during the last year. The focus of this planning has been not only to reorganize the publication strategy and procedures of the association's national office, but to develop a strategic plan to serve as a direction for the association as it approaches its centennial. This study focuses on the plan's impact on the staff, management, and association as a whole, with particular attention paid to the plan's effect on the publication process and how the writing and editing of the association is being "directed" by the document. However, instead of providing order to the association, especially an ordered connection between the association's management and its employees, the planning has instead emphasized the great schism between the management and the staff. By focusing on the impact of the plan, including the perceptions and perspectives of those affected, this study provides a glimpse of a culture comprised of discontented staff with an extremely high turnover rate and a management team unaware of the downwardly spiraling morale, trying to provide order and focus in a top-down, discursive strategic plan.

ELAINE—AN ETHNOGRAPHY OF A HISTORY WRITING COMPANY

In this ethnography, I examine the development of a fifteen-minute film (entitled "How the World Knows the Sterling Company"), produced by the History Place, a company that writes corporate histories. The video recounts the one-hundred-year history of advertising of a paper company. As I studied the culture and the writing of this workplace, I interviewed the writers and the chief executive officer, and I read the corporate history on which the script is based. The final script (and film) is vastly different from the first draft—it differs in length and tone and has gone from an academic study to a light-hearted advertising piece. In this paper I describe the history of this video, and report on the changes in the company which came about as a result of the controversies surrounding the script.

ELLA—DISSATISFIED LEGAL PROFESSIONALS: IS IT A LACK OF SUBSTANTIVE WRITING ASSIGNMENTS?

This is an honest portrayal of law firm life. This ethnography found that the majority of writing conducted within this litigation group of a large Washington, D.C., law firm is nonlegal. The group acts as national coordinating counsel for a large chemical company's asbestos premises litigation and works together with a team from the client company's legal department. This pairing offers a study in the aspects of client-attorney relationships when the client is an unwilling team member. The ethnography concludes that little substantive writing combined with poor client relations cause a growing number of legal professionals to become dissatisfied with their chosen careers.

EMMA—LIFE AMONG THE LITTLE PEOPLE: AN ELEMENTARY ETHNOGRAPHY

I studied the correspondence and writing practices of the faculty and staff of an area elementary school. The staff consists of 58 staff members including the principal, 3 secretaries, 12 resource and specialist teachers, 22 classroom teachers, and various other support staff. Through analysis of notes, memoranda, newsletters, and rhetorical notes on students' work, I observed how teachers' jobs and time constraints affected the kinds of writing they produced. I discovered that shorter, off-the-cuff forms of writing were prevalent in an environment where free time is scarce. The study suggests that the forms of writing, like the place from which they originate, are primarily educational in nature. Both handwritten and computer-generated forms of writing were analyzed for the ways in which they seemed to establish (or reduce) distance between writers and readers.

GARY—SNAPSHOT OF AN INTERNET BUSINESS: AN ETHNOGRAPHY

This ethnography describes the local culture of an Internet-based job recruitment company and how the department in charge of one of the company's products, a site on the World Wide Web, approaches writing. The ethnography describes the physical environment, the products and services the company provides, the people that I worked with, the actual work that I did at the company, and the writing process involved with that work. While I make no broad conclusions about writing in an Internet-based business, some of the more unusual aspects of the industry are described. Issues of authorship, audience, and nontraditional writers are all subjects of observation, particularly as rhetorical decisions are made in this fast-paced authoring environment. These concerns may become more prevalent in workplace writing in the future as this industry grows.

GEORGE—FOR SOMEONE ELSE'S SIGNATURE: AN ETHNOGRAPHY OF WRITING IN A MILITARY ORGANIZATION

This study examines the processes, products, and effects of writing, specifically ghostwriting, in the culture of one military headquarters organization. Ghostwriting, or writing for someone else's signature, is inherent in military cultures because of their authoritarian, hierarchical structures: Only those with proper authority may sign official documents although the signers often do not write the documents. Conducted using standard ethnographic techniques, the study illustrates how such research methodologies offer a structured framework for studying the writing done within a culture. The use of ethnographic techniques requires "triangulating" findings to draw conclusions that are substantiated by balanced data. Data collection methods used in the study include personal interviews, questionnaires, document analysis, and read-aloud protocols (to test ghostwriters' intents and readers' interpretations.) The study explores readers' responses to the texts to assess the effectiveness of the ghostwriting process in helping the members of the organization meet their goals. The readers' responses also provide an assessment of the efficiency of the organization's ghostwriting processes—from writing, revision, and signing to reading. Recommendations are provided on how this military organization's management might (1) help writers and revisors improve their writing processes to make reading more efficient (and the ghostwriting process as a whole more effective), (2) help revisors and signers improve the document review process to cut out wasted time, effort, and psychological pain, and (3) institute a new regime for signing that would allow authority to be shared more widely throughout the hierarchy.

GINGER—ETHNOGRAPHY OF STANLEY TROUT

This ethnography focuses on what role humor plays in the workplace, specifically in a law firm. The study of humor reflects back on that of the legal discourse in which the participant works and what it means for the employees who work there. There are many different ways of relating to impersonalizing legal discourse and humor is demonstrated to be one effective method. Different kinds of humor within the workplace are studied and demonstrated. It is also discussed how humor is used as a tool within legal discourse and for whom it actually works, the employee or the employer. Humor is studied as a much larger element within the workplace than would be thought at first glance.

GLORIA—DISTRIBUTING THE NATION'S "CHAMPAGNE": REFERENCE CORRESPONDENCE IN THE NEWSPAPER AND CURRENT PERIODICAL READING ROOM AS A REFLECTION OF LIBRARY MISSION AND CULTURE

This study investigates letter correspondence provided by reference staff in a reading room of the Library of Congress, the Newspaper and Current Periodical

Reading Room of the Serial and Government Publications Division. The tangible and intangible nature of correspondence is explored as a representation of the reference culture in the Library of Congress. Within this division, reference correspondence serves multiple purposes: as a representation of the library to the public, an educational tool for librarians, and as evidence of reference philosophy and practice. The implied authors of letters written in response to requests for research thus take on significance as singular representations of the library, even though frequently these letters are composed by several different researchers over the course of correspondence.

GRACE—EVOLUTION OF A FLAGSHIP PUBLICATION IN A PROFESSIONAL MEMBER SOCIETY: ORIGINS AND EXPLORATION

The researcher occupied the position of manuscript coordinator at the American Society for the Mapping Sciences, whose members come from government, industry, and the academy. Submissions for publication thus come from three very diverse sectors, and the manuscript coordinator was often confused by reviews that seemed to lack standard policies and guidelines, particularly concerning the academics. As part of her study of this local culture, she interviewed editors and directors of publications and engaged in participant-observation at the society's annual convention. She also conducted archival research on the history of the society and the evolution of its flagship publication, the *Journal of Mapping Sciences*. She discovered submission and review practices that had evolved as the field evolved and as the relationships among the three principal constituencies evolved—the government and industrial sector having shaped the field initially and the academic sector having enjoyed a more recent rise to prominence. The recent reviews of manuscripts that requested resubmission after revision (rather than flat rejection) came to make sense as a part of a knowledge-production process vital to academic writing.

GWEN—DOCUMENTATION IN THE WORKPLACE: HOW INTRIGUE CAN BECOME A PART OF DAILY LIFE

This study was conducted in the schizophrenia research branch of a federally funded psychiatric research hospital. The original goal of this study was to observe the conflict caused by impending personnel layoffs and their impact on office personnel as well as on office dynamics. It was found that, either as part of their daily routine or in response to the impending layoffs, four out of the five office members (including the author) keep some form of documentation on either their own actions or the actions of others for personal protection or career advancement. All of this documentation is largely being conducted without the knowledge of the other office staff. This hidden subculture was found to affect interpersonal relationships, office dynamics, and career advancement. Documentation was only one aspect of this subculture which, due to its concealed nature, is called "intrigue" throughout the paper. The reasons for documentation are discussed, and suggestions are offered for resolving some of the conflict and disparity between documenters.

HART—SEEKING THE FUTURE, RESPECTING THE PAST: COMMUNICATIONS AT MIDATLANTIC UNIVERSITY

The researcher conducted on-site observations and interviews with members of the communications office at Midatlantic University, with a focus on some of the publications produced by the office: the alumni magazine, special reports, and recruiting publications. Writers in the department cover regular "beats," which supply material for regularly issued press releases. The most challenging aspect of these assignments and those that contribute to the publications cited include articulating simultaneously a support of time-honored traditions on this sleepy southern campus as well as a forward-looking spirit that will attract students. Document analysis reveals recurrent tropes such as "aspiration" that reflect this dual appeal and frequent interplays between photos of campus red-brick colonial architecture and text that projects the environment represented by this period architecture into the future.

HEATHER—THE ENGINEERING ASSOCIATION: AN ETHNOGRAPHY

After moving its entire office from New York to Reston, Virginia, the Engineering Association had to hire a completely new staff. Problems existed in transition planning and a new staff was thrust into a foreign environment with little to no leadership. Instead of being inducted into an existing culture, the new employees were left to establish a culture on their own while learning a new job. This lack of existing culture created a disjointed staff where employees acted as individuals rather than as a cohesive team. A lack of social interaction pervaded the professional atmosphere as well, and editors rarely consulted with each other for opinions and suggestions. The result of this lack of interaction is an inefficient production cycle that fosters misunderstandings and resentment.

HELEN—EDITING: CHANGING TEXTS AND IMPLIED AUTHORS

I examined the types of interventions made by editors of a professional government magazine and how those interventions altered the implied authorship of the texts edited. I explored four types of interventions: factual text additions, creative text additions, rewriting, and text deletion. I found that the changes made enhanced the image of the implied author by adding the editors' expertise in written communication to the authors' expertise in the subject matter, thus creating an implied author who possessed both. Representing the authors in this way benefits the readers, the authors, the magazine, the magazine's sponsoring agency, and others.

HOLLY—THE WORKPLACE: FINDING YOURSELF IN THE PROCESS

As an MA student in English and a professional editor for three years, I took a personal perspective with this ethnography. In the course of the study, I lost the position which was my site and got a new job. I began to see this project as an opportunity to reflect on my experiences and education before moving forward; my undergraduate alma mater's alumnae magazine therefore fits as my publishing site. My study is an examination of how people fit into an editorial process. In particular, I focus on professional identity in authoring procedures marked by high turnover in personnel and gross discrepancies between work performed and wages garnered.

ITSY—ARC: AN ETHNOGRAPHY ON SMALL BUSINESS

The researcher studied ARC, Inc., a small business that manages two associations serving communicators and librarians. Parallels were drawn between the physical setting (a restored townhouse in Alexandria, Virginia) and the staff dynamics in this family-sized business consisting of a director, two staff members/writers, and the graphics specialist (whose office was located in the basement). Based on interviews and observations, the researcher concluded that a sense of family drove a commitment to excellent performance in addition to professional commitments.

JACKIE—REMEMBER THE MEMBER: STAFF-VOLUNTEER COLLABORATION IN WRITING FOR AN ASSOCIATION

This autoethnography centers on my work as an editor at a large trade organization, where I work with other staff writers/editors and association members who volunteer their time to produce periodicals and other publications. The Association for Engineering, where I have worked for one and a half years, emphasizes the importance of staff-volunteer relations. This theme—prevalent among all aspects of the association's projects, not just communications—poses unique questions about the management of corporate writing. With my background and experience in journalism and public relations, I find my current role unique in that it is often a reporter's job in an in-house and external public relations setting. The sometimes complementary and sometimes clashing interests between the reporting/PR aspects create unique management and member relations issues in terms of planning, job responsibility and accountability, delegation of duties, and editorial review. This work should be of interest and use to anyone interested in the writing process in a workplace setting, including organizational psychologists, professional writers and editors, educators association managers, and others who follow communications trends. On a more pragmatic note, this paper could especially benefit people who work (or want to work) in corporate communications, particularly for an association.

JAN—NEW ISSUE MANAGEMENT AT UMP: AN ETHNOGRAPHIC STUDY

As a part-time consultant to the insurance association where I had worked full-time for the past six years before being laid off recently, I conducted ethnographic inquiry into a new topic driving reorganization in the local culture: issue management. The association had just changed issue management practices from "functional" to "issue specific," and I used field notes and interviews, along with text analysis of memos on certain issues, to ascertain differences in organizational treatment of these issues. What this research revealed is that the personalities and dynamics among them were so entrenched in this culture that new structures suggested for issues management fell by the wayside; in the end, dominion established and maintained by particular players as part of their political maneuvering still drove issues management.

JANE—SELECTIVELY HONORING DEADLINES

Meeting deadlines can be detrimental to the success of documentation. In one government office, the ability or inability to meet deadlines seemed to correlate with the document's general significance, the authority of its intended reader, and the professional condition and attitude of its author. Although all documentation had to pass through a complex review process, items with a high-authority audience traveled through this process more rapidly. The perceived value of a document was also determined by the authority of the individual or department who initiated work on the assignment. If the production of a document were peripheral to an employee's main function, he or she might allow the project to languish and, eventually, perish. Deadlines also were missed as a result of individual tendencies to flout the review process. In such cases, the intent may have been to meet deadlines by forgoing lengthy review systems, but such oversight did not go unnoticed and, in the end, only exacerbated delays. In some cases of missed deadlines, no time frames had ever been clearly laid out for document production. The provision of specific deadlines to writers, reviewers, and editors could alleviate some issues of tardiness.

JANICE—FAMILY BUSINESS COMMUNICATIONS: THE DYING ART OF THE BUSINESS LETTER

I studied professional writing in a Washington, D.C., area family-owned and -operated turnkey fulfillment business that is about to pass to second generation control. Using recorded observations and interviews and writing samples including both the CEO's client correspondence and the second generation partners' form letter drafts, I recorded this business's dilemma as the CEO nears the last stages of terminal cancer. Of particular note in this study is the fact that none of the young partners have ever written any business letters geared toward client acquisition, and, to date, they only communicate with existing clients via e-mail and telephone. As a result, one added feature of this ethnography is my position as observer/activist, a nontraditional ethnographic role. In this capacity I proposed collaborative writing to the partners as one option to explore for the future.

JEFF—TECHNICAL EDITING: ADVENTURES IN CULTURE CLASH

People with technical and scientific backgrounds—civil engineers, for example— tend to exhibit a distinctive workplace writing style. They are fond of passive voice and agentless sentences ("The landfill liner was examined"). They nominalize, or "smother," their verbs ("an evaluation was performed"). They create long strings of modifiers ("the raw influent soluble phosphorus concentration"). Use of such constructions often makes meanings unclear, but it also serves to identify the author as a member of a professional culture and as a technical expert. The editor's attempt to assert his own expert status by decoding dense text and breaking up long modifier strings often is seen as an assault on the engineer's identity as a technical expert.

JEN—OFFICE STYLE AND WRITING STYLE IN A BIWEEKLY SUBSCRIPTION NEWSLETTER

This ethnography traces the history of JS, a biweekly subscription newsletter serving government employees and those seeking employment with the government. The study traces the history of this privately owned, twenty-two-person organization within an organizational psychology framework, in particular as "myths and legends" prevail, much of them related to the company founder and current president. Against this background, the study focuses on the selection and management of office decor as it becomes more regulated and controlled as one descends the organizational hierarchy. Parallels are drawn with latitude in prose style—as it is extended to those on the upper organization and withheld from those at lower editorial levels. The style of the editorial pages in this job announcement bulletin reflects this latitude and is analyzed here as "solicitous," appealing in particular to higher-end readers following trends in employment and thus occupying a similar professional class with that of company directors.

JIHAD—WRITE AN ESSAY, SELL FRIED CHICKEN

Ethnographic research on workplace writing explores new venues for writing instruction. My ethnographic study of writing in a fast food franchise entails the analysis of writing as it relates to the theory and practice of management and communication in this culture. Furthermore, I narratologically analyze the writing of certain individuals to shed some light on the formation of rhetorical positions and voices in this workplace. The study reveals that rhetorical discourse is contained within social and situational positions in the workplace. Moreover, the study results offer new insights to the teaching of writing in the classroom, particularly as writers' available positions are configured within genres such as the memo.

JILLIAN—FRAMING REALITY: AN ETHNOGRAPHIC STUDY
OF AN ELECTRONIC COMMUNITY

This ethnography draws on Erving Goffman's frame analysis and posits that electronic communities constitute one of the "multiple realities" described in his book. These communities should therefore be viewed "nonjudgementally" by the ethnographer, who should, as David Fetterman says, "suspend disbelief." The paper then goes on to describe Megabyte University, a list devoted computers and writing, of which the researcher is a member. Self-representations of members who post comments are discussed, using the qualified signatures of these members. The shift in membership over the years is discussed as a reflection of evolving approaches to list membership taken by people interested in composition and writing and active nationally in real and virtual discussions of scholarly life.

JOANNE—ETHNOGRAPHY OF A DOCUMENT
DEVELOPMENT PROJECT: A PROCESS OF CHANGE

A student ethnographer examines a documentation development project at a government contractor site, including the extensive changes in the project and the technology that had an impact on it. The original project had tightly defined requirements. After a year, the document standards, schedule, and delivery procedure had changed. The company involved, the student's employer, was a small disadvantaged business headquartered in a suburb of Washington, D.C. The documentation project required hiring new staff. The documentation team was then organized into a highly hierarchical organization. Persons at different levels of the hierarchy saw different factors as significant in the project. Communication among the various groups involved in the project required use of the Internet, e-mail, and local area network capabilities in addition to meetings and individual discussions, and was a key factor in developing the documentation. Preparation of the documentation schedule illustrates the planning, production, configuration management, and quality assurance involved in the project. The results of the study indicate that major technology innovations, new coding procedures, and the federal government's emphasis on providing useful products and services were instrumental in causing changes to the original plans.

JOE—THE CASE OF THE MISGUIDED STYLE MANUAL:
A STUDY OF CORPORATE WRITING AND REPRESENTATION

This study explores the corporate writing culture at Acme, Inc., a software development firm. To better update an old corporate style manual, an ethnographic study of the writers and writing styles at Acme was started to learn what types of written materials employees produced and where they felt they needed help with their writing. During the study, however, the author noticed a lopsided (mis)representation of the views of management versus the views of nonmanagement employees. In an effort to find out why a group of employees was misrepresented, this study-turned-mystery looks at the differences of the responses to surveys and questions answered by the two groups.

JULIE—THE RELATIONSHIP BETWEEN LOCAL CULTURES AND THE TEMPERAMENT OF STUDENT WRITING

This study explored the nature of the relationship that exists between various local cultures and student writing and found that a symbiotic relationship, as varied as the students and their cultures, exists between the two. The study focused on a second semester freshman composition class at a local community college. Data were also collected from various other student sources including a local businessman who is a part-time student and an art student attending an art and design school. Specifically, the study found that students do not carve their lives into separate spheres. There is overlapping between the various domains of students' lives in the following ways: students tend to transfer knowledge and skills from their work to their classroom writing, and their way of seeing and thinking about writing is heavily influenced by the disciplines they are studying. Several suggestions for ways to apply the research findings to teaching are included. These are a brief sketch of a plan to combine volunteerism and college writing, a suggestion that team teaching of block courses be encouraged, and a recommendation that schools need to offer more computer-based writing classes.

KALI—SINK OR SWIM: HOW EMPLOYEES STAY AFLOAT IN A NAVY CONTRACTING COMPANY

The Navy contracting industry is volatile, unpredictable, and offers little job security or recognition to its employees, which could affect the quality of their writing. None of the participants in this study agreed absolutely on the exact correlation between lack of job security and quality of writing, but all of the employees had an internal work ethic that stimulated them to work hard for personal satisfaction. This study gives a brief explanation of the ever shifting Navy contracting business, gives short biographies of the participants, and then discusses how the individuals perceive the effects of minimal job security on the quality of their writing.

KARLA—WRITING UP THE CORPORATE LADDER: AN ETHNOGRAPHIC EXAMINATION OF COMMUNICATIONS AT THE COSMETIC MANUFACTURERS AND RETAILERS ASSOCIATION

The purpose of this ethnography is to examine the impact of association infrastructure on internal communications between staff members and its effect on the association's external publications. The subject of study is the Cosmetic Manufacturers and Retailers Association's newsletter, *Snapshots,* and the activities of its editorial board. Class structure is a very important aspect of the culture of the association. The members of the editorial board subscribe to the tenet that information flows through CMRA from the top down. The members of the editorial board belong to a high-ranking level of staff within the association. It is at the top that the messages of the association are developed. The writers and editors are merely the conduits for moving the information out from CMRA to the members of the association, Congress, and the media. This ethnography considers how this phenomenon of circumventing creativity and voice affects the process of writing and editing in the association. All names (including the name of the association and any mention of its members) have been changed.

KATE—STRANGER IN A FAMILIAR LAND: A WRITING TEACHER'S ETHNOGRAPHY OF A UNIVERSITY WRITING CENTER

I observed tutoring sessions, workshops, staff meetings, and e-mail interchanges of the writing center of a local state university. The staff includes a full-time director, two full-time assistants (graduate students), a full-time instructor, and six part-time tutors (graduate students). The majority of tutorials are with undergraduate ESL students. Observations of tutorials revealed an array of interesting approaches for discussing writing with students, yet little expertise in actually teaching ESL students to become better writers. Nearly all of the tutors were graduate students in the MFA track, supported through this work-study arrangement; many of them were surprised to learn that the MA track in the teaching of writing and literature, in which I was completing my degree, existed. The study raises questions about staffing positions in the center, in light of expertise, career aims of graduate students, and needs of the writing center's clientele.

KELLY—REVISING A PUBLICATION'S PRODUCT ON PROCESS: EXAMINING THE TEAM CONCEPT

This study narrates the roles and responsibilities of a creative team, including writers, editors, graphic designers, and production/business managers, in producing informational and promotional material for a public university. Through a description of the work site, a description of the typical process of producing these documents from start to finish, interviews of participants, and an analysis of team concepts in business and publications settings, this ethnography uncovers some of the successes and difficulties of implementing Total Quality Management principles in a small publications environment. It also offers the participants' suggestions for continuous process improvement.

KIRSTEN—A DAY IN THE LIFE OF ASSOCIATION MAGAZINE STAFF

The life of a writer isn't necessarily a solitary process. Today writers work in environments which force them to interact, make choices, and face challenges—all for the publication of a quality product. In this study, I have tried to capture a "snapshot" of the typical work day of an association magazine staff in order to identify the duties and choices which one would not immediately associate with a writer. Included are observations on the use of e-mail to compose regular columns, conveying publications processes to other departments in order to garner information from them more effectively, scheduling feature stories well in advance, and review of bluelines, and meeting agendas. This "Day in the Life" compilation dovetails with findings on collaborative writing by researchers such as Janis Forman, Lisa Ede and Andrea Lunsford, and Cynthia Selfe; it will educate students who are considering a career as a writer. With a look at the typical day of an association magazine writer, students will be in a better position to determine if writing in an association is the career for them.

KOLAR—WRITING IN A U.S. SENATOR'S PRESS OFFICE

This ethnography follows several months in the career of a high-profile senator as he seeks reelection, written from my perspective as an assistant to the assistant deputy press secretary. It acknowledges the senator's savvy at garnering resources for and attention to his constituents, as well as findings by the Senate Ethics Committee that he has "conducted the business of his office in an improper and inappropriate manner." This business takes place among the "Tribes on the Hill" described by ethnographer Jack Weatherford, in which the new arrivals in Washington are socialized into the machinations of national government politics. As illustration of this socialization, this ethnography offers one writing practice in the senator's press office, regular fabrication of letters from constituents in response to a political opponent's faux pas, intended to bolster the senator's political position as a spokesperson for this constituency.

KYLE—PRODUCING *COMMON GROUND* MAGAZINE

This ethnography follows the production of the May/June issue of *Common Ground,* a magazine published by a nonprofit association in Alexandria, Virginia, and characterized by high turnover in staff. Historical background on the association is presented, including a shift in 1991 from a newsletter serving constituents to a full-blown magazine, along with the emergence in 1993 of the magazine's guiding philosophy of "service journalism." The researcher, who is also editor and sole full-time staffer of the magazine, retraces the scrambling to meet the deadline, which included frequent faxes and voice mail messages to contributing (unpaid) authors. He also enumerates his responsibilities, which include assigning and editing feature articles and departments, coordinating staff proofreading assignments, producing the annual editorial calendar, and working with the art director to develop design and art ideas. His own writing processes for the cover story are retraced, from the original idea (newspaper clips from Florida), through meetings with the art director, through revising of headlines and layouts, through drafts of the article evolving through plays on words, to the final issue. The work culture is interpreted as one that the editor can use to stoke the creative process.

LARA—THE IMPACT OF WRITING A SCHOOL PLAN

I observed collaborative writing efforts and the process of writing a school plan in an elementary school. Most of the staff are well established while the principal is fairly new to the school and to writing a school plan. (Plans are composed anew every three years.) Tensions between teachers, differing philosophies among the staff, and outside community influences impacted the writing of the school plan. Observations revealed that the school plan, in theory, has an enormous effect on the philosophy and direction of the school. However, in practice, at this particular culture, the school plan's impact is minimal at best and negative at worst, due to inadequate structuring of the collaborative writing sessions that resulted in affective conflict rather than substantive debate.

LEATHE—THE CULTURE OF A GOVERNMENT CONTRACTOR

The business culture at a northern Virginia company is examined through the announcement of a move, a description of the company's current building and offices, the dress code, employee access to the building and offices, and use of the paging system. The company's staff is described in terms of job titles, education levels, and number of foreign-born. Company documents are cited to establish how the staff is organized in task teams. Some of the ways the business culture affects teamwork are examined through a brief study of a Web site task team.

LEE—TECHNOLOGY IN THE COLLEGE WRITING CENTER: FINDING THE BALANCE

The researcher studied the use of educational software and the teaching of word processing as they enhanced students' writing skills in the writing center at Pleasantview Community College. This study was situated in an institutional context that had witnessed a recent relocation of the writing center from the English Department to the Campus Learning Resource Center and a decline in one-to-one conferences as computer-aided individualized instruction rose. Using participant observation (the researcher was the writing center director) and student surveys, it was found that students valued the computer work yet regretted the inavailability of one-to-one conference tutors for their drafts. (Tutors were volunteers, since the writing center budget made no provision for them.) The study concludes with a hope that the college will recognize the need for increased computer-supported instruction *and* one-on-one conferencing and budget accordingly.

LEIGH—SPEECH WRITING AT AGRA: WRITING IN THE TRENCHES

Drawing upon on-site observations, numerous interviews with writers, and analysis of speeches they have produced, this ethnography describes speech writing by four civil servants for the director of a high-profile government organization. These writers develop speeches that the director will present based primarily on three factors: the director's history and favorite dictums, popular metaphors of the time, and the administration's official position on topics addressed in each speech. Six people appear on the clearance sheet for each speech, to monitor an average of sixteen speeches per month. The writers' work is self-described as in the "trenches," since they write individually yet as a team, supporting one another regularly through reviews and edits, and particularly when any member is "crashing" on a speech. Part of their work entails listening to the director as he delivers speeches and taking notes on falters and strong moments. The personality of the speaker is the driving force behind work in this idea factory, which relies heavily on recycling ideas that have worked well in previous speeches.

LENA—PRODUCING A JOURNAL FOR SCIENCE EDUCATORS: AN ETHNOGRAPHY

This study provides some insight into the culture of a small staff who have the responsibility of producing one of the several magazines of a national association on science education. The study describes both the national association as well as the slick, four-color magazine the staff produces. Primarily through detailed description of each staff member and the role he or she plays in producing the publication, the author discusses the management philosophy of the managing editor, the harmonious interaction of the staff members, the challenge of editing articles by novice writers, the practice of hiring freelance graphic artists, and the association's concern about safety issues. Based on some of the comments made by the staff members, the document also contains a discussion of career advancement issues for those in writing, editing, and graphic design; for publications professionals, the author indicates that an employee's earning power may never increase dramatically unless the employee enters management and leaves writing, editing, and designing to the more poorly paid. The document concludes with a discussion of the application of the word "ethnography" to studies about nonethnic groups. The conclusion also contains a few comments about ways to obtain better, more complete, more interesting field data.

LISA—WRITING AT COMMUNITY NATIONAL BANK

To study writing at my place of work, a small year-old bank in northern Virginia referred to here as Community National, I used document analysis, interviews, and observations. Against a projected image of "family" (twelve eight-by-ten portraits of each of Community's employees hang on the wall of the "family room" where customers wait until bank representatives greet them), I analyzed a schism in management and writing styles between the bank's two principal divisions: Operations and Commercial Loans. Staffing of each division follows gender lines, Operations consisting of ten females and Commercial Loans of two males. Writing style in each division is markedly different, with Operations writing characterized by brevity, direct phrasing, and occasional colloquialisms and Loan writing characterized by wordiness, legal terminology, and formality. Analysis showed that these written styles, adopted from general styles within the industry, in this setting also melded with oral interactions among genders, in particular as males associated the discursive style of loans with banking tradition, to which women were perceived as newcomers.

LIZ—WRITING STYLE AT THE WORLD BANK: AN ETHNOGRAPHY

With approximately 9,500 staff occupying some 19 buildings in downtown Washington, D.C., the World Bank is the largest development bank lending to developing countries in the world. Staff at the bank fall into two categories, professional and support, separated by a glass ceiling and reflected in the title of an anonymously authored text, "How to Write Like the Rest of Us," in which the style of bank reports is parodied through wordiness, repeated nominalizations, and local jargon. This ethnography supplements this internal view with the opinions gained through interviews with report writing instructors in the training division, editors, and report authors. Based on these opinions and other materials gained as a participant-observer, the author concludes that the competitive, status-conscious environment seems to promote a ponderous, academic writing style in which staff display their knowledge by overwriting and, ironically, at the same time display their deficient mastery of the English language.

LOIS—WRITING CORPORATE CULTURE: AN ETHNOGRAPHIC STUDY OF CORPORATE CULTURES IN A VIRTUAL OFFICE ENVIRONMENT

The author, a graduate student of professional writing, performed an ethnographic study of the development of corporate cultures and countercultures within her employer's sales department during a time of extensive reorganization and reformulation of the corporate mission. These events occurred in a virtual (home-based) workplace environment where written documents were the principal means of communication within and between work groups. Her observations about the existence of imposed and reactive cultural products within the organization defines a gap where there is no intersection of the disparate corporate cultures. The maintenance of this gap consumes a significant amount of energy in the company. The author considers the impact of her position as a midcareer female manager on her data collection and evaluation activities.

MACK—PERZINE ETHNOGRAPHY

The personal magazine (Perzine) explosion has not gone unnoticed. From *Time* to *Seventeen* to *Playboy* to the *Chronicle of Higher Education* the phenomenon has been examined and commented upon. Much has been made of motivation: What drives people to bare their souls in writing for the entertainment of complete strangers? I've avoided entering a discussion on reasons and concentrated more on ways. How do the writers write? How do they put their zines together? How do they use language? How do they consider audience response? How do they edit? This ethnography begins with a brief examination of the respondents and their reading habits. Obvious connections exist that need more teasing apart. Next comes a look at the editing process, followed by short sections on audience response considerations, 'zine slang and conventions, production, and the 'zine look. An annotated bibliography concludes the paper.

MAGGIE—THE BATTLE OF THE BOOK: ONE EDITOR'S STRUGGLE

This study of a midsize book publishing firm, by following the production of a manuscript from idea to bound book, reveals a culture in which workers are largely autodidactic. The narrator—also the researcher and associate editor at the company operating from an office distant from the company's main hub—walks through the workplace experience, which include communicating with authors and colleagues in another city via e-mail, telephone, fax, voice mail, and overnight delivery service in order to bring a product to fruition. This piece offers to the first-time professional insider tips on the steps of the trade, the subtle nuances necessary to work with other employees, how to communicate with faceless authors, how to transform countless e-mail messages into a bound book, and, with a little luck and tenacity, how to do it right the first time.

MANDY—AN ETHNOGRAPHIC STUDY OF WRITING IN A CONSTRUCTION ASSOCIATION

While working as a secretary at Boston, a leading national trade association representing 8,000 general contractor firms and some 24,500 industry associate members in 102 chapters nationwide, I used participant-observation techniques to study writing as it was part of this local culture. This culture is almost exclusively white and male, reflected in a hierarchy that includes nonwhites only in administrative positions and in the mail room. The culture also includes many illicit maneuvers among certain middle managers as they attempt to finesse the bureaucracy for personal gain. This study focused on document production as it was affected by both the racism and sexism of the culture and by the finessing of one middle manager. Since document production followed highly irregular, interrupted, and unnecessarily reiterative paths, this study reveals a process rendered extremely expensive through the withholding of knowledge among divisions and ultimately wasteful of both human and material resources.

MARLA—COMMUNICATIONS WITHIN A HIGH SCHOOL: AN ETHNOGRAPHIC STUDY

Through the use of recognized ethnographic techniques, I have launched a study of how and what coworkers in a public high school communicate with each other. By carefully researching my own workplace, a setting I know well, I have tried to establish both insider and outsider views. Stemming from numerous interviews with certified staff, teachers and administrators, a few key issues emerged. Among the staff's concerns are a feeling of being ill-informed, a sense of powerlessness, and a desire to improve lines of communication throughout the ranks. Everyone with whom I conferred expressed a sincere wish to communicate in an efficient, effective manner. I believe that any flaws in the system are unintentional.

MARY—DEADLINES AND BYLINES: TIME AND COLLABORATIVE WRITING IN THE CORPORATE ENVIRONMENT

This study describes the role of organizational structure and hierarchy in the production of corporate documents. By examining a top management consulting firm that predicts the decline of corporate hierarchy as we know it, this paper discusses how the firm's unique nonhierarchical environment allows its employees to efficiently produce collaboratively written documents.

MAY—HOW MANY HANDS ARE ON THIS? A LOOK AT THE INFLUENCES ON THE PUBLIC RELATIONS WRITING AT CAPITOL HOSPITAL

This ethnography examines how the writing of the marketing and public relations department at Capitol Hospital (a pseudonym) impacted various members of the local work culture. I interviewed representatives from the hospital who were involved in the writing process as editors, those who provided quotes and background information or posed for photographs, and I share segments of these in-depth discussions in this study. Through my research an individualistic behavior is exemplified in the published hospital "beliefs" and mission statement produced by the executives and board members, where improving oneself and helping those in one's immediate area are spoken of in high regard; however, concepts such as teamwork are not directly addressed. Thus the marketing and public relations department's call for departments, subsidiary offices, off-campus physicians, and board members to band together to promote the hospital to the community and other professional services through written communication pieces was received passively, and in some cases, with a disgruntled attitude and even refusal. This ethnography draws conclusions regarding the reasoning for the culture's poor attitude for the work of the public relations materials, with an emphasis on upper management's experience and regard for the marketing and public relations department.

MEG—PROVING WORTH AND MANAGING EXPECTATIONS: THE CORPORATE MONTHLY REPORT

This study focuses on a global information corporation and its corporate departments' use of a monthly report to manage expectations, promote individuals' work, and reaffirm the worth of individuals and departments. The study also focuses on how in this corporate culture, effectively portraying work accomplished equals, to some extent, success. While many lower-level workers view the reporting mechanism as "jumping through hoops," other senior-level employees view it as a reflection on their management, hard work, and reason for existing within the corporation. The department I studied does not bring in revenue, and so in this case, the effective use of words equals dollar signs.

MEGAN—INTENTIONAL VAGUENESS IN DEVELOPMENT DISCOURSE

This ethnography is the continuation of an emerging discussion in academia regarding the purpose and necessity of vague language in particular situations. This paper focuses on the reasons why fund raisers need to be intentionally vague in some written documents and publications. The reasons include the need for time-less language to allow for the greatest degree of flexibility, broad language that allows a scholarship or program to be inclusive of as many potential student beneficiaries as possible, and personal letters that must be applied to a wide audience. Implications are drawn for a greater awareness and acceptance of strategic vagueness in academic, scientific, and professional writing.

NANCY AND ELLIE—HTO: AN ETHNOGRAPHIC STUDY OF WRITING IN AN EDUCATIONAL FACILITY PLANNING COMPANY

This study uses two researchers, one from inside the company and one from outside, to gain definite emic and etic perspectives at the start of the research process. They examined the writing of a small educational facility planning company and the environment that allows the writing to occur. They discovered that a family-type atmosphere had developed from the intense collaboration among the employees who were constantly striving to complete a project for a client. The limited number of employees causes the documents produced to be standardized to save time, so authorship and creativity are often lost. The question of who is an expert appeared repeatedly during the study. Each member of the company realized the importance of her own roles and the need for collaboration to produce a document.

NIDEAN—ASCRIBING MEANING TO MUSCLES: AN ETHNOGRAPHIC STUDY OF HOW A FITNESS FACILITY MANIPULATES WITH LANGUAGE

This study examines a fitness company owner's meaning-making language tactics, aimed strategically at ensnaring clients. It looks first at the way company documents linguistically pull clients in through subtle choices in document design and wording. Then it examines how gym discourse works to keep them "in," primarily through attributing power to a trim and toned body and sloth to a soft and weak one. Next, the study explores how fitness fanaticism has become a cultural panacea for those with marginal senses of self-esteem and thus how this company has made an easy entrance into this manipulation. Finally, it looks briefly at the fitness "rules" the company generates to codify beliefs in writing and to firm up client devotion.

NORMA—MEDICAL SHORTHAND

Writing in a doctor's office is not only affected by customary practice, but by time allocation. Medical shorthand, common in the medical field, is used by Dr. Dixon and his staff to document patient information. This shorthand is of a consistent style and finds its way into home and outside use. Moreover, the concise and to-the-point writing style that shorthand demands is also seen in letters, manuals, and reports written by staff. Time to write is the greatest challenge the office faces on a daily basis. Constant use of medical shorthand makes that time.

NYCK—WRITING A COMPANY'S IMAGE AND WORKERS' SELF-IMAGES

This ethnographic study explores the extent to which written documents encountered in the modern workplace affect a company's image and even the self-image of the employees within that workplace. It also examines how the *lack* of written documents in one workplace adversely affected the company image and led in several cases to internal conflict and poor self-images among employees. This study serves as a wake-up call for small businesses that have not yet developed an extensive written culture establishing formal written policies or setting goals and norms. In the course of this project the author composed several policies, now official, for his company.

PHOEBE—A PORTRAIT OF TWELVE ARTISTS AS A YOUNG 501C-3: AN ETHNOGRAPHY ON THE WORKPLACE CULTURE OF A NONPROFIT ORGANIZATION

This ethnography attempts to delineate some of the differences between a corporate workplace structure and a nonprofit workplace structure based upon the communication that takes place there. Ethnographic observations on organizational structures and corporate environments cannot be transposed to the not-for-profit sector. As this ethnography demonstrates, a principle reason for employees to choose to work in the nonprofit environment is knowing that their hard work is making a difference in another writer's life. It is the preservation of the craft of writing that is the cause, the driving force, behind their efforts. There are very different types of employees that are present in a nonprofit workplace, as a result. The nonprofit becomes a separate culture from other corporations because of this artistic backbone of its structure and the mission as priority as opposed to the almighty profit margin. As seen in the analysis of interoffice correspondence via Internet, memorandums, and voice mail messages, the personalities of these artists emerge. Staff members all have an idiosyncratic style and tone to their correspondence, reflecting their mood, attitude, and individuality, as well as their position within this unique structure.

RACHEL—THE WRITING CULTURE IN THE DEFENSE ATTACHÉ SECTION OF AN EMBASSY

This study relates the writing culture in a defense attaché section of a foreign embassy, in which much of the report writing is accomplished by attachés and foreign language assistants (FLAs). This section of the embassy employs fourteen military and ten civilian employees; because women may not serve in the country's armed forces, all of the military employees are male and all of the civilian employees are female. Because only attachés' names may appear on reports, those of the FLAs never appear, rendering much of their work invisible and the grounds upon which they might request increases in the pay scale unsolid. Because the local culture is anchored in a highly authoritarian tradition of the military, these issues of inequity are not likely to be resolved.

RAVI—CONVENTIONS: AN ETHNOGRAPHIC STUDY OF THE CORPORATE CULTURE AT "SOFTDEV"

In a business world where conventions such as working nine to five and having a set lunch break every day have become commonplace, it is difficult to imagine a corporate culture that diverges from this well-laid path. The stark, rigid angles of cubicle walls have become the foundation for America's corporate world, and the accepted conventions of working in this world have become nearly as rigid. Yet there are companies that enjoy a different sort of corporate culture—like SoftDev. The corporate culture of an organization can reveal itself to observers in many ways—but for this particular study, I focus on the topic of writing processes at SoftDev and outline how they can illuminate the nuances of this corporate culture in terms of office hierarchy, meetings, office hours, and dress code. I show that the deliberate flouting of conventions such as hierarchical culture and carefully structured meetings actually feeds collaborative processes in development and marketing writing.

RAY—POLICY WRITING IN A SMALL TOWN POLICE DEPARTMENT

My study of the implementation of a new vehicle response and pursuit policy for a small town police department mostly involved the observation of police department employees in their daily routine surrounding the policy's development. As the department's policy manual writer and editor, I was provided with the opportunity to observe closely the department's administrative staff as the policy moved toward completion. Observations of staff meetings to discuss policy and reflections on private meetings with the chief about this policy reveal a culture that is strongly oral, with stories used to solidify alliances within the culture. As a writer in this culture, I became positioned as the one who was *responsible* for the policy rather than the one who was consolidating decisions and mandates in written form.

RED—THE *SCRIBNER:* A STUDY OF NEWSROOM CULTURE

The *Scribner* is growing during a time when the newspaper industry is dissolving. Although the *Scribner* is growing, its newsroom faces internal and external pressures that have adversely affected morale and now threaten the quality of the *Scribner*'s chain of newspapers. This study shows how some of the pressures are uncontrollable because they have developed outside the company in the newspaper marketplace. But others have been misapplied by the *Scribner* owners and should be eliminated. And still others have developed inside the newsroom because of conflicting personalities and a lack of communication among the editorial staff. This ethnography presents an account of these pressures—how they originated, how they affect the people's writing and how they should be dealt with in this newsroom culture.

REX—THE BOUNDARIES OF LANGUAGE: INDEXERS' WRITING
CULTURE AT A NATIONAL MONTHLY MAGAZINE

Through observations and interviews, I studied the thirty full-time employees that index and abstract illustrations at a prestigious national monthly magazine. As the study progressed, it became clear that spatial boundaries established by work spaces in certain clusters were mirrored by linguistic boundaries established between veteran and novice writers. In particular, standards for captions among veterans dictated brevity, and transgressors of these standards (mostly novices) were regularly chided for producing "novelettes." In addition to these boundaries stood boundaries between administrators and abstracters, who occasionally parodied administrative jargon in jokes played upon one another.

SARAH—THE LONELINESS OF THE LONG-DISTANCE WRITER
AND OTHER MATTERS: FREELANCE WRITERS AT WORK

This project explores the working culture of freelance writers. Five writers were interviewed in person, one by questionnaire, and background research was done on the trend toward working at home. The following conclusions were reached: (1) getting a freelance business started is difficult and the best way to do it is to get a job as a writer and build up a freelance business part-time through those contacts; (2) while freelance writing offers a tremendous amount of freedom and diversity, the isolation of working alone at home is a problem for writers, even those who are self-described "introverts"; (3) the workplace is changing rapidly and new arrangements for getting the work done are gaining favor.

STARLA—CORPORATE COMMUNICATION OR
CORPORATE CONFUSION? AN ETHNOGRAPHIC STUDY

As an MA student in professional writing and editing, I undertook a three-month ethnographic study of my workplace culture while also operating as a full-time member of that workplace—the corporate communications department of a large financial services corporation. My study yielded observations of the confusion that abounds in a writing culture where the lines of authority are not tightly drawn as well as the confusion caused when the role of the corporate communications department, both as it relates to senior management and to internal communication to employees, is in question. My study also included observations regarding the exacerbating effect of immense change, both internal and external to the company I studied, on the above areas of ambiguity. The study concludes that, as communication is of utmost importance to the goals and objectives of a company, the lack of communication at the company I studied—and at corporations across the board—should be evaluated and addressed.

SUE—WRITING PROCEDURES AND MORALE
IN A GOVERNMENT/MILITARY FIELD OFFICE

From February to May 1996, I have been studying my workplace and identifying reasons why the morale has been so low there. There are many factors—personalities, management's mistreatment of its employees, personal problems, and so on—but the hardest hitting one is that the "systems" which have been set up to support us have broken down, and they have yet to be fixed. These systems have to do with the publication of reports, known here as Generic Documents (GD). Tracking these reports from inception to publication revealed numerous moments in the chain of command which allowed people to shirk their formatting and review responsibilities—in some cases for personal reasons and in others for reasons stemming from long-standing feuds in the local culture. When a shift from paper to paperless environment was introduced, some turnaround times within the office were reduced, but turnaround times among offices were actually heightened because of incompatible systems. This issue remains unaddressed, further undermining morale.

TESS—A WRITER'S SEARCH FOR MEANING IN THE WORKPLACE

This study is a reflective assessment of myself as a writer, whereby I compare two different cultures in which I worked. The first is HappyTravel, a travel agency serving primarily government, where I worked as a writer of internal publications in the communications department. Here I encountered a highly oral culture in which many of my routine questions such as "who is our audience?" were met with surprise and even suspicion. I was laid off from this job while conducting this study, prompting reflections on my former job as an assistant editor in the publications department of an association. There, the culture was more immersed in written production and knowledgeable of the intricate processes underlying good writing and editing. More significantly, perhaps, the association culture relied on written representations to sustain itself, whereas HappyTravel generated much of its business over the phone.

TOM—THE REVELATIONS OF ACADEMIC ADMINISTRATIVE MEMORANDA

In this brief paper the power-base relationships of a large community college system are revealed when the ethnographer attempts to analyze the written communications of the college senate. The senate is a body of employees formed from the three levels of employees—teaching faculty, administrative faculty, and classified staff—to represent the college community as a whole and to advise the college president of their issues and concerns. Memos composed by the senate chair (and edited by this researcher) reveal word choices subtly recalling earlier discussions of topics in full senate meetings yet situating these topics to leverage action on them now, selectively representing earlier discussions depending upon the audience for the memo.

WORKS CITED

Althusser, Louis. "Ideology and Ideological State Apparatuses." *Lenin and Philosophy and Other Essays*. Trans. Ben Brewster. London: New Left Books, 1971.

Anderson, Gary L., and Patricia Irvine. "Informing Critical Literacy with Ethnography." *Critical Literacy: Politics, Praxis, and the Postmodern*. Ed. Colin Lankshear and Peter L. McLaren. Albany: State U of New York P, 1993. 81–104.

Anson, Chris M. "Distant Voices: Teaching and Writing in a Culture of Technology." *College English* 61 (1999):261–80.

Barthes, Roland. *Image, Music, Text*. New York: Hill and Wang, 1977.

Behar, Ruth. "Introduction: Out of Exile." *Women Writing Culture*. Ed. Ruth Behar and Deborah Gordon. Berkeley: U of California P, 1995. 1–29.

Behar, Ruth, and Deborah Gordon, eds. *Women Writing Culture*. Berkeley: U of California P, 1995.

Belenky, Mary Field, Blythe McVicker Clinchy, Nancy Rule Goldberger, and Jill Mattuck Tarule. *Women's Ways of Knowing*. New York: Basic Books, 1997.

Belsey, Catherine. *Critical Practice*. London: Methuen, 1980.

Bennett, Tony. "Putting Policy into Cultural Studies." *Cultural Studies*. Ed. Lawrence Grossberg, Cary Nelson, and Paula Treichler. New York: Routledge, 1992. 23–37.

Bennett, Tony, and Janet Woollacott. *Bond and Beyond: The Political Career of a Cultural Hero*. New York: Methuen, 1987.

Berlin, James A. "English Studies, Work, and Politics in the New Economy." *Composition in the Twenty-First Century: Crisis and Change*. Ed. Lynn Z. Bloom, Donald A. Daiker, and Edward M. White. Carbondale: Southern Illinois UP, 1996. 215–25.

———. *Rhetoric and Reality: Writing Instruction in American Colleges, 1900–1985*. Carbondale: Southern Illinois UP, 1987.

———. *Rhetorics, Poetics, and Cultures: Refiguring College English Studies*. Urbana: NCTE, 1996.

———. "The Teacher as Researcher: Democracy, Dialogue, and Power." *The Writing Teacher as Researcher: Essays in the Theory and Practice of Class-Based Research*. Ed. Donald A. Daiker and Max Morenberg. Portsmouth, NH: Boynton/Cook, 1990. 3–14.

Bourdieu, Pierre, and Jean-Claude Passeron. *Reproduction in Education, Society, and Culture*. 2nd ed. London: SAGE, 1990.

Brady, Laura. "A Contextual Theory for Business Writing." *Journal of Business and Technical Communication* 7 (1993): 452–71.

Brandt, Deborah. "Sponsors of Literacy." *College Composition and Communication* 49 (1998): 165–85.

Braudel, Fernand. *The Identity of France.* Trans. Siân Reynolds. New York: Harper & Row, 1988.

Britton, James, Tony Burgess, Nancy Martin, Alex McLeod, and Harold Rosen. *The Development of Writing Abilities (11–18).* London: Macmillan, 1975.

Brodkey, Linda. "Modernism and the Scene(s) of Writing." *College English* 49 (1987): 396–418.

———. "On the Subjects of Class and Gender in 'The Literacy Letters.'" *College English* 51 (1989): 125–41.

Brodkey, Linda, and Jim Henry. "Voice Lessons in a Poststructural Key: Notes on Response and Revision." *A Rhetoric of Doing: Essays on Written Discourse in Honor of James L. Kinneavy.* Ed. Stephen P. Witte, Neil Nakadate, and Roger Cherry. Carbondale: Southern Illinois UP, 1992. 144–60.

Brown, Robert L., Jr. and Carl G. Herndl. "An Ethnographic Study of Corporate Writing: Job Status as Reflected in Written Text." *Functional Approaches to Writing: Research Perspectives.* Ed. Barbara Couture. London: Frances Pinter, 1986. 11–28.

Bureau of Labor Statistics. Table 2: Employment by occupation, 1996 and projected 2006. 4 July 1999. <http://www.fedstats.gov/index20.html>

———. Table 11: Employed persons by detailed occupation, sex, race, and Hispanic origin. 4 July 1999. <ftp://ftp.bls.gov/pub/special.requests/lf/aat11.txt>

Burnett, Rebecca E. "Substantive Conflict in a Cooperative Context: A Way to Improve the Collaborative Planning of Workplace Documents." *Technical Communication* 38 (1991): 532–39.

Chartier, Roger. *The Order of Books.* Stanford: Stanford UP, 1994.

Chatman, Seymour. *Story and Discourse: Narrative Structure in Fiction and Film.* Ithaca: Cornell UP, 1978.

Clifford, James. "Introduction: Partial Truths." *Writing Culture: The Poetics and Politics of Ethnography.* Ed. James Clifford and George E. Marcus. Berkeley: U of California P, 1986. 1–26.

Clifford, James, and George E. Marcus, eds. *Writing Culture: The Poetics and Politics of Ethnography.* Berkeley: U of California P, 1986.

Couture, Barbara. "Categorizing Professional Discourse: Engineering, Administrative, and Technical/Professional Writing." *Journal of Business and Technical Communication* 6 (1992): 5–37.

Crowley, Sharon. *Composition in the University: Historical and Polemical Essays.* Pittsburgh: U of Pittsburgh P, 1998.

———. "writing and Writing." *Writing and Reading Differently: Deconstruction and the Teaching of Composition and Literature.* Ed. Douglas Atkins and Michael L. Johnson. Lawrence: UP of Kansas, 1985. 93–100.

Dark, Ken A. *Theoretical Archaeology.* Ithaca: Cornell UP, 1995.

Davenport, Thomas. *Information Ecology.* New York: Oxford UP, 1997.

Debs, Mary Beth. "Corporate Authority: Sponsoring Rhetorical Practice." *Writing in the Workplace: New Research Perspectives.* Ed. Rachel Spilka. Carbondale: Southern Illinois University Press, 1993. 158–70.

Dias, Patrick, Aviva Freedman, Peter Medway, and Anthony Paré. *Worlds Apart: Acting and Writing in Academic and Workplace Contexts.* Mahwah, NJ: Lawrence Erlbaum Associates, 1999.

Eisner, Elliot W., and Elizabeth Vallance. "Five Concepts of Curriculum: Their Roots and Implications for Curriculum Planning." *Conflicting Concepts of Curriculum.* Ed. Elliot W. Eisner and Elizabeth Vallance. Berkeley: McCutchan, 1974. 1–18.

Elbow, Peter. "Closing My Eyes as I Speak: An Argument for Ignoring Audience." *College English* 49 (1987): 50–69.

Emig, Janet. "Writing as a Mode of Learning." *College Composition and Communication* 28 (1977): 122–28.

Faigley, Lester. *Fragments of Rationality: Postmodernity and the Subject of Composition.* Pittsburgh: U of Pittsburgh P, 1992.

Forman, Janis, ed. *New Visions of Collaborative Writing.* Portsmouth, NH: Boynton/Cook, 1992.

Foucault, Michel. *The Archaeology of Knowledge and the Discourse on Language.* New York: Pantheon Books, 1972.

———. "What Is an Author?" *Language, Counter-Memory, Practice: Selected Essays and Interviews by Michel Foucault.* Ed. Donald R. Bouchard. Ithaca: Cornell UP, 1977. 101–20.

Freed, Richard. "Postmodern Practice: Perspectives and Prospects." *Professional Communication: The Social Perspective.* Ed. Nancy Roundy Blyler and Charlotte Thralls. Newbury Park, CA: Sage, 1993. 196–14.

Frow, John. *Cultural Studies and Cultural Value.* Oxford: Clarendon Press, 1995.

Garay, Mary Sue, and Stephen A. Bernhardt, eds. *Expanding Literacies: English Teaching and the New Workplace.* Albany: State U of New York P, 1998.

Gere, Anne Ruggles. "Kitchen Tables and Rented Rooms: The Extracurriculum of Composition." *College Composition and Communication* 45 (1994): 75–92.

Goswami, Dixie, and Peter R. Stillman, eds. *Reclaiming the Classroom: Teacher Research as an Agency for Change.* Portsmouth, NH: Boynton/Cook, 1987.

Gregory, Kathleen L. "Nature-View Paradigms: Multiple Cultures and Culture Conflicts in Organizations." *Administrative Science Quarterly* 28 (1983): 359–76.

Haas, Christina. *Writing Technology: Studies on the Materiality of Literacy.* Mahwah, NJ: Lawrence Erlbaum Associates, 1996.

Hall, Stuart. "On Postmodernism and Articulation: An Interview with Stuart Hall." *Journal of Communication Inquiry* 10 (1986): 45–60.

Harding, Sandra. "Introduction: Is There a Feminist Method?" *Feminism and Methodology.* Ed. Sandra Harding. Bloomington: Indiana UP, 1987. 1–14.

Harvey, David. *The Condition of Postmodernity.* London: Blackwell, 1989.

Hayano, David M. "Auto-Ethnography: Paradigms, Problems, and Prospects." *Human Organization* 38 (1979): 99–104.

Henry, Jim. "Documenting Contributory Expertise: The Value Added by Technical Communicators in Collaborative Writing Situations" *Technical Communication* 45 (1998): 207–20.

———. "Teaching Technical Authorship." *Technical Communication Quarterly* 4 (1995): 261–84.

———. "Toward Technical Authorship." *Journal of Technical Writing and Communication* 24 (1994): 449–61.

Henry, Jim, and "George." "Workplace Ghostwriting." *Journal of Business and Technical Communication* 9 (1995): 425–45.

Herndl, Carl G. "Teaching Discourse and Reproducing Culture: A Critique of Research and Pedagogy in Professional and Non-Academic Writing." *College Composition and Communication* 44 (1993): 349–63.

Holmes, Urban T., Jr. "Transitions in European Education." *Twelfth-Century Europe and the Foundations of Modern Society.* Ed. Marshall Clagett, Gaines Post, and Robert Reynolds. Madison: U of Wisconsin P, 1966. 15–38.

hooks, bell. *yearning: race, gender, and cultural politics.* Boston: South End Press, 1990.

Hull, Glynda. "Hearing Other Voices: A Critical Assessment of Popular Views on Literacy and Work. *Changing Work, Changing Workers: Critical Perspectives on Language, Literacy, and Skills.* Ed. Glynda Hull. Albany, NY: State U of New York P, 1997. 3–39.

Jameson, Fredric. *Postmodernism, or, The Cultural Logic of Late Capitalism.* Durham: Duke UP, 1991.

Johannsen, Agneta M. "Applied Anthropology and Post-Modernist Ethnography." *Human Organization* 51 (1992): 71–81.

Johnson-Eilola, Johndan. *Nostalgic Angels: Rearticulating Hypertext Writing.* Norwood, NJ: Ablex Publishing Company, 1997.

———. "Relocating the Value of Work: Technical Communication in a Post-Industrial Age." *Technical Communication Quarterly* 5 (1996): 245–70.

Jolliffe, David. "Finding Yourself in the Text: Identity Formation in the Discourse of Workplace Documents. *Changing Work, Changing Workers: Critical Perspectives on Language, Literacy, and Skills.* Ed. Glynda Hull. Albany: State U of New York P, 1997. 335–49.

Katz, Steven. "The Ethic of Expediency: Classical Rhetoric, Technology, and the Holocaust." *College English* 54 (1992): 255–75.

Katz, Susan M. *The Dynamics of Writing Review: Opportunities for Growth and Change in the Workplace.* Stamford: Ablex, 1998.

Kenyatta, Jomo. *Facing Mount Kenya.* London: Secker and Warburg, 1938.

Kinneavy, James L. *A Theory of Discourse.* Englewood Cliffs, NJ: Prentice Hall, 1971.

Kirsch, Gesa. "Methodological Pluralism." *Methods and Methodology in Composition Research.* Ed. Gesa Kirsch and Patricia A. Sullivan. Carbondale: Southern Illinois UP, 1992. 247–69.

Kirsch, Gesa E., and Joy S. Ritchie. "Beyond the Personal: Theorizing a Politics of Location in Composition Research." *College Composition and Communication* 46 (1995): 7–29.

Kirshenblatt-Gimblett, Barbara. "Mistaken Dichotomies." *Journal of American Folklore* 101 (1988): 140–55.

Kleimann, Susan. "The Reciprocal Relationship of Workplace Culture and Review." *Writing in the Workplace: New Research Perspectives.* Ed. Rachel Spilka. Carbondale: Southern Illinois UP, 1993. 56–70.

Kliebard, Herbert M. *The Struggle for the American Curriculum, 1893–1958.* New York: Routledge & Kegan Paul, 1987.

Kondo, Dorinne. "Bad Girls: Theater, Women of Color, and the Politics of Representation." *Women Writing Culture.* Ed. Ruth Behar and Deborah Gordon. Berkeley: U of California P, 1995. 49–64.

Kushner, Tony. *Angels in America: A Gay Fantasia on National Themes. Part One: Millennium Approaches*. New York: Theatre Communications Group, 1993.

Lacan, Jacques. *Ecrits: A Selection*. New York: Norton, 1977.

Lanham, Richard. *The Electronic Word: Democracy, Technology, and the Arts*. Chicago: U of Chicago P, 1993.

Lather, Patti. *Getting Smart: Feminist Research and Pedagogy with/in the Postmodern*. New York: Routledge, 1991.

Lay, Mary M. and William M. Karis, eds. *Collaborative Writing in Industry: Investigations in Theory and Practice*. Amityville, NY: Baywood, 1991.

Lay, Mary M., Billie J. Wahlstrom, Carolyn Rude, Cindy Selfe, and Jack Selzer. *Technical Communication*. 2nd ed. New York: McGraw-Hill, 1999.

Leggo, Carl. "Questions I Need to Ask before I Advise My Students to Write in Their Own Voices." *Rhetoric Review* 10 (1991): 143–52.

Lionnet, Françoise. "Autoethnography: The An-Archic Style of *Dust Tracks on a Road*." *Reading Black, Reading Feminist*. Ed. Henry Louis Gates. New York: Meridian Press, 1990. 382–414.

Lunsford, Andrea Abernathy. "Rhetoric, Feminism, and the Politics of Textual Ownership." *College English* 61 (1999): 529–44.

Lunsford, Andrea, and Lisa Ede. "Collaborative Authorship and the Teaching of Writing." *The Construction of Authorship: Textual Appropriation in Law and Literature*. Ed. Martha Woodmansee and Peter Jaszi. Durham: Duke UP, 1994. 417–38.

————. *Singular Texts/Plural Authors: Perspectives on Collaborative Writing*. Carbondale: Southern Illinois UP, 1990.

Lyotard, Jean-François. *The Postmodern Condition: A Report on Knowledge*. Trans. Geoff Bennington and Brian Massumi. Minneapolis: U of Minnesota P, 1984.

Martin, Henri-Jean. *The History and Power of Writing*. Trans. Lydia G. Cochrane. Chicago: U of Chicago P, 1994

McBeth, Sally. "Myths of Objectivity and the Collaborative Process in Life History Research." *When They Read What We Write: The Politics of Ethnography*. Ed. Caroline B. Brettell. Westport: Bergin. 1993. 145–62.

Miller, Carolyn R. "Learning from History: World War II and the Culture of High Technology." *Journal of Business and Technical Communication* 12 (1998): 288–315.

————. "What's Practical about Technical Writing?" *Technical Writing: Theory and Practice*. Ed. Bertie E. Fearing and W. Keats Sparrow. New York: MLA, 1989. 14–24.

Miller, Richard E. "Fault Lines in the Contact Zone." *College English* 56 (1994): 389–408.

Miller, Susan. *Textual Carnivals: The Politics of Composition*. Carbondale: Southern Illinois UP, 1991.

Miller, Thomas P. "Treating Professional Writing as Social Praxis." *Journal of Advanced Composition* 11 (1991): 57–72.

Morgan, Meg, and Mary Murray. "Insight and Collaborative Writing." *Collaborative Writing in Industry: Investigations in Theory and Practice*. Ed. Mary M. Lay and William M. Karis. Amityville, NY: Baywood, 1991. 64–81.

Odell, Lee, and Dixie Goswami, ed. *Writing in Nonacademic Settings*. New York: Guilford, 1985.

Parker, William Riley. "Where Do English Departments Come From?" *College English* 28 (1967): 339–51.

Phelps, Louise Wetherbee. "Audience and Authorship: The Disappearing Boundary." *A Sense of Audience in Written Communication*. Ed. Gesa Kirsch and Duane H. Roen. Newbury Park, CA: Sage, 1990.

Piwowarczyk, Mary Ann. "The Narratee and the Situation of Enunciation: A Reconsideration of Prince's Theory." *Genre* 9 (1976): 161–77.

Porter, James E. "Developing a Postmodern Ethics of Rhetoric and Composition." *Defining the New Rhetorics*. Ed. Theresa Enos and Stuart C. Brown. Newbury Park, CA: Sage, 1993. 207–26.

Porter, James E., and Patricia Sullivan. "Working Across Methodological Interfaces: The Study of Computers and Writing in the Workplace." *Electronic Literacies in the Workplace*. Ed. Patricia Sullivan and Jennie Dautermann. Urbana: NCTE, 1996. 294–322.

Pratt, Mary Louise. "Arts of the Contact Zone." *Profession 91*. New York: MLA, 1991. 33–40.

Prince, Gerald. *A Dictionary of Narratology*. Lincoln: U of Nebraska P, 1987.

———. "Introduction to the Study of the Narratee." *Reader Response Criticism: From Formalism to Post-Structuralism*. Ed. Jane P. Tompkins. Baltimore: John Hopkins UP, 1980. 7–25.

Reagan, Sally Barr, Thomas Fox, and David Bleich. *Writing With: New Directions in Collaborative Teaching, Learning, and Research*. Albany: State U of New York P, 1994.

Reich, Robert. *The Work of Nations*. New York: Vintage, 1992.

Rosaldo, Renato. *Culture and Truth: The Remaking of Social Analysis*. Boston: Beacon Press, 1993.

Russell, David R. *Writing in the Academic Disciplines, 1870–1990: A Curricular History*. Carbondale: Southern Illinois UP, 1991.

Schein, Edgar H. "Organizational Culture." *American Psychologist* 45 (1990): 109–19.

Selber, Stuart A. "Beyond Skill Building: Challenges Facing Technical Communication Teachers in the Computer Age." *Technical Communication Quarterly* 3 (1994): 365–90.

Selber, Stuart A., Dan McGavin, William Klein, and Johndan Johnson-Eilola. "Issues in Hypertext-Supported Collaborative Writing." *Nonacademic Writing: Social Theory and Technology*. Ed. Ann Hill Duin and Craig J. Hansen. Mahwah: Erlbaum. 257–80.

Selfe, Cynthia L. "Theorizing E-mail for the Practice, Instruction, and Study of Literacy." *Electronic Literacies in the Workplace*. Ed. Patricia Sullivan and Jennie Dautermann. Urbana: NCTE, 1996. 255–93.

Selfe, Cynthia L., and Richard J. Selfe Jr. "Writing as Democratic Social Action in a Technological World: Politicizing and Inhabiting Virtual Landscapes." *Nonacademic Writing: Social Theory and Technology*. Ed. Ann Hill Duin and Craig J. Hansen. Mahwah: Erlbaum. 325–58.

Selzer, Jack. "Intertextuality and the Writing Process: An Overview." *Writing in the Workplace:New Research Perspectives*. Ed. Rachel Spilka. Carbondale: Southern Illinois UP, 1993. 171–80.

Silverman, David, and Brian Torode. *The Material Word: Some Theories of Language and its Limits*. London: Routledge, 1980.

Slack, Jennifer Daryl, David James Miller, and Jeffrey Doak. "The Technical Communicator as Author: Meaning, Power, Authority." *Journal of Business and Technical Communication* 7 (1993): 12–36.

Slevin, James. "Disciplining Students: Whom Should Composition Teach and What Should They Know?" *Composition in the Twenty-First Century: Crisis and Change*. Ed. Lynn Z. Bloom, Donald A. Daiker, and Edward M. White. Carbondale: Southern Illinois UP, 1996. 153–65.

Society for Technical Communication. Special Section: Measuring the Value Added by Professional Technical Communicators. *Technical Communication* 42 (1995): 23–83.

Spellmeyer, Kurt. "Foucault and the Freshman Writer: Considering the Self in Discourse." *College English* 51 (1989): 715–29.

———. "Inventing the University Student." *Composition in the Twenty-First Century: Crisis and Change*. Ed. Lynn Z. Bloom, Donald A. Daiker, and Edward M. White. Carbondale: Southern Illinois UP, 1996. 39–44.

Spilka, Rachel. "Influencing Workplace Practice: A Challenge for Professional Writing Specialists in the Academy." *Writing in the Workplace: New Research Perspectives*. Ed. Rachel Spilka. Carbondale: Southern Illinois UP, 1993. 207–19.

Stewart, Donald C. "Two Model Teachers and the Harvardization of English Departments." *The Rhetorical Tradition and Modern Writing*. Ed. James J. Murphy. New York: MLA, 1982. 118–29.

Sullivan, Patricia A. "Feminism and Methodology in Composition Studies." *Methods and Methodology in Composition Research*. Ed. Gesa Kirsch and Patricia A. Sullivan. Carbondale: Southern Illinois UP, 1992. 37–61.

Sullivan, Patricia A., and James E. Porter. "Remapping Curricular Geography: Professional Writing in/and English." *Journal of Business and Technical Communication* 7 (1993): 389–422.

Taylor, Frederick W. *The Principles of Scientific Management*. New York: Harper & Brothers, 1911.

Trimbur, John. "Writing Instruction and the Politics of Professionalization." *Composition in the Twenty-First Century: Crisis and Change*. Ed. Lynn Z. Bloom, Donald A. Daiker, and Edward M. White. Carbondale: Southern Illinois UP, 1996. 133–45.

Tufte, Edward R. *Envisioning Information*. Cheshire: Graphics Press, 1990.

Van Maanen, John, and Stephen R. Barley. "Occupational Communities: Culture and Control in Organizations." *Research in Organizational Behavior*. Ed. B. M. Straw and L. L. Cummings Greenwich, CT: JAI Press, 1984.

van Slyck, Phyllis. "Repositioning Ourselves in the Contact Zones." *College English* 59 (1997): 149–70.

Virilio, Paul. *Speed and Politics: An Essay on Domology*. Trans. M. Polizzotti. New York: Semiotext(e), 1986.

White, Hayden. *The Content of the Form: Narrative Discourse and Historical Representation*. Baltimore: Johns Hopkins UP, 1987.

Winsor, Dorothy. "Owning Corporate Texts." *Journal of Business and Technical Communication* 7 (1993): 179–95.

Woodmansee, Martha. "On the Author Effect: Recovering Collectivity." *The Construction of Authorship: Textual Appropriation in Law and Literature*. Ed. Martha Woodmansee and Peter Jaszi. Durham: Duke UP, 1994. 1–14.

Yates, JoAnne. *Control through Communication: The Rise of System in American Management*. Baltimore: Johns Hopkins UP, 1989.

Young, Richard E., Alton L. Becker, and Kenneth L. Pike. *Rhetoric: Discovery and Change*. New York: Harcourt, 1970.

Zebroski, James Thomas, and Nancy Mack. "Ethnographic Writing for Critical Consciousness." *Social Issues in the English Classroom.* Ed. C. Mark Hurlbert and Samuel Totten. Urbana: NCTE, 1992. 269–82.

Zuboff, Shoshana. *In the Age of the Smart Machine: The Future of Work and Power.* New York: Basic Books, 1988.

INDEX

Adam, 39, 40, 41, 55, 85, 97, 103, 105, 124, 187, 189, 211, 221

Adria, 40, 42, 55, 73, 76, 79, 85–86, 95, 101, 103, 187, 189, 211, 221

agency: as circumscribed by cultural and discursive practices, 2, 28, 45–46, 120, 151; as implied, 124; intermediary, 155–58; obfuscation of, 149; in stabilization and change, 86, 89; among subject positions, 97, 125–26

Albert, 37, 42, 55, 58, 73, 95–96, 103, 135, 153, 187, 189–90, 214, 221–22

Alice, 37, 38, 39, 63, 85–86, 95, 99, 176, 188, 190, 218, 222

Althusser, Louis, 16, 123

Amy, 95, 100, 187, 190, 211, 222

Ana, 27–28, 58, 75, 79, 82, 85, 87, 95, 101, 103, 105, 187, 190, 214, 222

Andrew, 41, 42, 63, 85, 187, 191, 218, 223

Angels in America (Kushner), 161, 172, 182

Anita, 37, 39, 41, 58, 75, 95, 101, 105, 187, 191, 215, 223

Ann, 29–31, 39, 40, 54, 75, 76, 95, 97, 100, 105, 174, 187, 191, 211, 223

Anne, 15, 20, 21, 63, 87, 95, 103, 188, 192, 218, 223–24

anthropology: applied, 163; epistemology of, 1, 7–9, 50–52

archaeological digs: and classification of shards, 35; and hypertext excavations, 10; processes for conducting, 9; shards in, 9

audience: advocacy for, 147; and authorship, 131, 170–71; multiple, 63, 65; public as, 57, 58, 65; serial, 63, 65. *See also* reader

author: death of, 16, 142; function, 26, 118; implied, 12, 19–22, 26, 74, 144, 148; real, 19–22, 112, 146, 148, 165

authorship: and audience, 131, 179–81; and authority, 12, 134; collaborative, 38, 42, 59, 81, 117, 133, 153; organizational, 172–73, 182, 183–84; and ownership, 45; as a sociological function, 30, 143; technical, 143, 145; theories of, 12, 16–17, 19–20, 29–34, 45, 142

autoethnography, 49–67, 92–93, 126, 131, 130

Barthes, Roland, 16, 142

Behar, Ruth, 24, 162

Belenky, Mary Field, et al., 174

Belmont Report, 7

Belsey, Catherine, 122, 124, 167

Bergoffen, Debra, 9, 24

Berlin, James, 2, 7, 115, 117

Bernie, 37, 42, 60, 61, 75, 87, 101, 103, 139–40, 187, 192, 216, 224

Bourdieu, Pierre, and Jean-Claude Passeron, 164

Branden, 15, 21, 25–27, 39, 57, 58, 79, 95, 100, 105, 183, 188, 192, 215, 224

Brandt, Deborah, 174

Braudel, Fernand, 130

Brenda, 37–39, 41, 58, 60, 76, 79, 80, 95, 187, 192, 216, 224

Britton, James, et al., 147

Brodkey, Linda, 38, 91, 123, 173

Bureau of Labor, 32, 44

Burr, Zofia, 179, 181

Carolyn, 41, 42, 55, 75, 79, 95, 97, 103, 187, 188, 192, 211, 225

Cass, 37, 41, 42, 57, 58, 82, 101, 105, 187, 193, 215, 225

Challis, 43, 61, 62, 85, 95, 126, 151, 187, 188, 193, 216, 225

Chatman, Seymour, 20, 147

Chet, 39–41, 54, 76, 79, 97, 103, 105, 187–88, 193, 211, 225–26

Clifford, James, 1, 3, 166

cognitive mapping, 71–72

collaboration, xiii, 42, 44, 58, 59, 64, 81; and collective reports, 58; and individual contributions, 58. *See also* authorship, collaborative; composition, collaborative

Communications Decency Act, 172

community colleges, 86, 177

composition: and affect, 39–43, 102–5, 112, 121–22; collaborative, 38, 42, 58–59, 132–34, 154–55; computerized, 134–36; current-traditional, 2–4, 30–32; curricular alternatives, 128; deficit models of, 18; and discursive experience, ix–xi, 3–4, 31; expressivism, 112–13; epistemology, 4, 6, 17, 30–32, 43–46, 65, 108, 117, 140–42, 183; and *ethos,* 126, 149; as a field, 16, 119; and hypertext, 130–31; in modernist modes, 120; in postmodern modes, 120–27, 135; process pedagogy, x, 120–26; and research papers, 3

Conference on College Composition and Communication, 149, 183

contact zones, 51, 119, 126, 180–81

Corinne, 39–42, 60, 87, 95, 97, 187, 193, 217, 226

Crowley, Sharon, 2, 30–32, 120, 122, 126, 128, 142, 183

cultural reproduction, 98, 151

cultures, codex, 4

curriculum: "academic rationalist," 127; and "extracurriculum," 176–77; "geographies of," 32–33, 118; of professional writing, 127–36; and "self-actualization," 127–128, 164; "social-efficiency," 4; social reconstruction, 164

Daisy, 37, 39, 40–42, 76, 79–80, 95, 103, 187, 194, 211, 226

Debs, Mary Beth, 69, 70, 139, 156, 177

Department of Commerce, 27, 57

Derrida, Jacques, 15, 181

Diane, 41, 60, 75, 82, 95, 98–99, 101, 103, 105, 187, 194, 217, 226–27

discourse: academic, 95; administrative, 105; analysis, xi; authoritarian, 104; community, 82, 94, 99–100, 107; critical relationship with, 15, 184; definitions of, 92; effects of, 102–6; events of, 9; first-person, 4; and formations, 26; forms of, 94–102; heterosexist, 101; instrumental, xi, 11, 106; management, 101–3; market, 101; modernist theories of, 114–16;

"multilayerdness" of, 114; multiple forms of, 98–100, 123–24, 151–52; official organizational, 100; "performative" model of, 114; and points of application, 26; political, 58–59; postmodern theories of, 91–92, 114–15; and practices and traditions, 16; products, 97–98; racist, 93, 101; sexist, 93, 101, 103; sites of, 9; specialists, 119; studies, 120–27; of surveillance, 80, 104, 129; twentieth-century, 10, 20; underlying, 100–102, 123–24, 151–52; unities of, 24, 88–89, 93; vague, 63, 73–74, 87, 96

discursive constructions: of the "I," 4, 15–16, 31, 121–26, 165–68; of the "other," 125–26, 136, 166; of the "self," 16–18, 20, 26, 125–26, 133, 136, 166

discursive formations, 16, 26, 36–46, 119, 132, 180

Doak, Jeffrey, 69, 70, 143–44

document processes, 78–81, 89, 153–55

domain of professional authorship, 146–49

Ede, Lisa, 132–33

Elaine, 40, 55, 73, 82, 95, 97, 99, 103, 188, 194, 212, 227

Ella, 41–42, 55, 75–76, 79, 82, 87, 95, 103, 105, 167, 194, 212, 227

Ellie, 39, 54, 73, 76, 79, 95, 187, 205, 213, 241

Emma, 37, 39, 63, 82, 95, 176, 195, 218, 228

English: and *belles lettres,* 3; departments of, ix–x, 3, 32–33, 129, 137

ethnography: performative, 162, 179; theory, 50–52

ethos, 126, 149–58, 167

expressivism. *See* composition

Faigley, Lester, 2, 28, 118

feminism, 23, 162, 174, 182

folklore, 65–66

Foucault, Michel, xi, 8–10, 24, 26, 29–30

Frow, John, 44, 111–13, 119, 125, 159, 169

Gary, 37, 39, 55, 73, 87, 95, 97–98, 101, 146, 170, 188, 195, 212, 227–28

General Accounting Office, 154

George, 37, 40, 57–59, 75, 79–80, 100–101, 103, 105, 158, 175–76, 187, 195, 215, 228

Ginger, 40–42, 55, 75, 82, 87, 98, 105, 187, 195, 212, 228
Gloria, 39–42, 57–58, 73, 82, 95–97, 176, 187, 196, 215, 228–29
Grace, 37–38, 41, 73, 79–80, 82, 95, 105, 187, 196, 217, 229
Gwen, 37–39, 41–42, 58, 73, 75, 95, 103–4, 121, 154, 187, 196, 215, 229

Hart, 37, 39, 63, 82–83, 95, 97, 156, 187, 196, 218, 229–30
Harvard model, ix, 3
Harvey, David, 178, 180
Hayano, David, 49, 89
Heather, 37, 60, 75, 85, 103, 105, 187, 197, 217, 230
Helen, 30, 41, 58, 61, 73, 79–80, 95, 97–98, 176, 187, 197, 215, 230
heuristics, in interpreting data, 11
hierarchy: flattened, 116–17, 134, 171; and information flow, 81, 88, 152, 185–86
Holly, 39, 41, 55, 57, 79, 85, 95, 103, 105, 187, 197, 212, 230
Hurston, Zora Neale, 51–52, 66, 126

identities: subjective, 52; subjective work, 52, 66
ideology: as symbolic representations, 124–27, 156; zero-sum, 88
"informating," 134
information workers, 111, 113
"interdiscursivity," 124
intertextuality, 132, 146
intervention, 161–84
Itsy, 37, 60, 95, 187, 197, 217, 230–31

Jackie, 39, 41–42, 60–62, 76, 79–80, 82, 85, 95, 97–99, 105, 187–88, 197–98, 217, 231
Jan, 37, 60–61, 75, 85, 87, 95–96, 101, 187, 198, 217, 231
Jane, 42, 58, 75, 79, 82, 95, 103, 105, 185, 198, 215, 231
Janice, 37, 39, 54, 73, 85, 87, 95, 188, 198, 212, 232
Jeff, 40–41, 55, 73, 75–76, 82–83, 95, 98–99, 105, 154, 175, 187, 198, 212, 232
Jen, 40, 55, 95, 97–99, 156, 187, 198–99, 212, 232
Jihad, 95–96, 105, 188, 199, 212, 233
Jillian, 39, 41, 63, 85–86, 95, 176, 188, 199, 219, 233

Joanne, 40, 42, 55, 73, 76, 79, 82, 95, 187, 199, 212, 233
Joe, 39, 42, 55, 76, 95, 97–98, 187, 199–200, 212, 233–34
Johnson-Eilola, Johndan, 44, 130, 134–35, 153
Jolliffe, David, 124
Jones, Grace, 161–62, 182
journals, 87, 121, 124. *See also* self-documentation
Julie, 63, 95, 99, 176, 188, 200, 219, 234

Kali, 58, 75, 82, 87, 95, 101, 103, 178, 187, 200, 215, 234
Karla, 38, 40, 60, 75, 79–80, 95, 97, 101, 105, 187, 200, 217, 234–35
Kate, 63, 73, 82, 87, 95, 99, 188, 200–201, 219, 235
Kelly, 39, 41–42, 63, 76, 79–80, 82, 85–86, 103, 187–88, 201, 219, 235
Kenyata, Jomo, 50
Kirsten, 37, 39, 41–42, 60–61, 73, 76, 79, 82, 95, 101, 103, 187, 201, 218, 235
Kolar, 58–59, 73, 75, 85, 87, 95, 101, 105, 187, 201, 216, 236
Kondo, Dorinne, 161–62, 179
Kushner, Tony, 161, 182
Kyle, 37–39, 41, 60, 62, 73, 79–80, 95, 97, 103, 105, 176, 187, 201, 218, 236

Lacan, Jacques, 16
Lara, 63, 82, 95, 188, 201–2, 219, 236
Lather, Patti, 122, 181
Leathe, 41, 55, 73, 76, 82, 95, 97, 116, 187, 202, 213, 236–37
Lee, 39, 42, 63, 86–87, 95, 176, 188, 202, 219, 237
Leggo, Carl, 123
Leigh, 39, 41, 58–59, 73, 75–76, 79, 95, 100, 103, 184, 187, 202, 216, 237
Lena, 60, 75, 79–80, 95, 97, 101, 105, 159, 187, 203, 218, 237–38
liberal humanism, ix, 3, 108
Library of Congress, 57, 96, 176
Lionnet, Françoise, 51
Lisa, 39, 42, 55, 82–83, 95, 96, 101, 103, 175, 187–88, 203, 213, 238
literacy: demands in high-volume workplace, ix, 5; projects, critical, 11, 177; sponsorship of, 174
Liz, 40, 57–58, 73, 75, 82, 187, 203, 216, 238

logs. *See* journals
Lois, 39, 42, 54–55, 82, 95–96, 98–99, 101, 105, 187, 203, 213, 238
Lunsford, Andrea, 45, 132–33
Lyotard, Jean-François, 10–11

Mack, 40–42, 54–55, 95, 103, 187, 203–4, 213, 239
Maggie, 38–39, 41–42, 79, 95, 97, 103, 105, 187–88, 204, 213, 239
management: scientific, 4; systematic, 4
Mandy, 28, 37, 39, 60, 75, 79, 91–93, 101, 103, 105, 187, 204, 218, 239
Marla, 42, 63, 82, 105, 176, 187–88, 207, 219, 239–40
Martin, Henri-Jean, 131
Mary, 41–42, 55, 72, 79, 82, 95, 100, 103, 105, 116, 187–88, 204, 213, 240
May, 38, 42, 55, 75, 82, 95, 187, 205, 213, 240
Meese, Ed, 161, 172
Meg, 37, 55, 73, 95, 101, 103, 105, 187, 205, 213, 240
Megan, 63, 73, 87, 95–97, 100, 187, 205, 219, 240–41
Miller, Carolyn, 144, 152, 165
Miller, James, 69, 70, 143–44
Miller, Susan, 2, 28, 117
Miyake, Issey, 162
Moylan, Tom, 111, 113

Nancy, 37, 54, 73, 76, 79, 95, 187, 205, 213, 241
narratology, 19–22
New Criticism, 31
Nidean, 15, 20–21, 42, 54, 73, 87, 95, 101, 105, 187, 206, 213, 241
Norma, 37, 39–40, 73, 95, 98, 187, 206, 214, 241
Nyck, 37, 39, 41, 55, 75–76, 85, 95, 103, 175, 187, 206, 214, 241–42

Odell, Lee, and Dixie Goswami, 7
organization: charts, 5, 168, 172; information flows in, 81, 88, 152, 155–56; in national context, 5
organizational studies, 128–30

petits recits, xi, 70–72, 92, 171
Phelps, Louise Wetherbee, 147, 157, 166
Phoebe, 38–39, 41, 63–64, 95, 98–99, 105, 187, 206, 219, 242

policy, writing of, 58–59
Porter, James E., 11, 22, 32–33, 118, 147, 149–50
post-Fordism: and "flexibility" of labor, 43, 76, 111, 113, 178
postmodernism, xi, 1–2, 11, 16–17, 91–93, 114–15, 163; theoretical tenets and daily life, 2
Prague Linguistics Circle, 147
Pratt, Mary Louise, 51, 162, 180
Prince, Gerald, 12, 19, 148
professional managerial class, 180
professional writing: and civic humanism, 174; curricula, 127–36; as a field, 33
property, intellectual, 45

Rachel, 38, 40, 58, 75, 82, 95, 101, 103, 187, 207, 216, 242
Ravi, 40–41, 55, 73, 76, 82, 87, 95, 101, 187, 207, 214, 242–43
Ray, 40, 58, 73, 82–83, 95–96, 99, 103–5, 187, 207, 216, 243
readability, 11, 144
reader: implied, 19–20, 144, 148; real, 19–20, 148; response theory, 58. *See also* audience
reading formations, 132, 180
Reagan, Ronald, 172, 192
Red, 37, 39, 55, 73, 75–76, 79–80, 82–83, 95–96, 103, 131, 175, 187, 207, 214, 243
Reich, Robert, 5, 12, 115–16, 119, 129, 132–33
relationality, and social interests, 46, 157
representational practices, 45–46, 157–58, 179–80; and misrepresentation, 98; politics and poetics of, xi, 1, 50–52, 65–66, 161, 182; and "self" and "other," 113
research: grounded, 23; informed intersubjective methodology, xi, 7; reflexivity and, 66, 125; teacher, 7; on workplace writing, xi, 7
Rex, 39, 55, 73, 82–83, 95, 175, 187, 208, 214, 243
rhetoric: current-traditional, 3; departments of, 3; postmodern, 3
Rosaldo, Renato, 1, 156

Sarah, 39, 41–42, 54–55, 73, 79, 103, 187, 208, 214, 243–44
Schein, Edgar H., 25, 224
Selber, Stuart, 134

self, as constructed through discourses. *See* discursive constructions, of the "self"

self-documentation, 74, 103–4, 121. *See also* journals

Selfe, Cynthia L., 136, 171

Selfe, Cynthia L., and Richard J. Selfe Jr., 124, 167, 173

Silverman, David, and Brian Torode, 123

Slack, Jennifer Daryl, 69, 70, 143–44

Smith-Bermiss, Michelle, 126

social constructionist theory, x, 8, 89

Society for Technical Communication, 33, 115

Spellmeyer, Kurt, 15, 16, 20, 181

Starla, 38–39, 55, 69–70, 76, 79, 88, 95, 135, 156, 175, 187, 208, 214, 244

subject formation: and autoethnographic subject positions, 50–52, 66; and discourses, 10, 91–108; and relationality, 121–27

subjectivity: as articulated to ideologies, 123–24; economic, 127; ideological, 124–27, 136; panopticon, 81, 129; political, 16, 122–24, 136; as positioned in interpretation, 50–52, 66, 93; psychological, 16, 17, 121–22, 136; and semiotic constructions, 16, 125; as shaped by state and surrogate institutions, 17; and sites, 66–67; sociological, 121–22; student, 4, 21, 145; technological, 167; theories of, x, 16

Sue, 39–40, 58, 73, 79–80, 101, 103–5, 187, 208, 216, 244

Sullivan, Patricia, 11, 22, 32–33, 118, 147

symbolic analysts, 115–22, 132, 134–35

Taylor, Frederick W., 4

Taylorization: and time-motion studies, 4; and work organization, 4, 5, 12, 44, 116, 131, 136, 164

Tess, 38–39, 41–42, 55, 57, 82–83, 99, 105, 187, 208, 214, 244

Tom, 37, 39, 63–64, 95–96, 187, 209, 220, 245

Tufte, Edward R., 10

usability, 11, 71

value added, 115

virtual forums, 124–25, 169–71

voice, 123, 158

WAC (writing across the curriculum), 140, 147

workplace: high-value, x, 5, 108, 115–19, 125, 130, 134, 152, 170; high-volume, x, 108; and literacy demands, 45–46; managers, 141

workplace cultures: and alliances, 183; and cognitive mapping, 71–72; and "continuous quality improvement," 85; counterproductivity in, 93; and disciplining, 103; discursive features, 91–108; and gender lines, 96; and heterosexism, 101; organizational divisions, 96; organizational features, 69–90; organizational goals, 86–88; organizational memory, 79; and racism, 93, 101; and sexism, 93, 101, 103; stabilization and change, 84–86, 89; subcultural dynamics, 81–84, 89

workshops, 121–22, 125

World Bank, 57

World Wide Web, 55, 58, 59, 87–88, 95–98, 135, 146, 170

writers: and affect, 31, 39, 104, 112, 121–22; as arbitrators, 147; and "block," 122; in Bureau of Labor statistics, 32, 44; and collaboration (*see* collaboration); and cultural histories and traditions, 130–32; as end-user advocates, 59, 175; and expertise, 5, 108, 140, 149–53, 162; as functionaries, 75–76; and knowledge and behavior, 105–6; as liaisons to exterior, 76–77; as lookouts, 175; as mediators, 107; as "mediums," 39; as negotiators, 147; as nodes, 135, 157; as an "occupational community," 33; and organizational studies, 128–30; as a professional class, 88, 111–13, 125, 126, 145, 179; profiles of, 134–46; psychology of, 102–5; as robots, 143–62; roles of, 76–78, 88; skills of, 72–74, 89, 106; status of, 74–76, 106–7, 140, 162; and systems thinking, 129; and turnover, 55, 57; and ways of knowing, 83

writing: and autodidacticism, 38; in businesses and corporations, 54–57, 211–14; and career change, 42; collaborative (*see* composition, collaborative); computer-mediated, 134–36; and creative/critical binary, 179; and deadlines, 41, 79; difficulty of, 39; and diplomacy, 42; and document design, 73, 145; in educational and nonprofit institutions, 62–64, 213–20; as eliciting emotions, 40, 43; as encounter with the world, 39; as engage-

writing, *(continued)*
  ment, 39; as exposing oneself, 39; ghost-writing, 58–59; in government agencies and institutions, 57–60, 214–16; and hypertext composing, 130; impersonal, 4; kinds of, 94–97; as learned, 36–41; as linked to feelings, 39; as literary authorship, 39; as a livelihood, 40; as a mode of learning, 6, 107; as organizational product, 97–98; and other people's metaphors, 73; and other people's texts, 41; as personal, 40; and power, x, 117–19; in professional associations and societies, 60–62, 216–18; and project management, 41; and publication, 39; as rep-resenting the organization, 135; review processes, 58, 65; and schooling, 38–39; and skills development, 37; socialization into, 85; solicitations and acknowledgments, 95–96; speeches, 79; and talent, 37; and teaching, 42, 54, 63; teams, 65, 76–78, 81, 83, 152, 159, 169 (*see also* composition, collaborative); and technology studies, 131; and utilitarian ends, 42; and value, x, 115–17

Yocom, Margaret "Peggy," 66, 91

Zebroski, James, and Nancy Mack, 166–67
Zuboff, Shoshana, 6, 12, 134, 170

Jim Henry holds degrees from Princeton University, the Université de Genève, the Institut Universitaire d'Etudes du Développement, Webster University in Geneva, and the University of Pennsylvania. He is an associate professor of English at George Mason University, where he develops curricula for the MA program in professional writing and editing. His essays have appeared in *College English* and in numerous professional writing journals.